George M. Blue, James Milton
& Jane Saville (eds.)

Assessing English for Academic Purposes

PETER LANG

Oxford · Bern · Berlin · Bruxelles · Frankfurt am Main · New York · Wien

Die Deutsche Bibliothek – CIP-Einheitsaufnahme

Assessing English for academic purposes / George M. Blue ... (ed.) –
Oxford ; Bern ; Berlin ; Bruxelles ; Frankfurt am Main ; New York ; Wien :
Lang, 2000
ISBN 3-906765-98-9

British Library and Library of Congress Cataloguing-in-Publication Data:
A catalogue record for this book is available from *The British Library,*
Great Britain, and from *The Library of Congress,* USA

Cover design: Thomas Jaberg, Peter Lang AG

ISBN 3-906765-98-9
US-ISBN 0-8204-5316-1

© Peter Lang AG, European Academic Publishers, Bern 2000
Jupiterstr. 15, Postfach, 3000 Bern 15, Switzerland; info@peterlang.com

Printed in Germany

Contents

Part Four: Non-Traditional Forms of Assessment

Part Five: Students' Views of Assessment

George M Blue, James Milton and Jane Saville

Introduction: Assessing English for Academic Purposes

1. Introduction

In the last few years the theme of assessment has been growing in importance in all areas of education, not least in language education. The numbers of students studying through a language other than their mother tongue have multiplied and this is, in part, due to the repeated call for universities to be more 'international'. As a result, the assessment of language as a medium for study has also become increasingly important.

International students often find the learning experience in British, North American and Australasian universities quite difficult, as the conventions and study modes may be very different from what they are used to. However, they generally find it an enriching experience, at least until they come to be assessed. Assessment, whether of language or the subject of study, can often cause more severe problems as, unlike the learning experience, there is little time to adjust to new conventions and expectations, and of course the consequences can be very far-reaching. Initial tests of language proficiency may deny students a place in higher education or point to the need for further language study, usually in the form of a pre-sessional course. On the other hand, being the imperfect instruments that they are, they may fail to predict very real difficulties that some students will encounter because of their inadequate command of English for academic purposes (EAP). Work that is done at university may be assessed for language (often by non-specialists) as well as for content, and often the label 'inadequate language' is applied when in fact the real issue is not so much one of grammar and vocabulary as of genre and rhetorical structure or inadequate study skills. Students in higher education often need to be able to structure an argument, to criticise a point of view, to evaluate different possibilities, etc. in a way that requires a very sophisticated use of language.

Both in EAP and in other subject areas there has been a growing interest in non-traditional forms of assessment, and students may be expected to play some part in assessing their own work or that of their peers. They often have responsibility for completing a portfolio of work for assessment, or for choosing their best work to submit. These are important areas to consider, as looking through the whole photograph album, as it were, rather than at a single snapshot may help us to form a more accurate assessment of students' achievement and of their abilities. In this context, it is also important to consider students' views of assessment and, as far as possible, to take them into account. Nevertheless, for many international students, adapting to the norms of the host academic community will remain an essential part not only of learning but also of achieving a successful outcome. This is an area in which EAP practitioners are able to give valuable help.

It is a feature of the current state of assessment in EAP that there is a growing division between high-stakes, formal testing for university entry and low-stakes, less formal assessment undertaken in universities for a variety of other reasons. The high-stakes examinations in this field, such as IELTS and TOEFL, now have a prominence and significance they have not had before as an integral part of the university admissions process (see for example, CVCP, 1992). Numbers taking these exams are increasing: a four-fold increase in six years in the case of IELTS (UCLES, 1998: 4). Superficially this area appears very professional. The low-stakes assessment systems appear, by contrast, varied and unfocused, and this is an area Alderson (in this volume) suggests requires attention. It might be more complete and accurate, however, to suggest that both areas deserve closer attention and the papers in this volume are part of such a process.

2. An Overview of EAP Assessment

High-stakes assessment in EAP centres chiefly on IELTS and TOEFL, the two examinations designed explicitly to provide potential students with evidence of their ability in English language for the purposes of academic study. Both have undergone considerable recent change. TOEFL is now available through computer delivery (Educational Testing Service, 1998) and a computerised version of IELTS will be available from 2001 (UCLES, 1999). While there are certain procedural advantages, such as the ability to give all testees a different sequence of questions, the motivation must in no small part be the cost advantages which come from computer delivery and marking. We are led to believe that these developments are simply following the trend in global education. However, EAP teachers will be aware that not all students are *au fait* with computers and it may be important to consider whether some candidates are disadvantaged by computerised tests. Since question forms can be the same as those of the paper tests it is difficult to see any major progress at the level of theory here. Computer testing is an area which deserves closer investigation and Fanning and Hale (in this volume) attempt this.

At the same time as introducing computer testing, IELTS has switched from a situation where it was possible to take an exam which reflected the student's academic specialisation to a single, general series of papers in English for study. This represents a major change. The whole point of having different papers for different disciplines in ELTS and IELTS was the belief that language, and particularly vocabulary, can be highly subject specific and that a student's fitness for study required knowledge of this specialist language. There is anecdotal evidence (Alderson, this volume) that testees taking IELTS have this belief and feel the general IELTS may have been inappropriate. And yet there has been no objection to this change from the EAP community. It is worth asking why, when EAP teaching recognises the value of both English for general academic purposes (EGAP) and English for specific academic purposes (ESAP) (see Blue, 1988), high-stakes EAP testing now seems to find itself firmly in the EGAP camp. We may wonder too why the two predominant examinations in this field are so very different, to the point where very little can be meaningfully compared in tests of concurrent validity (see Bachman et al, 1995). The answers almost certainly lie in the use now made of these tests. The original design of the examinations may have been the product of a concern with content and construct validity (Criper and Davies, 1988) but formal, high-stakes assessment in EAP is now concerned with other things. Some indication of this can be seen in the range of examinations, not necessarily directly related to EAP knowledge, which universities will now accept to satisfy their language requirements (see, for example, Bool et al, 1999). High-stakes formal assessment in EAP now requires institutional and predictive validity. Institutional validity because university admissions departments must have a qualification from a credible institution or organisation to justify the offer of a place. Predictive validity because admissions officers are less concerned with what students know before entry and are more concerned with whether students' examination scores are good predictors of subsequent academic success. It might be thought that this whole area has more an appearance of professionalism and quality than substance. Criper and Davies' conclusion about ELTS (1988: 112) was that it predicted '...as well as (no more than/no better than) other English language proficiency tests ...with r's of about 0.3 for about 10% of variance '. This is extremely modest but not very surprising given that language proficiency tests, even when they appear to test identical qualities of language, often correlate only moderately with one another (see Alderson in this volume for a summary of recent research in this area). Criper and Davies report (1988: 113) that in ELTS a critical point is reached at band 6 since below that level a failure rate of 30% or higher is predicted, but despite this universities can vary their admissions requirements considerably, often below this figure. Universities, it seems, adopt entry qualifications by imitating other universities rather than drawing on empirical evidence (Boldt and Courtney, 1997). Perhaps this is due to a lack of reliable empirical evidence. Only now, for the first time in 10 years, is research into the predictive validity of examination scores being undertaken (for example, Cotton and Conrow, 1998, and Green, this volume).

Low-stakes, less formal assessment is undertaken in and often by universities themselves. It can take many different forms. There are computer tests batteries (for example Fanning and Hale, this volume), pencil and paper tests (Morley, this volume), various forms of continuous assessment including portfolios (Gray and Cresswell, both in this volume) and self-assessment batteries (Freeman and Blue, both in this volume). There are even computer programs, devised at Swansea, which have trained neural networks to grade written assignments in English as a foreign language, which is potentially a huge step forward in the standardisation of assessment of written language. These forms of assessment reflect the many different aims and uses to which they are put. Universities typically need to test for placement on entry, for progress and sponsors' reports, for level (to offer advice to students and departments on remedial work that may be needed), for aptitude (to advise learners and department on subject choice), and to provide feedback to learners (to help them intelligently to plan their own learning). Tests generally need to be easy to use and flexible in delivery. Variety, and increasing variety associated with technical change, are the hallmarks of assessment in this area, and not surprisingly it is difficult to establish hard and fast standards. The first step, as Alderson (this volume) points out, is to be absolutely clear as to the purpose of the tests that are used and the qualities of validity and reliability which the tests have. Too often, as is seen in the high-stakes aspect of EAP testing, tests designed for one purpose are used for another and this is inevitably unsatisfactory. As this volume shows, this is a concern in the EAP profession and efforts are being made to put these problems right.

3. The Papers in this Volume

These papers are a selection from the BALEAP (British Association of Lecturers in English for Academic Purposes) conference held in Swansea in the spring of 1997 with the title *Assessing English for Academic Purposes*, and they consider many issues in both high-stakes and low-stakes assessment. Some of the chapters report on particular work in a local context, whilst others are more general in their scope. All of them, though, are of relevance beyond the particular circumstances in which they were written, and they should inform good practice not only in the United Kingdom but anywhere where students receive part or all of their higher education in a language other than their mother tongue. The papers are divided under five headings: Language testing in an EAP context; Language testing in EAP departments; the Requirements of different academic departments and institutions; Non-traditional forms of assessment; and Students' views of assessment.

3.1 Language testing in an EAP context

The first section deals with language testing in an EAP context. Charles Alderson opens the section with an overarching view of testing in EAP, discussing the purpose of different tests (proficiency, progress, achievement, ...) and traditional concepts of validity. EAP testing is put into its historical context and a comprehensive overview of current research, especially that surrounding IELTS, is provided. Finally, Alderson calls for more development of progress and achievement tests and counsels against the misuse of proficiency tests to measure progress or achievement.

This provides an essential backdrop to the other two chapters in this section, which investigate specific tests. Morley examines the Chaplen Test, which has been in use since its development in the late 1960s. The issue of validity is considered, and results of the discrete item grammar and vocabulary test are compared with holistic scores given for writing continuous prose. It is concluded that, with some provisos, the Chaplen test can still have a part to play in the testing of newly arrived international students. In contrast Fanning and Hale's chapter on the use of the UCLES Computer Adaptive Test examines state-of-the-art assessment. Although there are weaknesses in the test, which they discuss in some detail, there are also many advantages in using a computer adaptive test for screening or placement purposes.

3.2 Assessment and the requirements of academic departments

The second and third sections of the book deal with the requirements of different academic institutions and departments. The second section focuses specifically on language assessment, whilst the third section takes a broader look at the requirements of academic departments. Section Two starts with Daborn and Calderwood's discussion of written reports in Electrical Engineering. They compare the grading criteria used by English language tutors with those of the Electronics and Electrical Engineering staff and then examine the scores given to both home and international students by the two sets of staff. This kind of collaboration is an important part of good EAP practice and is seen to be of benefit in this case to EAP staff, engineering staff and, above all, students.

Of course, it is not only international students who have difficulty in using language accurately and appropriately in academic contexts. In Cutting's chapter the writing of international and home students is examined, focusing particularly on the types of errors that they make. Although international students tend to make different errors from home students it is concluded that high-flying international students can in some cases outperform their British peers, even when the latter are students of Linguistics!

The third section of the book looks in more detail at the requirements of academic departments. Hartill's chapter, which is in many ways central to the theme of the book, challenges the *status quo* and reports on a research project to determine what are the assessment tasks that postgraduate students can expect to encounter during their studies, and what are the expectations of staff in different departments. Although this chapter lends some support to established EAP practice there are also a few surprises as assessment patterns can vary considerably between different disciplines.

Green's chapter is also very wide-ranging in its scope, as the experiences of students who have taken a pre-sessional EAP course are described once they have embarked upon their main studies. Green investigates whether pre-sessional grades are a good predictor of academic success, considering academic tutors' assessment of students, students' self-assessment and final degree results. The factors that have helped or hindered academic performance are also investigated.

Errey's chapter focuses on a narrower area, specifically what academic assessors expect of their students' writing in different subject areas. A number of factors relating both to content and to language are investigated and it is concluded that, although there are certain common trends, there seems to be considerable variation in what is acceptable in different subject areas and possibly even by different assessors within the same subject area. Sensitising both EAP specialists and other subject specialists to this variation may help not only in raising awareness but also in bringing about a greater degree of consistency and, above all, making the criteria more explicit for the students.

In the final chapter of this section Meldrum turns her attention to an area that many international students find extremely difficult: being critical of their own and other work in their fields. Teaching students how to think analytically and critically, and also how to express their criticism appropriately, form important components of much EAP work, and it is therefore fitting that the ability to criticise should form part of the assessment in EAP as well as in the disciplines concerned.

3.3 Non-traditional forms of assessment

The fourth section of the book considers a number of non-traditional forms of assessment. Gray's chapter provides an overview, relating trends in assessment to trends in education more generally. The effects that alternative approaches to learning have had on assessment are examined, including collaborative learning, working on e-mail, resource-based learning, focusing on skills, competencies, abilities and capabilities rather than, or as well as, knowledge. A number of learner-centred approaches to assessment are explored, especially projects, group work, portfolios and learner diaries.

Portfolio-based assessment is considered in much greater detail in the next chapter by Cresswell, who sees it as an important way of bringing about a closer correspondence between teaching and assessment. A pilot project to explore the feasibility of portfolio assessment on a full-time EAP course is described, addressing many of the issues which need resolution here. Although there are a number of questions that have yet to be resolved, portfolio-based assessment shows great promise in assessing the process that students go through in writing and charting the progress that they make.

The last two chapters in this section deal with self-assessment, a form of assessment that has for many years appeared to have great potential yet one which is still relatively untried in terms of mainstream assessment. Freeman describes a self-assessment instrument based on communicative 'can-do' scales. His trialling of the instrument with British and international students leads him to claim that it demonstrates adequate reliability and validity, and he suggests that it could be used primarily to guide students in their learning, helping them to formulate and develop their own goals. Blue's chapter is more sceptical. Although convinced of the usefulness of self-assessment, Blue is much less convinced of its accuracy. Data drawn from a much wider range of national and cultural backgrounds result in different conclusions as to the accuracy and reliability of self-assessment. Nevertheless it is accepted that self-assessment can be very useful as a way of guiding students in their learning, encouraging them to think about their strengths and weaknesses and playing an important role in defining learners' needs.

3.4 Students' views of assessment

Assessment is often viewed as something that is done *to* students, not generally *by* them and not necessarily *for* their benefit. It is important, therefore, to redress the balance, and the final section considers students' views of assessment. Atherton reports on a study that has been carried out with international students, investigating their attitudes towards feedback and error correction. It is shown that students are generally aware of their areas of difficulty and are very appreciative of all forms of feedback (including correction of errors) that help them to identify their weaknesses. However, they do not appear to work systematically through the feedback that they receive in order to learn from it. Atherton therefore suggests a strategy for helping students to take more note of the feedback that they receive and to self-correct or proof-read their own writing more effectively.

The final chapter, by Jordan, reports on a survey of students' attitudes towards assessment in EAP. He asks about the types of assessment that students prefer, what they think should be assessed, when assessment should take place, how long tests should be, what is the purpose of assessment and how useful it is. Of course, students' views and attitudes have to be weighed carefully against those of the experts. Nevertheless, Jordan concludes, and this is a fitting conclusion to the book as a whole, that we should pay more attention to students' opinions and, very importantly, that our assessment procedures should be carefully explained to the students.

4. Conclusion

This collection ranges over a wide variety of topics in the assessment of EAP, and although there is no particular 'party line' that emerges there are a number of common threads running through the book. In particular, it aims to define and to demonstrate good practice in all the different facets of EAP assessment, both high-stakes and low-stakes. As EAP practitioners we aim to help students to deal with all the requirements of assessment, whether on their language courses or in their study of other disciplines, whether it is the language or the content that is being assessed. In order to do this we often need to help students to adapt to the Western academic culture in which assessment takes place and to the specific requirements of their discipline. As EAP specialists we cannot afford to work in isolation (or in ignorance) and it is very important to maintain close contact with our colleagues in other disciplines and to be sensitive to the experience and the opinions of our students. Equally important is the need to sensitise our colleagues in other departments as to the requirements and the limitations of the overseas students they tutor. It is the hope of all the contributors that this volume will clarify thinking on assessment in EAP and that many of the approaches described will provide models that can be replicated or modified for use in other contexts.

References

Bachman L F, F Davidson, K Ryan and I-C Choi (1995) *Studies in Language Testing 1: An investigation into the comparability of two tests of English as a foreign language*, Cambridge: Cambridge University Press

Blue G M (1988) 'Individualising academic writing tuition', in Robinson P (ed) *Academic Writing: Process and product*, Oxford: Modern English Publications in association with the British Council

Bool H, D Dunmore and A Tonkyn (1999) *The BALEAP Guidelines on English Language Proficiency Levels for International Applicants to UK Universities*, BALEAP Occasional Paper, March 1999

Boldt R F and R G Courtney (1997) *Survey of Standards for Foreign Student Applicants*, TOEFL Research Report RR-57, August 1997, Princeton: Educational Testing Service

Cotton F and F Conrow (1998) 'An investigation into the predictive validity of IELTS amongst a group of international students studying at the University of Tasmania', *IELTS Research Reports*, Volume 1, ELICOS Association and IELTS Australia Ltd

Criper C and A Davies (1988) *ELTS Validation Project Report*, Research Report 1(i), Cambridge: The British Council and the University of Cambridge Local Examinations Syndicate

CVCP (1992) *The Management of Higher Degrees Undertaken by Overseas Students*, CVCP Guidance document, September 1992

Educational Testing Service (1998) *Computer-Based TOEFL Score User Guide*, Princeton: Educational Testing Service

UCLES (1998) *IELTS Annual Review 1997/98*, Cambridge: University of Cambridge Local Examinations Syndicate

UCLES (1999) *IELTS Annual Review 1998/99*, Cambridge: University of Cambridge Local Examinations Syndicate

Part One:

Language Testing in an EAP Context

J Charles Alderson

Testing in EAP: Progress? Achievement? Proficiency?

1. Introduction

In this paper I discuss traditional concepts of validity and test purpose, and begin to problematise these, both by reference to case studies relevant to the testing of EAP, and by reference to developing theory in educational measurement and associated research. I shall discuss cases of test misuse: where proficiency tests are used to measure achievement or even progress, and argue that increasing pressures of accountability and value for money on EAP programmes run the danger that tests will increasingly be misused in the future. I will suggest that as a profession, EAP specialists need to pay much more attention to the measurement of progress and achievement, not only for accountability purposes, but also for professional reasons. I begin with a practical example of test use.

In the mid-1970s I was an impoverished PhD student in Edinburgh, and one way I earned some extra cash was by administering tests on language improvement programmes. This was usually at the request of the programme organiser, who also specified which test was to be used. The most frequently requested test was the English Proficiency Test Battery – EPTB, or the Davies test. It was probably the most frequently requested, not simply because three versions of the test had been developed at Edinburgh, but because it was the best known English language proficiency test in the 1970s – it was to be replaced as a screening test for English-medium study by the ELTS test in 1980. In other words, it was a proficiency test, with a very similar purpose to that of the current IELTS test, however different its content and method. However, I was required to administer it as a measure of learning during language programmes: a pre-test was given at the beginning of the programme, and a post-test – sometimes the same test, sometimes a different version – at the end. The courses varied between one and two months in length, and with hindsight the results were not surprising: average gains were very small, largely uninterpretable, and many students – up to a quarter, as I recall – showed no gains at all, or even regression. The backsliding I glibly explained as being due to the standard error of measurement – no test is 100% reliable – but of course I might equally validly have explained small *gain* scores as due to unreliability!

Sponsors were disappointed by the small amount of improvement, and I came to explain this, to myself at least, as due to the stability of the trait of proficiency. I argued that proficiency tests were intended to measure a trait which was relatively stable, at least over relatively short periods of time, certainly for learners who had been studying the language already for several years, as most EPTB candidates indeed had. Since the test was often administered up to nine months in advance of a student coming to the UK, it should not be susceptible to short-term changes, but should instead faithfully reflect the level of proficiency that a student might be expected to have on entry to a UK university. In other words, EPTB was designed as a proficiency test, by sampling across a wide range of language, and by being aimed at a very heterogeneous group of students, and was highly unsuitable for use as a measure of achievement. With the best of intentions, the test had been misused.

Why? Partly because it was felt important to use well-known measures rather than home-grown ones. This is what Davies (1982) called institutional validity: if a test is associated with a prestigious institution or name, it will be preferred to another, less well-known one that may be more appropriate. Partly because nobody really understood the differences between proficiency tests and achievement tests in terms of sensitivity to gain: indeed, I am not sure we fully understand this even now. And partly, and importantly in the context of BALEAP, because it was available. Other tests were not. There simply were no tests of achievement geared to the particular learning circumstances of the students I was testing. And, of course, sponsors were not willing to pay to get one developed. (I shall return to this, but they were, almost by definition in setting up the courses, willing to pay for the development or aggregation of suitable learning materials.

But not tests. Why, they might have argued, are they necessary? We have the Davies test!)

2. Test Purpose: Axioms

It is commonplace in language testing to say that a test can be valid for one purpose, but not another. Thus a test may be designed to measure whether students have sufficient English to study in an English-medium university, and yet it would be quite inappropriate to use such a test to measure how much students have learned on a given syllabus. Achievement tests are typically designed to measure how much of a syllabus a learner has mastered, and thus they are only valid to the extent to which the content of the test matches the content of the syllabus. A placement test is typically designed to see where in an institutional curriculum a learner might most appropriately be entered, but to use such a test to measure what a student has learned after placement would almost certainly under-represent learning and achievement.

Test validity is classically defined as the extent to which a test measures what it is intended to measure. The intention of the test designer may, however, not always be quite so clear cut: what is the intention of UCLES's FCE? It is presumably not designed to be a measure of achievement within a specific syllabus or institutional context, since it is offered world-wide in a large variety of different contexts. Is it then a proficiency test, intended to see how much language a student has for a given purpose? Since it is not claimed to relate to the world of work, or the world of higher education, it is hard to see how such predictive power could be claimed. Indeed, its likeliest purpose might be defined as to establish whether students have achieved the level of FCE. In other words, it could be said to have no particular purpose, other than to define a level of achievement/proficiency, but defined not in terms of any curriculum, but in terms of its own specifications, and internally justified largely in terms of its relation to other tests in the same series: easier than CAE, harder than PET. How then might be the validity of such a purposeless test be established? In content terms, presumably, by showing that the test covers relevant aspects of English at the appropriate level, which is hopefully defined in the test specifications. In empirical terms, presumably, by showing that the test is harder than PET but easier than CAE, by giving students both (or all three) tests. Or by showing that students perform on this test similarly to the way they perform on an equivalent, non-UCLES test. The problem is, of course, which measure is that? How do we know that it is equivalent, especially if it cannot be shown to meet the same purpose (which in the case of FCE is undefined)? Of course, given that there is an enormous textbook publication industry surrounding FCE, then perhaps the test's validity is established by matching the test to the textbooks. This creates a curious circularity, however, since the textbooks were no doubt created to match the test, and so if the test's content and method do not match the textbooks, is that because of poor test design, or poor textbook design? In short, whilst the relation between validity and purpose is clear theoretically, and purpose must be paramount, in practice it is often hard to decide how best to validate a test against its purpose.

3. Traditional Validities

Traditionally, it has been commonplace to distinguish five different types of validity: face, content, construct, concurrent and predictive (although face validity was frequently dismissed as not really validity – what Doug Stevenson (1985) called pop validity – that is, beliefs about a test held by people who know nothing about testing). These four or five validities were typically associated with certain distinct test purposes: proficiency tests had to predict future performance and so they needed predictive validity; achievement tests had to cover a syllabus and so they needed content validity; aptitude tests were based on a theory of language learning and so they needed construct validity, and so on. Distinctions were typically made between *a priori* and *a posteriori* (Weir, 1983) validities, with face and content seen as being established *a priori* – that is, in advance of a test ever having been administered – whereas empirical validities required performance on a test to be recorded and compared with performance on some other measure, be it a test, an attitude questionnaire, a teacher's assessment, and so on. Whilst this distinction was clear in theory, in practice it was recognised that the gathering of appropriate criteria against which to measure the test in question was not so straightforward: another 'valid' test may not exist, teachers' assessments may have doubtful reliability or objectivity, the accuracy of self-assessments is known to vary by the culture of the learner and by their level of proficiency, and so on. In other words, finding criteria against which to judge an unknown test that were themselves criterial – that is, in which we could have faith – was far from easy.

We see, then, that concepts taken as basic and axiomatic in testing are in fact rather difficult to pin down when we look at specific and familiar examples. Recently, testing theorists have begun to re-examine familiar concepts in the light of some of the inadequacies discovered in practice, and have refined them somewhat. Before going into detail of the changes in theory, let me illustrate with the case of an EAP placement test.

Wall et al (1994) illustrate the difficulty of validating a test by describing a case study of an attempt to establish the value (if not validity) of a placement test for EAP courses at the Institute for English Language Education in Lancaster. We gathered data on the relationship between the test and the teaching programme, teachers' and students' assessments of students' reading, writing, listening and speaking abilities, students' comments on the relationship between their placement test scores and their abilities, and their opinions of the test, student take-up of and attendance at the courses to which the test had assigned them, language teachers' views on whether students were well placed, and subject department tutors' of students' abilities. All these data were related to students' placement test scores, and the placement test itself was analysed in terms of internal reliability, inter-subtest relationships, item performance and marker reliability. We also attempted comparisons with students' performances on other language tests they happened to have taken (IELTS and TOEFL). One problem we had was the lack of convincing external evidence against which to validate the test. Few students had taken the same test in advance of attending the course, so the sample size for any comparison was small. In addition, the language teachers' and subject tutors' judgements were necessarily gathered several months after the test had been administered, and were therefore likely to have related to a different proficiency than that measured in the test, and in any case it was unclear that such opinions are the best basis for judgements about the quality of the test.

What we show, I believe, is that no one criterion can be seen to be more important than another, or, rather, that no one piece of validity evidence is strikingly more convincing than any other. Correlations are unsurprisingly moderate, opinions vary, or are very difficult to gather at an appropriate time from suitable informants, and so on. The real world is messier than theory leads us to expect and we conclude in the paper that we had done all we possibly could to gather suitable evidence for our test's validity, but that the evidence we had gathered was difficult to interpret, and certainly not overwhelmingly supporting any claim that our test is the best placement test ever. The most we could claim is that we had failed to uncover evidence that the test was seriously inaccurate or inappropriate, and most evidence provided moderate support for its validity. The test is still used!

What we had done, in a rather constrained and semi-rigorous way perhaps, is seek multiple sources of evidence for validity. Rather than taking one sort of validity as supremely important, we recognised the practical if not theoretical difficulty of clearly and uncontroversially establishing validity evidence, and so sought evidence from as many sources as was possible.

4. Construct Validity and Multiple Perspectives

What we had done corresponds, roughly, to what theorists now call construct validation. Construct validity used to be seen as the extent to which a test is based on an appropriate theory (in this case, of language). How it was to be measured was always something of a problem. By inspection, if we had a clearly operationalisable theory like language aptitude, often taken to consist of traits like sensitivity to sound differences, sensitivity to grammatical form, ability to remember unknown words, and so on. By statistical means, if possible: multi-trait, multi-method convergent-divergent validation was one such statistical technique used in the 1980s, where fairly sophisticated analyses were conducted to see whether tests that in theory ought to relate to each other did in fact so relate more than to tests that in theory were distinct. In practice, however, such studies were hard to carry out for operational tests (rather than as doctoral theses) and were rarely done.

Recent conceptions of construct validity see it, however, not as one sort of validity in parallel to the other ones I have briefly discussed, but rather as an overarching concept, with different sorts of empirical evidence being eligible to support or question its existence. What is most important is that the test should be theoretically sound: it should be shown to be based on appropriate theory, it should therefore have appropriate statistical properties consistent with that theory, it should adequately cover the construct being measured and not omit significant or important elements of that construct (construct under-representation, in the jargon), and scores on the test should not be contaminated by irrelevant abilities or knowledge (construct irrelevance).

All well and good, no doubt, and not radically different, despite the jargon, from what was believed, if not practised in the past. What is different is that any and all sources of evidence for construct validity, be they from a content, concurrent, predictive or other perspective, are now seen as contributing to a test's validity. There is no one best validity any more than there is one best test or best test method. The responsibility of test developers now is therefore to gather all available evidence to support the case for a test's validity.

It follows from this that no one traditional validity is adequate on its own. This is especially true of face validity since it represents only one (albeit according to some people powerful, according to others trivial) source of evidence. Communicative language testers like Keith Morrow and Brendan Carroll used to delight in outraging conservative testers like me by declaring that face and predictive validity are the only two validities that matter. Allwright and Banerjee (1997) show that predictive validity is itself highly problematic, and so from a

Morrow or Carroll perspective, that would leave us only with face validity to trust. (Actually, Keith Morrow (1986) declared that washback validity was the most important validity of a test, but I shall return to this concept shortly in order to argue that washback validity is a nonsense, and is based upon a hugely naive misunderstanding of human motivation and attitude.)

5. Face Validity

I have argued, with my colleagues Dianne Wall and Caroline Clapham (Alderson et al, 1995) that traditional views of face validity, such as those represented by Doug Stevenson (op cit), are probably overstated and need problematising. Testing experts used to dismiss face validity, as I have already said, by claiming that it simply represents beliefs about a test held by people who know nothing about testing. To put it more charitably, face validity is the lay person's version of content validity. If a test appears to be valid, from a superficial inspection, to people who are not experts (interestingly often defined as including students and teachers, and not just the general public) then it has mere face validity. Alderson et al (1995) argue that such opinions may actually be important to other aspects of test validity: in particular to response validity. If learners think a test looks like a sensible test, they are arguably more likely to put effort into taking the test, they will take it more seriously, and therefore the ability the test measures will be more likely to reflect the learners' best efforts, or as Swain (1985) put it, the test will bias for best.

Actually, this is an assertion on our part: a statement of belief, albeit plausible, and one for which we have little evidence. We would probably argue, for example, that the IELTS test looks like an EAP test appropriate for its intended purpose, and therefore students will take it more seriously. Anecdotally, I have found that overseas students coming to Lancaster are actually rather critical of the IELTS as a result of the experience of taking it, because they found the listening test too fast, or the reading texts too remote from their own interests or subject areas: in short, because they do not feel they have been best measured by the test. Whether this is affected by the appearance of the test is hard to determine, and a useful research study would investigate that systematically. My usual counter is the lame one: well, surely it looks more like a test of EAP than TOEFL? In other words, I counter their face validity arguments by other face validity arguments. However, perhaps we need to reconceptualise the students' reactions as being something other than face validity. Since they have the experience of taking the test, are they not arguably at least as well-informed as an expert in testing who may not have actually taken the test under operational conditions, and for whom the test was not intended in the first place? In which case, perhaps their reactions are truly response validity, or at least responses in the light of responding to items and tasks, and not just superficial inspections.

Perhaps we should investigate the bases for such (student *and* teacher) judgements: there is evidence that students might be more influenced by the perceived difficulty of tasks and tests than by their content (which is what is normally, at least implicitly, alluded to in discussions of face validity). Watanabe (1997) found that students do not prepare for those aspects of the Japanese university entrance exams that they perceive as undiscriminating, that is, those that are either too easy (often the listening tests) or those that are too difficult, or those that they consider to be insufficiently weighted to make any difference to the outcome anyway (for example, the famous paper-and-pencil pronunciation tests). Lewkowicz (1996) found to her surprise that her Hong Kong students thought that a practice TOEFL test corresponded more to what they thought an EAP test ought to measure than did a test which was designed by their own EAP teachers to reflect the curriculum as closely as possible. Authenticity, in this case, had to be redefined in relation to who was making the judgements of authenticity, and those judges' expectations of what a good language test should contain (as well, arguably, as their views on what sort of test they might be better able to pass). Indeed, it is conceivable that the consequences of the test to the test-taker will be more important than any consideration of test method or test content, much less of whether the test is based on an appropriate theory, and may well have powerful effects on response validity – as yet unresearched, albeit frequently asserted. Alderson and Hamp-Lyons (1996) report teachers believing that they have to teach TOEFL classes the way they do because 'students expect it that way'. However, interviews with students revealed quite different views on the most appropriate way to prepare for TOEFL, including such unexpected things as going to the movies, having American friends, and using the library a lot.

In other words, face validity is probably a more complex matter than used to be thought, and it needs further problematisation and investigation. However, under the new conceptualisation of construct validity, it would still not be sufficient to rely solely on face validity evidence, however reconceptualised, in order to assert a test's validity. All possible sources of evidence would need to be gathered, and this would include statistical data as well as judgemental data and data gathered by more qualitative means (like test-taker introspections, and the like).

A recent study of the claims of face validity and their relation to construct validity is a PhD thesis at La Trobe by Anh (1997). In brief, Anh investigates the rival claims of TOEFL and IELTS, or, more accurately, the proponents of the tests, and the language testing traditions they are based upon. She argues that authenticity, however this is defined (and she uses Bachman's 1990 situational and interactional distinction to good effect), is not the same as validity. Authenticity may be a desirable component of test content, according to some proponents, and depending upon how it is defined, but it is not the same thing as test validity.

Anh (1997) reports a study in Vietnam, where apparently teachers and others find themselves in two different camps: those who favour a TOEFL or American-type approach to EAP testing and those who favour an IELTS or British-type approach (the polarisation is an exaggeration, of course). She found that the Reading test of IELTS correlated at only a moderate .5005 (n=300) with the Reading (and vocabulary) component of TOEFL. Her factor analyses showed more overlap across the two tests, especially in reading and vocabulary (IELTS summary completion and TOEFL vocabulary) but there was evidence that whereas TOEFL measured reading for main idea, details and inferences, IELTS did not, showing however a distinct 'ability to read numbers and statistics' factor. One interpretation is that this is a passage effect; the other is that whereas TOEFL appears to measure reading ability broadly defined, IELTS shows both method and text effects, despite, or maybe because of, the difference in 'authenticity'. In short, Anh (1997) shows the value of empirical analyses of test comparisons, and the danger of relying upon impressions of text and task authenticity as indicating 'validity'.

Griffin (1990) reports correlations of TOEFL with the IELTS reading modules at surprisingly high levels: '.804 (n=66); .879 (n=15) .866 (n=21) and .704 (n=18) for modules A, B, and C respectively (sic)' (cited in Anh, 1997). Anh quotes Griffin as saying: 'The evidence is encouraging for the IELTS battery in terms of criterion validity. It is clear that IELTS is measuring language proficiency in the same domain measured by similar test batteries' (Anh, 1997: 117). As Anh points out, however, given the differences in construct and subject specificity, these correlations are worrisomely high.

Buell (1992) compares the reading sections of TOEFL and IELTS (Module C). TOEFL and IELTS seemed to be more similar than they look: r = .554 (n=68). Despite predictions that IELTS would correlate better with teachers' ratings than would TOEFL, the correlations were in fact remarkably similar (TOEFL: teachers' ratings = .499; IELTS and teachers' ratings = .516).

Geranpayeh (1994) shows correlations for the complete IELTS with TOEFL total as .667, (n=103), for students who were familiar with TOEFL, and .829 (n=113), for students who were unfamiliar with either test. Interestingly, this study showed a differential test preparation effect: for students familiar with TOEFL (who had taken TOEFL preparation courses) band 6 on IELTS was shown to be equivalent to TOEFL 600, whereas for students unfamiliar with either test, 6 on IELTS was equivalent to 550 on TOEFL. Geranpayeh concluded that 'score comparisons across TOEFL and IELTS are possible', although he warned of the possible effects of test preparation on test performance (Anh, 1997: 120).

Criper and Davies (1988) report correlations of .81 (n=435) between overall ELTS and EPTB (Version D), despite the low (.41 – .44) correlations between cloze and grammar and M1 (Study Skills = Reading, or G1 (Grammar in continuous text) at .57 and .61 respectively. They also report correlations of ELBA and ELTS Total as roughly .77, and ELBA Reading with ELTS M1 (Study Skills) as

.50 and with ELTS G1 (Reading) as .69. Despite intentions, the relationship between the new ELTS and the old discrete-point language-focused EPTB and ELBA is surprisingly high.

The draft IELTS grammar test also showed remarkably high correlations with Reading: between .64 and .76, whereas the different reading modules correlated with each other at roughly the same levels: between .59 and .74. Indeed, the correlations between supposedly parallel tests within each subject module (A, B and C) at .64, .69 and .81) were in some cases lower than the correlation of the reading test with a grammar test. Alderson (1993) concludes that 'the relationship between the new grammar test and the new reading test is at least as close as that between the new reading test and the old reading test!' (p. 215). 'Such a result must begin to cast doubt on the separability of reading tests from grammar tests' (loc cit).

Clapham and Alderson (1997) report correlations between the old ELTS test and the IELTS which relaced it, as being surprisingly low. Of course, the two tests were different in the sense that the Study Skills/Reading modules in particular are designed for a wider audience in the case of the IELTS. However, a correlation of .39 between ELTS Study Skills Physical Sciences and IELTS Reading Physical Sciences and Technology, shows little parallelism. Although the correlation of ELTS Social Sciences Study Skills and IELTS Reading Business and Social Sciences is much more encouraging, at .76, the latter Reading module correlates almost exactly the same (.75) with the old ELTS Grammar test (labelled Reading), with which it is not supposed to be parallel. Interestingly, the new IELTS Module A correlated at .53 with the ELTS Total, yet IELTS Module C correlated at .80. The low correlation can be taken as evidence of lack of parallelism, that is, lack of validity, or as evidence for the validity of a largely revised IELTS. However, the opposite is the case for IELTS Module C: the high correlation, suggesting closeness between the two, could be evidence of the lack of need for a new IELTS, or for concurrent validity of the new test compared with the old one, since both are intended to do a similar job.

In short, it will be apparent from these studies that the establishment of test validity is no simple matter, that frequently conflicting results will appear, that tests which might be thought to be different may in reality be more similar than anticipated, and judgement will always have to be called upon in order to balance or weight evidence from different perspectives. Construct validation involves the careful and systematic gathering of evidence from all possible angles, not just the accumulation of opinions and prejudices. Above all, test validation implies the suspension of prejudice in the hope of its confirmation but in the expectation of the unexpected.

In the real world, much of this may seem unrealistic. Who has time to gather so much evidence, from so many angles, in the expectation of being proved wrong anyway? Despite the obvious and important practical and logistical constraints (which can however be exaggerated and used as an excuse for inaction rather than seeking to overcome the constraints), it is clear that test developers have an ethical and professional duty to ensure that they investigate as fully as possible the validity of any test that has important consequences for test-takers. Paradoxically however, much of this evidence can only become available once the test is in use. It is impossible to gather data on a test's impact before it has actually been given the opportunity to create impact – that is, be used. Whilst concurrent validity evidence may be available during the trialling stage of test development, predictive validity evidence is unlikely to be available until after the test is used operationally, and (as Allwright and Banerjee, 1997, show) test researchers then face the problem of truncated samples, namely that the only students they are able to follow up in predictive validation are those who have 'passed' the test, not those who have 'failed' it and therefore whose lives have already been affected. The fact is that it is impossible fully to establish the validity of a test before it is introduced. Further validation will always be needed once a test has been introduced. Responsible test developers obviously should not launch a test whose reliability is known to be doubtful or whose validity is suspect, especially if it is a high stakes test; but ultimately testers necessarily take a leap of faith in putting their test into operation. They gather the best evidence they can at the time, and then reach a judgement as to when a test can safely be launched. What is of crucial importance is the establishment of a test monitoring function, to enable ongoing evidence to be gathered as to the test's validity in operation. I shall shortly illustrate this with the IELTS test.

6. Validation and Test Use: Consequential Validity and Washback

But first I shall introduce and discuss a second new aspect of the theorizing of test validity, and that is the development of the notion of consequential validity. Unlike construct validation, which I have argued is essentially a development from long-standing concerns for the relation of evidence for validity to test purpose, the development of the notion of consequential validity is recent. Morrow first coined the phrase 'washback validity' in 1986 (to my knowledge), and Frederiksen and Collins first used a similar concept, which they called 'systemic validity', in 1989. The term 'consequential validity' has been developed in the past few years, and it is currently being used a great deal, especially in the USA, in contexts where performance-based assessment is influential. (Interestingly we have here a belated echo in general education of the phenomenon in language testing in the UK in the 1980s, where it was argued that communicative tests – being performance-based – were automatically more valid than traditional tests, and had more beneficial washback – assertions yet to be substantiated. It is a pity that the US performance testing movement has not looked more critically at its British antecedents!)

The notion of consequential validity is intended explicitly to focus test developers' minds on the consequences of their instruments: the uses to which they are put, the impact they have, and the consequences of the test for test users. Whilst in need of further refinement, the focus on consequences and use is a salutary reminder of the dangers of test misuse, and reflects a growing concern among measurement specialists for the ethics of testing, the need to develop codes of practice for fair testing, and the need for better definitions of what is meant by fairness. This debate is very current: some holding that validity itself encompasses fairness, if not always explicitly, and others arguing that fairness goes beyond traditional validity to include issues like gender, linguistic or ethnic bias. I will not enter the debate here, other than to say that it is a healthy issue to be discussing, and it should be encouraging for anybody who uses tests, not just those who develop or research them, that testers are debating such concerns.

However, whilst not wishing to diminish the importance of the debate, having introduced the notion of consequential validity, I need to problematise it, as it seems to me to be in need of further development. At present, there is a risk among some testers, and the wider applied linguistic audience, of an uncritical, politically correct adoption of the term 'consequential validity'.

Tests have consequences: the existence of consequences is undeniable, and hardly controversial. Tests are often designed because consequences are needed: access to higher education has to be limited, and thus those who fail the test suffer the consequences of the decision to have a test. Achievement tests are designed to measure what students have learned, and if students cannot be shown to have learned what should have been learned, there are consequences for the student, the teacher, the institution and indeed society at large. Society decides that it needs tests, or decides that it does not (as in the case of the new South Africa, where the use of tests to select for entry to higher education has been severely restricted recently). Such decisions are often taken because of restricted resources, but also for ideological reasons, or reasons of social engineering. Opinions on the desirability of test use will vary, and will rarely be uncontroversial. The test developer's job is to develop the best possible instrument for the purpose for which society has decided it needs a test. Not all test consequences are life-threatening or associated with gate-keeping encounters, but many are, and such high-stakes tests should be all the more open to scrutiny and criticism. Low-stakes tests undoubtedly also exist, and may have consequences, which are by definition not life-threatening. However, not unreasonably, high-stakes tests command the greatest share of resources for test development and validation, and so low-stakes tests are less frequently scrutinised, criticised or even validated. This is of course a great pity, because there is probably a great deal to be learned about test development, and the relation between language and learning theory and tests as operationalisations of these, in low-stakes settings, where the minimal consequences do not risk distortion of test performance by cheating, test preparation practices, and the like. I have long lamented the lack of attention paid to the development of achievement and progress tests, and will come back to this in the BALEAP context, but if such tests do not have important consequences, they will not get much attention, and therefore will command few resources for their development – and our knowledge of what gets learned in EAP programmes will be all the poorer for such lack of attention and development.

To summarise, I agree that tests have consequences. The question is whether test developers are responsible for these, or 'society'. I do not believe that test developers can be held responsible for the consequences of their instruments, unless these can be clearly shown to relate to the design of the test and associated procedures. I maintain that it is the developers' task to produce the best possible instrument in the circumstances for the purposes for which it is intended. They may even be justified in issuing warnings of test misuse – although this rarely happens at present. However, I find it hard to envisage a situation where test developers can *prevent* their instrument being misused, and therefore I find it unreasonable to hold test developers responsible for misuse.

Yet since validity is a property of test design, this is precisely what the concept of consequential validity proposes: test consequences are seen as part of test design, and I disagree. This is far too simplistic. Tests can be misused, and unforeseen consequences can ensue. Yet I cannot imagine a test developer knowingly designing a test to have undesirable consequences, or knowingly encouraging its misuse, even for the basest of commercial reasons. If such happens, it should of course be exposed, and the test developer should be warned accordingly. If steps are not taken to prevent such misuse, by changing the test design, then clearly the developer is culpable. However, I still have difficulty in seeing this as part of test validity rather than the encouragement of misuse.

Recent years have seen a rapid growth in washback studies: studies of the supposed impact of tests on teaching, as part of a larger notion of test impact on a variety of layers of society. What has already clearly emerged from the empirical studies of supposed washback is that nothing is as simple as is claimed. The effect of tests on teaching that has been researched has been shown, fairly convincingly to me, to vary. It varies according to content and method – tests seems to impact more on what teachers teach than on how they teach it (Alderson and Wall, 1993). It varies according to teacher – some teachers change how they teach to accommodate the test, in some sense; others do not (Alderson and Hamp-Lyons, 1996). Some teachers teach their regular classes as if they were test preparation classes, others change the way they teach in test preparation classes in comparison with normal classes.

A particularly interesting facet of this teacher effect appears to be that not all teachers know why they change the way they teach. Some may have given it serious thought, and have good pedagogic or professional reasons for doing what they do in test preparation. The evidence we have gathered (Alderson and Hamp-Lyons, 1996), however, suggests that many teachers have *not* given much thought to the most appropriate way to teach towards a test, indeed many have given *no* thought to that, and simply assume that the best way is test practice, lectures on grammar, perfunctory provision of correct answers, and so on.

Test preparation textbooks give few methodological rationales or even guidelines (Hamp-Lyons, in preparation); teacher training courses rarely give teachers advice on how best to prepare their students for tests, even high-stakes tests. The overall impression one gets is that the language education profession as a whole has given little or no thought to such matters. Yet if passing a test like TOEFL is the most important thing that a student can do, surely we need to be more professional than this and offer students the best possible way of preparing to take such tests. The evidence is that this is simply ignored. When teachers were asked (Alderson and Hamp-Lyons, 1996) what they liked most about teaching TOEFL, a common answer was: not having to prepare lessons, and not having to mark homework. Imagine: teachers like best those lessons they do not have to think about in advance and where they do not need to give learners feedback on what they have learned! Hardly the hallmark of professional responsibility.

Yet can the TOEFL test itself be blamed for this? Can poor or unthought-through test preparation practices be the fault of ETS? Surely not. Surely the individual teacher or teaching institution bears the greatest responsibility for this. You might want to argue that the TOEFL programme might at least give teachers advice on the best way to prepare students for their tests and this would certainly be an interesting and doubtless lucrative research project. But I still resist the notion that ETS have damaged the validity of their test by not providing advice on test preparation.

Where test preparation practices can be evidentially linked to the design of the test and associated procedures (rather than to lack of thought on the part of teachers, or other factors unrelated to test design), one could argue that better test design should be attempted in order to influence the test preparation practices. However, even this position is a statement of belief, and is not based upon much empirical evidence that better test preparation practice will result. Wall (1996) shows clearly that attempts at inducing better test preparation practice by improving test design were naively (rather than ill-) conceived simply because they took no account of the nature of innovation, and what makes people, including teachers, change their behaviour. She briefly discusses the innovation literature in order to argue that what brings about successful change has much more to do with contextual factors, than with test design. The degree of understanding that teachers have of the nature of the test, the amount of support and advice they are given on how to proceed, the extent to which they own the innovation and feel responsible for its success, the origin of the innovation and its subsequent ownership: all these and many more factors impact greatly on whether a test will have washback. To claim that negative, or the lack of positive, washback is a direct consequence of the work of the test developers, as is suggested in the concept of consequential validity, flies in the face of the evidence gathered to date, of common sense, and of the studies of innovation and change in education, as well as of the influence of teacher thinking on teacher style. The concept of consequential validity is naive, and harmful if it results in all participants laying the responsibility for how teachers teach for tests, and the consequences that tests have, at the door of test developers rather than elsewhere in society.

None of which is to argue that test developers should not monitor the effects that their tests have, especially if they are high-stakes tests. To date, studies of washback, or impact more generally, by test developers have been extremely rare. However, there is evidence that the situation is changing. At Lancaster, Jay Banerjee and I have been involved in developing a series of instruments for UCLES to enable them to investigate the impact that IELTS might be having on a number of constituencies. This Impact Study is now in the piloting stage, where UCLES intend to validate the instruments we have developed. In the near future I would expect to see either a research project or, even better a regular monitoring study, set up where previously validated instruments will be used to study the effect of the IELTS test. As currently conceived, there are four sub-projects within this Impact Study, which involve a number of instruments.

Project One involves a lengthy checklist style instrument to facilitate the analysis of textbooks intended to prepare students for IELTS. Comparison of the completed checklist (designed to indicate to what extent the textbook teaches IELTS relevant abilities) with the same checklist completed after analysing a TOEFL test preparation textbook should show the potential differential impact of the two tests, and comparison of the analysis of IELTS textbooks with ordinary communicative textbooks, including those intended to promote study skills in EAP, should reveal the extent to which a focus on IELTS results in different textbooks.

Project Two looks at IELTS preparation classrooms and includes three instruments: a classroom observation schedule and separate questionnaires for students and teachers administered after classroom observation. Again, it will be possible to analyse IELTS classes in detail and to compare IELTS classes with non-IELTS classes.

Project Three investigates attitudes to IELTS, and involves several questionnaires: to teachers preparing student for IELTS; teachers teaching students who have already taken IELTS (typically in the target country on pre-sessional or in-sessional courses); students who are preparing for IELTS; students who have taken IELTS; administrators who deal with IELTS testing and IELTS test preparation; subject teachers and admissions officers who receive students' IELTS scores. Not only will these instruments enable the gathering of important attitudinal data and a comparison across different informant groups, they will also allow changes in attitudes to IELTS to be monitored over time.

Project Four involves the development of an In-depth Candidate Information Sheet, which candidates complete before taking IELTS and which is intended to gather data on students' motivation, their learning and communication strategies, and their test-preparation practices. This will enable comparisons of candidate characteristics with test performance to see to what extent IELTS is biased in favour of or against particular types of candidates.

Whether or not such studies can be conceptualised as part of test validation, I believe that they are important things for test developers to be doing, in order to help us understand what effects tests have and how they might have these effects, as well as to provide evidence that might enable us to mitigate any negative effects that such tests might have. To the extent that the advent of the notion of consequential validity has hastened such studies, I welcome the concept, despite its theoretically ill-founded name.

7. Accountability

I now turn to issues of accountability of EAP programmes. The case is speculative, but probably very real. In the 1980s, when I was involved in EAP teaching, sponsors like the ODA and the British Council came under increasing financial pressure, and the value of pre-sessional EAP training was frequently questioned. Clearly, where budgets were tight, a course of one, two or three months preparation, in the UK rather than the home country, seemed like an expensive item, if not a luxury. Questions were frequently asked of the kind: how much language improvement can be expected from a four-, eight- or twelve-week pre-sessional course? And, of course, since the sponsors used ELTS, later IELTS, to screen candidates they not unnaturally thought of language improvement in terms of ELTS/IELTS band scores, and usually overall band scores at that. The pressure, then, was to evaluate student improvement in terms of ELTS/IELTS scores. As might be guessed from my opening anecdote, my position is that this is an inappropriate question based on a misunderstanding of language tests and test development. However, sponsors regarded such reactions as typical academic indecisiveness, and had little patience with them. I do not know whether any studies were in fact carried out to investigate what sort of IELTS-based improvement might be possible over such periods, but whilst interesting, they would have been inconclusive, and almost certainly damaging to EAP. ELTS/IELTS is not designed to measure such gain, and should not be used that way. But that is only part of the response that a responsible profession ought to give to sponsors. Fortunately, as far as I am aware, the pressure reduced simply because British and other sponsors stopped sending students to the UK, initially on pre-sessional courses, but then soon after, at all. So the need to show what our EAP courses were capable of achieving was removed, and the opportunity of investigating what students were actually learning receded.

This is most unfortunate. Although it was a relief, I am convinced it is only temporary. Budgetary constraints are now much closer to home: they are not just in the ODA, they are in our own institutions, and we are faced with the imminent likelihood of the need to demonstrate the value of the EAP teaching that goes on. Now of course, we are all skilled operators, not just in designing learning materials and helping students learn, but also in manipulating our political contexts, in marshalling to our defence friends in the academic departments with whom we have contact, and in referring to BALEAP inspections and codes of practice, UKCOSA recommendations, and the general view in higher education that academic support for overseas students is 'a good thing'. But how long this will last, I do not know, and I suspect that sooner or later we will be obliged to demonstrate what students do learn, and how our activities do actually benefit them. Already, institutions are seeking to lower their language proficiency entry requirements, and are asking for evidence that students with IELTS scores of less than, say 6.0, really do have greater problems than students with higher scores – as Allwright and Banerjee (1997) report. The fact is of course that we must be ready for such threats, not just politically, but academically. The professional need to understand what the outcomes of our EAP programmes are, what benefits students gain, has always been there. We have not always faced the challenge squarely. Last time I believe we got off the hook as ODA sponsorship simply dried up. The next time the threat may be much closer to home, and we need to be prepared. EAP programmes will need to pay much more attention to the development of appropriate measures of progress and achievement, if they are to avoid serious test misuse, or worse, shrinkage or closure.

Of course, the full answer to this demand for accountability is not simply to develop tests or, worse, to misuse existing tests. Clearly there are other sources of information about EAP achievement, including course evaluations, receiving department evaluations, student follow-up, and evidence and pressure from external agencies. However, test data is part of the answer, and an increasingly required one. Yet if we were to look for evidence of good practice in the assessing of EAP, I personally do not know where to look to find good tests. Where are the EAP achievement tests that can be used to justify the existence of an Academic Support programme, or an EAP unit?

8. BALEAP Survey

In 1986 BALEAP conducted a survey of its members, to identify testing practices, and that survey was updated in 1989, and published in *Language Testing Update* (Clapham and Wall, 1990). The survey found very few achievement or progress tests, much less any measures that had been properly researched and validated, and in whose results one could have a modicum of confidence. If that survey were to be repeated – and I would, certainly recommend such a replication – I suspect one would find little change. Yet I would argue that we need to take seriously the need to measure achievement, to explore and demonstrate what can be measured, and if we cannot demonstrate achievement and progress, then we need to be clear about why not. It is not satisfactory to blame the tests, or to blandly state that learning takes time. The question will be: is the time that we resource you to take language training, worth it? and without an answer, we are going to look silly, as academics and professionals as well as colleagues. The temptation will be to use existing tests, and that means proficiency tests. And I strongly advise against that, not only from a theoretical point of view, but from bitter experience. The results will be confusing and damaging.

The history of EAP in the UK has had a strong materials focus: it is no coincidence that BALEAP used to be called SELMOUS (Special

English Language Materials for Overseas University Students), with the stress on materials. Of course, part of the reason for the materials focus was that few commercially available materials were suitable for our circumstances, and with the publication of more EAP and Study Skills materials, things have changed somewhat. It is nevertheless interesting to reflect on the fact that very few of the materials that were developed, and those that were published, were tests, or even had tests associated with them. How much focus is there now on developing academic purpose progress measures? And, since the question is intended to be rhetorical, let me follow it, and draw to a close, with a real question: why not?

The BALEAP Survey offers some interesting suggestions. In answer to the question 'If you do not test your students during the term, is there a reason for not doing so?' there were four main responses. One was that there was neither time nor expertise to develop such tests; the second was that there was no time for students to take tests, as the EAP courses were voluntary and were squeezed into already crowded timetables. The third reason was that outside agencies did not require tests, and therefore tests were not needed, and the fourth was a feeling among some respondents that it was inappropriate to test students, either because tutors already knew their students' strengths and weaknesses, or because students themselves are already aware of their inadequacies from the experience of studying in an English-medium environment.

There is recent evidence, for example from the conference from which this volume is derived, that things might be changing, and that EAP teachers are beginning to take in-course assessment more seriously. Gray's paper 'Moving Away from Traditional Models'(this volume) suggests that teachers may be thinking of new ways of assessing students. Several papers addressed self-assessment and portfolio assessment. Whereas self-assessment has been advocated for some time in EAP contexts, the use of portfolio assessment is increasingly common in first language writing, and now appears to be spreading to ESL. Within EAP courses, the gathering of portfolios of drafts of writing, or various completed pieces, would allow the evaluation of student progress over time and across task types. Similar records of performances in their academic subjects, together with records of subject tutor comments, would prove valuable evidence of student learning and progress.

BALEAP has always been known for its interest in innovative approaches to teaching and learning and so it is encouraging to see that attention now appears to be paid to new ways of assessment. Yet Bob Jordan's paper (this volume) entitled 'Is the Customer Sometimes Right?' offers a salutary corrective to this in considering student views on assessment in EAP. One such traditional student view is that tests are useful and necessary indicators of progress. The BALEAP Survey suggested that teachers were less moved by such opinions and were more likely to take a teacher-centred view that there was no need for external measures, or that teachers knew best anyway, or that students were being constantly tested in their academic settings and had no need for measures of improvement. As reported above, a common objection to the use of progress tests was that there simply was no time during in-sessional courses for them, and so, since no external agency or sponsor required such measures, it was much more beneficial to students to devote time to teaching and not testing.

However, since 1990 technology has begun to change things. The wide availability of networked PCs, and the increasing availability of the Internet, and especially Web-based teaching materials, indicates the possibility of IT-based testing, which need not interfere with any teaching schedules. Students could take progress tests outside class, whenever they wish. Tests could be designed to provide diagnostic feedback to students on their strengths and weaknesses, and offer advice on how best to improve in particular areas. Tests can be tailor-made to particular groups, or to levels of achievement or performance, through computer-adaptive engines. The most common adaptive test of this type administers items at appropriate levels of difficulty, but others could enable the delivery of adaptive tests according to content area as particular weaknesses are revealed, and could indeed branch students out into learning routines as the necessity was diagnosed. Thus, the disruptive and perceived de-motivating aspects of testing could be avoided through IT based testing. In fact, a European Project funded by LINGUA is currently underway to design just such diagnostic assessment measures for fifteen European Community languages. The Project, known as DIALANG is funded by Socrates – LINGUA and designed for all adults, rather than EAP specifically, but there is no reason at all why its methodology could not be adapted for use in EAP. DIALANG incorporates an important element of self-assessment and self-evaluation, and the use of both of these could be explored in EAP as well. DIALANG will allow students first to self-assess their abilities on specific tasks, and then to compare their self-assessment with their actual performance. This will hopefully result in improved self-assessment and learner awareness. DIALANG also plans to allow IT-based assessment of writing and speaking abilities, in which students will record their performances on particular tasks, and then be offered benchmark performances by sample learners at a range of levels, as well as by competent native speakers, against which to compare their performances. Such benchmark performances will contain hotspot-based hidden commentaries on features of the performance, so that learners can look at the grammatical features of particular benchmarks, or their organisational features, or pronunciation, or spelling, and so on.

In short, we are facing the possibility of exciting new innovations in assessment in EAP, both in methods of assessment and in validation of instruments. These innovations offer the opportunity truly to explore the assessment of progress and achievement, and not to confine ourselves to estimates of proficiency or to the invalid use of proficiency tests. Hopefully, the pressure of increased accountability will then offer an opportunity to innovate, and not a threat of misuse.

References

Alderson J C (1993) 'The relationship between grammar and reading in an English for academic purposes test battery', in Douglas D and C Chappelle (eds) *A New Decade of Language Testing Research*, Alexandria, Va: TESOL

Alderson J C and L Hamp-Lyons (1996) 'TOEFL preparation courses: a study of washback', *Language Testing* 13.3, pp 280 – 97

Alderson J C and D M Wall (1993) 'Does washback exist?', *Applied Linguistics* 14.2, pp 115 – 29

Allwright J and J Banerjee (1997) 'Investigating the accuracy of admissions criteria – a case study in a British university', Paper presented at BALEAP Conference, April 1997

Anh Vu Thi Phuong (1997) *Authenticity and Validity in Language Testing: Investigating the reading components of IELTS and TOEFL*, Unpublished PhD Thesis, La Trobe University, Melbourne, Australia

Bachman L F (1990) *Fundamental Considerations in Language Testing*, Oxford: Oxford University Press

Buell J G (1992) 'TOEFL and IELTS as measures of academic reading ability: an exploratory study', Paper presented to the 26th Annual International Convention of TESOL, Vancouver, Canada, 4 March, cited in Anh (1997)

Clapham C M and J C Alderson (eds) (1997) *Constructing and Trialling the ELTS Test: IELTS Research Report 3*, London: The British Council, UCLES, and IDP Australia

Clapham C and D M Wall (1990) 'Report on a BALEAP questionnaire to British universities on the English language testing of overseas students', *Language Testing Update*, Issue 7, pp 2 – 24

Criper C and A Davies (1988) *ELTS Validation Project Report*, Research Report 1(i), Cambridge: The British Council and the University of Cambridge Local Examinations Syndicate

Davies A (1982) 'Criteria for evaluation of tests of English as a foreign language', in Heaton B (ed) *Language Testing*, London: Modern English Publications

Frederiksen J R and A Collins (1989) 'A systems approach to educational testing', *Educational Researcher* 18.9, pp 27 – 32

Geranpayeh (1994) cited in Anh (1997)

Griffin P (1990) 'Characteristics of the test components of the IELTS battery: Australian trial data', Paper presented at the Regional English Language Centre Annual Seminar, Singapore, 9-12 April 1990, cited in Anh (1997)

Hamp-Lyons L (in preparation) 'Ethical test preparation practice: the case of the TOEFL'

Lewkowicz J (1996) *Authenticity in Language Testing*, Unpublished PhD Thesis, Lancaster University

Messick S (1996) 'Validity and washback in language testing', *Language Testing* 13.3, pp 241 – 56

Messick S (1989) 'Validity', in Linn R L (ed) *Educational Measurement* (3rd edition), New York: Macmillan

Morrow K (1986) 'The evaluation of tests of communicative performance', in Portal M (ed) *Innovations in Language Testing*, Windsor, Berks: National Foundation for Educational Research

Portal M (ed) (1986) *Innovations in Language Testing*, Windsor, Berks: National Foundation for Educational Research

Stevenson D K (1985) 'Authenticity, validity and a tea party', *Language Testing* 2.1, pp 41 – 47

Swain M (1985) 'Large-scale communicative language testing: a case study', in Lee Y O, A C Y Fok, R Lord, and G Low (eds) *New Directions in Language Testing*, Oxford: Pergamon

Wall D M, C Clapham and J C Alderson (1994) 'Evaluating a placement test', *Language Testing* 11.3, pp 321 – 44

Wall D M (1996) 'Introducing new tests into traditional systems: insights from general education and from innovation theory', *Language Testing* 13.3, pp 334 – 354

Watanabe Y (1997) *The Washback Effects of the Japanese University Entrance Examinations of English – Classroom based research*, Unpublished PhD Thesis, Lancaster University

Weir C J (1983) *Identifying the Language Problems of Overseas Students in Tertiary Education in the United Kingdom*, Unpublished PhD Thesis, University of London

John Morley

The Chaplen Test Revisited

1. Introduction

The Chaplen Speeded Grammar and Vocabulary Test has been used by the English Language Teaching Unit at Manchester University since the early 1970s. It is used to identify recently arrived overseas students at Manchester who will probably experience difficulties in their academic work due to less than adequate levels of English language proficiency in reading and writing. Where such students are identified, they are advised to attend appropriate in-sessional English language support classes. The Chaplen Test is not used as an admissions test. In fact, all prospective overseas students are asked to submit an IELTS grade when applying to the university. Many do not, however, and it is the Chaplen Test which is used to identify weak students once they are 'in the system'. The test is also used, in conjunction with other assessment methods, to place students in groups on our pre-sessional courses.

Developed in the late 1960s, the test reflects the structuralist description of language and methods of language testing. Using a multiple-choice format, the Grammar (10 minutes) and Vocabulary (18 minutes) sections test students' knowledge of a range of individual items of structure and lexis in 'everyday educated English' (Chaplen 1970:174). For each section there are 50 questions, consisting of a sentence with a word or phrase omitted. The test taker must choose the correct filler from the list of possible answers provided. There is a choice of three possible answers in the Grammar section and five possible answers in the Vocabulary section. The short amount of time allowed for each section means that students work under considerable pressure of time and only the more proficient students manage to complete all the questions. The total number of correct answers is presented as a percentage score. A score of less than 40% is interpreted as indicating that the student has an inadequate level of English language proficiency for their academic studies. In these cases, the receiving department is informed, and students may be advised to postpone their studies in order to join a pre-sessional course. A score of less than 70% but more than 40% is interpreted as indicating that the student will probably experience difficulties with their studies and in-sessional support classes in academic writing and grammar are recommended. Where students score over 70%, they are advised that they should not need to attend classes, but they may attend if they feel that these would be useful. The full range of score interpretations is given in Appendix 1. In practice, the advice given to students also takes into consideration an assessment of a sample of their continuous writing.

The theoretical assumption that underpins the Chaplen Test is that adequate control of the general language system as measured by the test can serve as a reliable indication of a student's ability to apply this knowledge in academic situations. The extensive trials that the test underwent during its development would appear to support this (Chaplen 1970). In addition, in two follow-up studies, the test has been shown to have reasonable predictive validity. James (1980) showed that of a group of 34 recently arrived overseas postgraduate students (out of a total of 140) who scored below 40% on the Chaplen Test, 22 did in fact go on to experience difficulties with their academic work according to the subject tutors. The 12 students who did not experience difficulties had either attended a pre-sessional course prior to their academic studies or were engaged in work which might be 'classified as minimally language dependent'. Of those students who scored more than 40% (n=106), only 10 went on to experience difficulties with their studies. The majority of this latter group, though, had still scored poorly on the Chaplen Test (41% – 55%), and many were doing work which was 'heavily language dependent'. More recently, in a post-course evaluation, O'Brien (1993) found that of 7 students who had scored below 40% on the Chaplen Test, 6 were reported by the receiving department as having experienced difficulty during their first year of registration. Although these studies tell us little about students who score above 40% on the Chaplen Test, many of whom may experience difficulties without these being recognised by their subject tutors, the 40% cut-off score does seem to be a fairly reliable predictor of academic difficulty.

2. The Problem

As the person responsible for administering, marking and reporting on the test results to the students and their departments, and also being in a position to assess samples of the students' continuous writing, I have begun to question the interpretation of the scores on the Chaplen Test for certain groups of students. For example, although there would appear to be a general correspondence of the Chaplen Test scores with assessments of the students' writing, I have sometimes come across cases of students who perform very badly on the Chaplen Test (below 40%), but who appear to be reasonably proficient academic writers. Conversely, I have known certain students who perform quite well on the Chaplen Test, then produce a very weak piece of writing. In other words, a prediction of their future academic performance derived from their writing is at variance with the prediction given by the Chaplen Test. A marked lack of correspondence would seem to be apparent in about 7% of cases.

In addition, when placing students on our pre-sessional courses, teachers have tended to treat the Chaplen Test data with a degree of scepticism, and generally give more weight to other indicators of a student's proficiency, which include samples of student writing and interviews. It is generally felt that these performance-based methods of assessment have greater validity and are more useful measures of students' language proficiency; they are holistic in nature and assess language production rather than mere recognition. There also exists a perception that, although there is a general correspondence between the Chaplen Test scores and the other methods of assessment, there are too many instances where this is not the case.

A further source of unease is the poor face validity of many of the test items and/or their contexts, which are decidedly 'unacademic' in nature. Consequently, the test does not look as if it can provide valid information about a student's proficiency in academic English. Two examples, of 'unacademic' items, one from each paper, are given below:

> 13. She gave a cry of ...... when her pencil broke.
>   A. dismay   B. disuse   C. discourage
>   D. disclaim   E. discharge
> 35. He will make ....
>   A. for her a good husband   B. her a good husband
>   C. to her a good husband

In fact, the vocabulary items selected by Chaplen, when constructing the test, were drawn from readers' letters to *The Times* newspaper, and the grammar items were drawn from contemporary ELT coursebooks.

3. The Objectives

After more than a quarter of a century of its use, and in light of the aforementioned concerns, it was felt that there was a strong case for reassessing the Chaplen Test. This study, therefore, had the following objectives:

1. To find out more about the nature and strength of relationship between students' scores on the discrete item Chaplen Test and a holistic assessment of their ability to produce continuous discourse in written academic English.
2. To demonstrate how this relationship might be affected by a student's country of origin.

Significant lack of concurrence between the two methods of assessment would certainly raise serious questions about the current score interpretations and the recommendations based on these, and, where this was shown to be extreme, call into question continued use of the instrument. On the other hand, where reasonable concurrence was demonstrated, advice given to students who took the test would be based on a more informed understanding and interpretation of the scores.

An additional, but longer term, objective of this study is to improve the face validity of the test by replacing items which are obviously 'unacademic' in nature with items which are more convincing. However, this second stage of the project would depend on the results of the first stage.

4. Method

Samples of continuous writing produced under test conditions and Chaplen Test scores were obtained for 153 newly arrived overseas students. All the scripts had been produced at the same time as the students had sat for the Chaplen Test on different occasions over a three-year period. For each student, therefore, a Chaplen Test score was available together with a piece of writing. The countries represented were China, Iran, Italy, Korea, Greece, Turkey, Malaysia and Japan, and there were similar numbers of students for each country (19 – 20). The main sampling criteria were that the students were postgraduates who came from countries which were well represented in our pre-sessional course and in-sessional intake. In addition, for each country, the aim was to select students purposively so that a complete range of Chaplen Test scores was represented. The writing task (30 minutes), which can be seen in Appendix 2, required students to write about their academic and/or professional backgrounds, their current academic studies, and their future academic and professional plans.

The written scripts were assessed using a 0–9 scale of band descriptors similar to those employed in the IELTS writing subtest. Two IELTS trained assessors assigned bands, composed of an aggregate score for readability and the range and accuracy of vocabulary and sentence structure, to each script. The scripts were not assessed in terms of their quality of argument or ideas because the writing task did not require students to produce an argumentative text; in this respect the holistic bands employed in this study were different from those used in the IELTS writing subtest. An additional difference was that although IELTS writing scores are normally only given as whole bands, in this study it was decided to permit the assessors to use .5 of a band. This allowed discrimination between, for example, a band 6 and a 'good' band 6. Where the first two assessors disagreed on a grade by more than one whole band, the scripts were passed to a third examiner for assessment. This was done 8 times. The inter-rater reliability coefficient for the first two examiners using the .5 band scale was a satisfactory .87.

The scores for the written scripts and the three Chaplen Test scores (Grammar, Vocabulary and the total score) were entered into a file using SPSS. Analysis included comparisons of mean scores, correlation studies, regression analysis and the production of scatterplots.

5. The Results

A summary of the correlations between the holistic writing assessments and the Chaplen Test total scores, and the Chaplen subtest scores, is given in Table 1. The ranking correlation coefficient between the writing assessments and the overall Chaplen Test scores was a relatively high .812. The vocabulary subtest correlated slightly more positively with the writing than did the grammar subtest, .809 compared with .696. These results might suggest that range and control of vocabulary contributed more to the assessors' evaluations of the pieces of writing than knowledge and control of language structure.

Table 1. Spearman ranking correlations between Chaplen Test(s) and holistic writing

TESTS	WRITING	CHAPLEN (total)	GRAMMAR
CHAPLEN (total)	.8120		
GRAMMAR	.6964	.9254	
VOCAB	.8092	.9452	.7753

No of cases 153. All correlations significant at $p < .001$ (1-tailed)

Another possible interpretation of this, however, might lie in the nature of the grammar subtest. The grammar subtest requires students to choose between only three possible answers to complete each question, unlike the vocabulary subtest's five answers. As a result, simply by guessing, a student may obtain a higher score on the grammar subtest than on the vocabulary subtest where a similar number of answers are guessed. In fact, the mean grammar score for all students (63.4%) was higher than the mean vocabulary score (49%) even though the mean completion scores were very similar (90.6% and 91% respectively). The possible presence of a higher number of guessed correct answers would reduce the validity of the scores on the grammar subtest, and this could explain the slightly lower correlation.

The scatterplot generated by SPSS revealed a broad linear pattern reflecting the high positive correlation between the Chaplen Test total scores and the holistic writing assessments. However, considerable dispersion of the Chaplen Test scores around each writing band occurs. Students whose writing was assessed at band 6.5, for example, scored between 34% and 90% on the Chaplen Test. Looking at the data the other way round, students who scored around 50% on the Chaplen Test, for example, had writing assessments which ranged from band 4 to band 7. The results clearly show, therefore, that, even allowing for some unreliability on the writing assessments, a significant number of students may score quite well on one measure of English language proficiency but relatively poorly on the other.

Regression lines were produced for all students and for each group of students. Discounting the extreme scores and working within the 95% confidence level, certain patterns of prediction were identified. The data suggests that students who score less than 30% on the Chaplen Test should have a writing score of 5.5 or less. The results also indicate that students who score less than 40% may have a writing score of 6 but will probably be below this. On the other hand, students who score above 70% on the Chaplen Test are extremely unlikely to have a writing score of less than 6.5. Where students score between 40% and 70% on the Chaplen Test, however, writing band predictions are much less certain, and this is significant since about 50% of students fall into this group.

When analysed in terms of national groups, the mean Chaplen Test scores of students who obtained writing bands 6 and 6.5, pooled for statistical reasons, revealed certain marked differences. These scores are given in Table 2 below.

While the mean score for most groups is between 56% and 61%, noticeable exceptions are the Koreans (mean = 69%) and the Malaysians (mean = 49%). Interestingly, only cases from these groups were situated outside the 95% confidence level lines. Prediction lines for Iranian and Turkish students, as with the Malaysians, fell markedly below the prediction line for all students in the study, but with these groups, unlike the Malaysians, all scores were well within the 95% confidence level lines.

Table 2. Mean Chaplen Test scores for writing bands 6/6.5 by country

Country	Mean %	Std Dev	No. of cases
China	59.9	11.1	7
Greece	60.5	10.8	6
Iran	56.0	9.7	5
Italy	61.0	13.5	11
Japan	58.0	9.5	5
Korea	69.5	12.5	11
Malaysia	49.5	12.6	7
Turkey	56.0	12.5	8
All students	59.9	12.7	60

It is interesting to speculate on the reasons for the marked differences in the Chaplen Test scores for the Koreans and the Malaysians. We do know of course that for many Malaysians English is a widely used second language, particularly in urban areas. The low scores on the discrete item structural test in relation to their communicative proficiency as measured by the holistic writing assessments may reflect this. Anecdotal evidence from Korean students suggests that language teaching in that country is still very structural in orientation, and this may explain the relatively high Chaplen Test scores. The low Chaplen Test scores for the Turkish and Iranian students, in relation to their writing assessments, however, are less easy to explain. Cultural and educational factors may play a part, along with age and level of study. All the Iranians and most of the Turkish students were mature students who were planning to study at PhD level. It may be that in-depth familiarity with a particular subject allows a student to write about his/her subject quite proficiently even though the underlying general language competence is weak. Of course, one has to be careful not to deduce too much from these observations given that they are based on relatively small numbers of students from each country. Nevertheless, certain tendencies do seem to have emerged.

6. Conclusion

This study has shown that, although the Chaplen Test correlates quite strongly with the assessment of students' holistic writing, the precise interpretations currently used with the Chaplen Test scores have been found to be suspect. At any given band of holistic writing, students have been shown to score very differently on the Chaplen Test. The study has also shown that students of different nationalities, with similar levels of proficiency in written English, have tendencies to perform differently on the test. These findings lead us to consider the question: 'Is there still a good case for continuing to use the Chaplen

Test?' I would suggest that the answer to this question is 'yes' for the following reasons.

It has been shown that the test can be used to identify students who clearly have inadequate levels of written English for academic purposes (below 30%), and those who quite probably have inadequate levels of English (below 40%). This would seem to support the findings of James (1980) and O'Brien (1993), which I discussed earlier. The test also has the power to identify the group of students who are likely to encounter few serious difficulties with language in their studies (over 70%). In this respect, the test serves as an easy to administer screening instrument, allowing the assessor to identify quickly groups of students who need separate consideration. Between the extreme scores, however, it would seem necessary to take students' written English into account before coming to any firm conclusion about language proficiency and probable future difficulties with academic work.

Secondly, where it is evident, for example, that a student scores well on the Chaplen Test but poorly on a written performance-based task, we might conclude that there is a mismatch between the student's knowledge of the language system and their ability to express themselves in written English. With such students, the kind of information revealed by the Chaplen Test is particularly useful when advising students about their English language needs or when placing students in appropriate groups on our pre-sessional courses. For example, it may help when advising students whether they should attend classes in academic writing or grammar.

A final reason for continuing to use the test has to do with the way it is perceived by both students and receiving departments. Despite the low face validity of many of its items, the test would seem to provide an objective and reliable balance to the subjective assessments of the students' writing. It has what might be described as a high degree of perceived methodological validity in the eyes of those it is designed to test. Of relevance here are the results of a small survey I conducted recently, which revealed that a significant number of students felt the Chaplen Test was a useful indicator of their ability to use English in their studies.

Of course, continued use should be dependent on changes in a number of areas, which are as follows:

- it should be made clear to students that the Chaplen Test is a test of their lexical/structural competence rather than a test of their communicative competence in their proposed fields of study, and that these may be at variance,
- the interpretations of the Chaplen Test scores on the current test report form should be expressed more cautiously, in terms of probabilities rather than certainties,
- the test report form should be reformatted to include a section on the students' writing so that this information can be formally included in test feedback.

In addition, as discussed earlier, continued use requires an improvement in the face validity of many of the test's questions. This will involve the inclusion of more 'academic' items in realistic contexts. An additional improvement that is also worth considering is the inclusion of a greater number of answers for each question in the grammar subtest. This should improve the subtest's discriminatory power, and we may find that a higher correlation with students' writing can be achieved. Of course, permission to make these changes will need to be obtained from the test author.

In this study the relationship between Chaplen Test scores and measurements of students' performance on only one language subskill was examined. Correlations between Chaplen Test scores and reading performance may be much stronger, and it may be possible to make more confident predictions based on the test. This would certainly be an interesting area for further investigation, along, perhaps, with comparing Chaplen Test scores with assessments for listening and speaking. In addition, further collection and analysis of data on the comparative performance of different national groups would seem worthwhile.

Given the small scale and rather specific nature of this research, we have to be careful about drawing more general conclusions from these findings. Nevertheless, it is plausible to suppose that the demonstrated lack of concurrence between the multiple choice Chaplen Test scores and the more holistic performance based writing assessments may be found with other discrete item multiple choice tests, and that it is dangerous to rely only on a discrete item multiple choice assessment of a student's proficiency.

References

Chaplen E F (1970) *The Identification of Non-Native Speakers of English Likely to Underachieve in University Courses through Inadequate Command of the Language*, Unpublished PhD Thesis, University of Manchester

James K (1980) 'Survey of University of Manchester overseas postgraduate students' initial level of competence in English and their subsequent academic performance: calendar year 1977', in Greenall G M and J E Price (eds) *Study Modes and Academic Development of Overseas Students*, ELT Documents 109, London: The British Council

O'Brien J P (1993) 'English for academic purposes: the role of the subject tutor', Paper presented at NATESOL, University of Manchester, 26 January 1993

Appendix 1
Current Chaplen Test Report Form

UNIVERSITY OF MANCHESTER ENGLISH LANGUAGE TEACHING UNIT

English Language Test (Chaplen) Results

Name.. **Date**..............

Chaplen Speeded Vocabulary Test: ___ out of 50 (___ attempted)

Chaplen Speeded Grammar Test: ___ out of 50 (___ attempted)

Total: _____ %

Note: This document is not to be used as a language proficiency certificate outside the University of Manchester

The scores below need to be interpreted. Some subjects are more language dependent than others. Law, for example, will require a higher test score than, say, Computer Science. Generally, however, the following guide should give a rough idea as to how strong a basis you have in English grammar and vocabulary from the point of view of reading and writing academic English.

	85%+	You are approaching native-speaker standard. The majority of the problems you will have are likely to be shared by native speakers.
	70%+	You have a good basis in grammar and vocabulary. You will normally be able to communicate your meaning satisfactorily though you may have the occasional problem in minor points of grammar and/or fluency or style.
	60%+	You have an adequate basis to achieve effective communication, although you are likely to find it hard to do so on occasions, and you may make the occasional serious mistake in grammar or vocabulary.
Classes	50%+	You have a barely adequate basis to make a start on your studies. You are likely to make fairly frequent grammatical mistakes and to be restricted sometimes in what you can express because of lack of vocabulary.
are	40%+	Your basis in grammar and vocabulary is very weak and ill seriously limit your ability to communicate.
recommended	-40%	You have an inadequate basis to start on University studies

Appendix 2
Writing Task

Write three paragraphs, one on each of the following:

- Your work/study before coming to Manchester University

- Your course/research at Manchester University

- How your course/research at Manchester will help you when you return home.

Paul Fanning and Lynne Hale

Screening New Students with the UCLES Computer Adaptive Test

1. The Need for Testing

It has not been common in British universities for every single new student possessing a first language other than English to be subjected to a language test on first arrival. Traditionally, testing has been confined to students on pre-sessional English courses, usually for the purposes of placement and/or course evaluation. International students entering a university directly without a pre-sessional course tended not to be tested because usually they had already performed adequately on an external test (such as IELTS) that an internal test could do no more than duplicate. Practicality has also been a factor in deciding who to test. Even if the number of non-pre-sessional students is small, locating and communicating with them in order to arrange a test, and finding a place and time suitable for all, presents a significant logistical challenge. The need for blanket screening of new arrivals, however, is growing. The massive increase in the number of non-native English speakers entering British universities, particularly at undergraduate level, means that the number who start their academic courses without, or only just with, the minimum acceptable level of English is becoming significant.

One factor here is the continuing expansion in the range of English language qualifications that are proffered. It is inevitable that the equivalence of some of these qualifications to well-known measures like IELTS will be uncertain. A further factor is an increase in the number of 'home' undergraduates who do not in fact speak English as their first language. Often such students are not even asked, when applying, to prove their competence in English, because it is taken for granted that they are native speakers (these being often deemed, despite growing evidence to the contrary, to be fully equipped linguistically for tertiary study).

Assuming that the practicalities of large numbers can be overcome, the main justification for a compulsory cross-university test of newly arrived non-native speakers is threefold. Most obviously, a test allows early identification of students with serious language weaknesses, giving them the chance to take remedial action before it is too late. (It is too late at the next likely opportunity for a student's weaknesses to become apparent: the first formal academic assessment). The second value in having everyone tested at the outset is that in-sessional language support staff and classes can be further publicised and given reality in students' minds. Thirdly, a university-wide test raises the profile of the English Support Unit in the university as a whole, perhaps encouraging more student referrals by concerned academic colleagues.

Our use of the minimal term 'screening' reflects the first of these purposes. It means nothing more than separating sheep from goats. Of course there are other possible purposes of a blanket test, most notably diagnosis of language needs. The initial emphasis, however, is on screening, because information gained for other purposes will often be wasted as a result of students choosing not to attend the subsequent voluntary language support classes. Procedures like diagnosis are perhaps best left to the tutors of particular language support classes, whose exact participants will be fairly predictable.

At our university there has been an obvious need for blanket screening for many years. What has prevented it has always been the practicalities of dealing in one short week with hundreds of students taking a wide range of subjects on six widely-separated campuses. For many years we simply concentrated on the Business School, the single campus with the largest number of non-native speakers. We ran a traditional 2-hour test of English for academic purposes (EAP), consisting of a tape-recorded lecture with questions, and an integrated reading/writing task.

In 1995, however, we were presented with the opportunity to acquire a computer-adaptive test of general English from UCLES (University of Cambridge Local Examinations Syndicate). We decided that, despite one or two worries about the content of the test, here at last was a chance to experiment with testing right across the university.

2. Computer Adaptive Testing (CAT)

Interest in computer adaptive testing started to grow in the late 1970s (cf Kreitzberg et al, 1978). Tests involve on-screen presentation and answering previously classified questions. Each new question is selected from a database according to the candidate's response to the one immediately before: a correct response brings a slightly more difficult following question; an incorrect one has an easier follow-up. Every candidate starts with a question of middling difficulty (chosen randomly from a set of such questions in order to maximise variety and unpredictability), but very quickly moves into a unique pathway through the test. Nobody is presented with all of the questions in the database - candidates see only enough for the computer to 'decide' their overall level with the prescribed degree of accuracy. This means that the combination of test questions is likely to differ for every candidate. It also means that CAT tests tend to require fewer candidate responses than usual since, as Tung (1986: 3) points out, there is less need to waste time on items that are too easy or too difficult. CAT results, like those of any fully computerised test, can be provided immediately after the test has been completed, with or without feedback on answers.

The UCLES test uses questions from past Cambridge examinations. The difficulty levels are thus linked to standard Cambridge categories (PET, FCE, CAE etc) and range from near beginner to native speaker. There are tests of grammar, vocabulary, reading and, to some extent, writing (by means of sentence transformations). The 1997 Windows version, which we did not have at the time, also incorporates listening. Besides the sentence transformations, the question types include multiple choice and cloze. They thus bear out claims that CAT might not or will not lead to innovations in test method or test content (Canale, 1986; Alderson,

1990). Before starting, candidates answer a few practice questions (one for each question type in the test) in order to minimise the effect of the unfamiliar test procedure on overall validity. During the test candidates are allowed as much time as they need to answer the questions. At the end the candidates are informed of the Cambridge level that they have demonstrated, and can read both their own and the correct answers to all of the questions.

Two changes that we were able to make to the software in order to adapt the test to our own needs were to disable the longer reading test (which we found to be rather cumbersome), and to rewrite the results screen. We preferred to use more transparent level descriptors, such as 'intermediate', and we wanted to make reference to our own English Support Service.

3. Expected Strengths and Weaknesses of the UCLES Test

In the rest of this paper we first describe what we thought would be the advantages and disadvantages of using the UCLES test, and then we relate our actual experiences.

There were five expected advantages. Firstly, we expected to save time on both test preparation and marking. It was, of course, this expected advantage that made CAT attractive to us in the first place, since it would allow us to extend our testing across the university. The main preparation chore no longer necessary is the printing and distribution of question papers. Marking, obviously, is eliminated by the CAT's ability to provide instant on-screen results (and to store them for future reference in a data file). This same ability would, as a second advantage, enable candidates to receive immediate advice about follow-up study without the need for a few days' wait, during which interest might cool off. The third expected advantage was that the variability of CAT questions promised to ensure test security. This is an important consideration when the test is likely to be used repeatedly in order to cope with geographically separate campuses and staggered student arrivals (late registrations seeming particularly to affect students arriving from abroad). Fourthly, a test that used questions from tried and tested Cambridge examinations could be expected to short cut the need for piloting and validation that any in-house alternative would have. And fifthly, the matching of questions to candidates' levels and the consequent shortening of test content would save more time for both invigilators and students.

Inevitably, we believed that there would be disadvantages too, but not enough to put us off. Firstly, mass computerised testing requires mass availability of computers in high-capacity rooms. There were certainly enough computers (their availability being assisted by the timing of the test: at the start of the academic year, before serious computing instruction got under way), but room capacity tended to average only 20-30, making the number of test sessions (each lasting 60 minutes) greater than we would have liked.

Secondly, we were not particularly keen on the indirect, non-communicative style of question in the UCLES test. We agree with Bachman (1990: 306) that, however professional a test is psychometrically, it ought also to take account of contemporary ideas of language use. There was also the worry, first expressed by Carroll (1961), that discrete point items may not be testing the same thing as direct tests. To put it in terms of today's cognitive theories of second language acquisition, success with a discrete point item may result from either declarative or procedural knowledge, whereas success with a more direct test will more likely indicate only procedural knowledge. We thus preferred to include tests of a more direct kind, like essay writing and note making, at least alongside indirect tests. However, we realised at the time that we were unlikely to acquire the CAT format and direct testing as well, and there was also a feeling that if the questions worked for UCLES then they were worth a try by us.

A third worry about the test was that it was not focussed on English for academic purposes. We subscribe to the 'increasing agreement among testers that language proficiency tests should, where possible, be related to candidates' future language needs' (Clapham 1996: 1). The concern was that information provided by the UCLES test – that is, candidates' ability or inability to use English for any and every purpose – would be no real indication of their ability or inability to use English for academic study. Two different mismatches can be visualised: candidates might pass CAT but be unable to use EAP, or they might fail CAT but still have EAP ability. Mismatches may be considered by reference to both the language and the content of the test. Thinking in terms of language, failing CAT but still being able to use EAP seems more logically likely than the opposite. This is because it is quite easy to visualise a candidate failing the test as a whole because of inadequate performances in most aspects of the language, yet performing adequately with a significant amount of the language with especial importance in EAP. It is less easy (but not impossible) to believe that a candidate who demonstrates ability to use English for any and every purpose (that is, who passes CAT) can be inadequate with EAP. Indeed a case for the reality of the former scenario can be made on the basis of experience with speakers of Romance languages. French speakers, for example, have little problem with much of the vocabulary used in academic textbooks because it is of Latinate origin, and thus likely to have cognates in their native language. However, these same students, able to read academic texts without much difficulty, may well be lost when it comes to reading texts from a wide range of other sources, for example, tabloid newspapers, with a much wider and more idiomatic vocabulary. On the face of it, then, if there is any potential language-based problem with using a general test instead of an EAP one, it is more likely to be a denial of worthy students than the redemption of unworthy ones. In considering test content, the two mismatches mentioned above seem less of a worry. This is partly because of the finding by Tan (1990) that linguistic proficiency is a greater predictor of EAP success than subject familiarity, but also because contextualised topics were not a major feature of the test that we used. With the longer reading component of the test disabled, we were left with a series of single-sentence items, plus two to three short cloze passages (of around 200 words each). Despite arguments such as the above against using a general purposes test for EAP screening, we were happy to go ahead. The shortcomings had not been definitely proven, and we hoped we might eventually be able to contribute some new empirical findings to the EAP/General Purposes debate. To make use of the test, moreover, would be to act in line with the established university admissions practice of accepting UCLES CAE and CPE passes as alternatives to IELTS.

The fourth perceived disadvantage of the CAT was its lack of oral and aural components. Although UCLES now do supply a listening component, we had none. This was a worry not just because oral/aural skills are so central to academic study, but also because, in the absence of such a thing as unitary competence (cf Cummins, 1979; 1980a), they are unlikely to be an exact reflection of reading/writing proficiency. To rely on reading/writing scores as an indicator of overall EAP competence is thus unreliable, to say the least. What we hoped, however, was that the CAT score would usually indicate overall competence. We reasoned that if students had an acceptable CAT score, any deficiency in listening/speaking skills was not a worry. Experience had shown that students with a high level of 'declarative' grammatical and lexical knowledge quickly overcame listening weaknesses once they needed to understand lectures on a regular basis. On the other hand, if the CAT score was low but the student actually had strong speaking/listening skills, then the low score would not be a major injustice because the need for help with reading and writing would still exist. As Cummins (1980b; 1983) points out, literacy does not develop automatically from skill with the spoken language.

A final disadvantage of adopting the UCLES CAT was its cost. A home-grown EAP test would bring no extra cost to the university. UCLES, however, rightly expected to be reimbursed for their services. The agreed fee of £1,200 was within our budget, but naturally prevented purchases elsewhere.

4. Using the Test

The actual strengths and weaknesses of the CAT were quite close to what we had expected. With regard to the strengths, we certainly achieved our aim of testing on every campus, although the time required for this was not that much less than testing by traditional means would have taken. The number of students that we subsequently met in our in-sessional EAP classes and tutorials increased, presumably as a result of both the test's wider reach and the improved counselling opportunity provided by instant result-giving. (An additional factor here might have been a greater street credibility of computer testing, something that seemed evident from occasional student comments). The profile and standing of our unit within the university was also definitely raised. Our academic colleagues seemed to like both the fact that we were testing more students and our involvement with computers. The security of the test was, furthermore, as good as expected, so that we were able to repeat it even more frequently than we had anticipated. We found, for example, that many individuals who had missed the sessions in the first week of term wanted us to arrange special extra sittings. We eventually allowed individuals to take the test at their own convenience in the computer centre with minimal support from us, and we found that they always seemed to manage satisfactorily. If there was any real disappointment with the test, it was with imperfections that emerged in the UCLES questions and scoring.

There were a number of ways in which the time taken to administer the CAT was spun out. Firstly, the number of one-hour test sessions was even greater than expected, particularly second time around, owing to increased student numbers. With a paper-based test, a single sitting can often take many additional, unexpected students; but the usual room capacity of 20 for the CAT allows no such flexibility.

Secondly, there were unanticipated preparation needs. Installation of the test on the university-wide computer network proved to be a major undertaking for our colleagues in the computer centre. Even in the second year a great deal of time was required to ensure that everything was working properly on an upgraded network. Moreover, the inflexible sizes of test groups created a need for a signing up system for candidates, so that we would not have to turn away large disgruntled crowds from the more popular sessions. We found also that there are still many students out there who have no or very little familiarity with computer keyboards and associated terminology such as *Enter, Tab, Spacebar, Shift*. We therefore felt a need for paper handouts labelling the standard keys, and these had to be photocopied and distributed. We also prepared OHP transparencies to support the pre-test briefing.

Thirdly, the collation and distribution of the test results proved more time-consuming than expected. Every test grade across the university was initially stored automatically in a single centralised data file. In the first year we sought to convert this central list of names and scores into six campus-based sublists for distribution to relevant EAP staff and subject academics; but matching student names to campuses and transferring them from one list to another proved to be a major operation. In year 2 we arranged for each candidate's test result to be recorded on the university's central student database (under 'entry qualifications'), and asked interested colleagues simply to look scores up for themselves. Even this arrangement, however, necessitated a fair amount of manual computer inputting.

The problems with UCLES's questions and scoring should not have been so unexpected, given that even for UCLES the CAT was still in an early developmental stage. To begin with, we found the practice test a nuisance. It took students longer to complete than we expected (sometimes as long as the test itself), and they did not always appreciate its practice status. Invigilators expended a great deal of energy moving from candidate to candidate hurrying them through the practice test and explaining that their answers were not being recorded. If the practice test could have been got through more quickly we would have been able to have test sessions lasting 45 minutes instead of 60. However, it is not easy to see how things could have been speeded up, and a practice test is certainly necessary.

Another problem with the test itself was that the original results screen gave candidates a grade on a scale from 0 to 6. Grade 0, however, was a low-intermediate Cambridge level, and not an indication of absolute or false beginners. Inevitably, some of our students 'achieved' this grade, and were not best pleased. The following year we renumbered the scale 1–7 instead of 0–6.

A further problem with the results was that on balance they seemed to underestimate our students' ability by about one level. We had two main sources of evidence for this. Firstly, we asked every candidate to fill out a form telling us the names and grades of any English Language qualifications that they had previously acquired, and we very often found that, for example, a candidate who claimed to have passed CAE had been judged by the CAT to be of FCE level. Sometimes we found even greater discrepancies than this. Secondly, we obtained a short writing sample from some of the students and compared our impressions of the level shown there with what the CAT indicated. This rather subjective check again suggested that some students could communicate more successfully in English than the CAT had indicated.

There are various possible explanations for such discrepancies. The simplest is that the CAT might not be finely tuned enough and that with a little adjustment it would accurately assess candidates' levels. More probably, however, the above-mentioned worries about the range of question types and the non-academic focus have some foundation.

The absence of an oral/aural component of the test might explain why some candidates scored lower than their actual qualifications would predict. This explanation would apply to candidates who had a very strong oral command of English but who experienced problems with reading and writing. Such a combination sometimes arises with people who have lived for many years in an English-speaking environment but who have had very little recent experience of formal English-medium education. Bilinguals whose schooling has been in their other language might fall into this category, as might inhabitants of countries where English is a widely-spoken official language (for example, Nigeria or India), who left school early or long ago, and who have been accepted into higher education as 'mature' students. Students of this type will perform reasonably well overall in a test of all four language skills, because their oral ability will compensate for their written weaknesses. However, when only written English is involved, the overall average will be low.

The third possible cause of candidates' under-scoring is the fact that the CAT focuses on General English rather than EAP. An explanation has already been advanced of how such a focus might be to the disadvantage of some prospective EAP users. It could be that students who performed better than predicted on our short writing task possessed a level of EAP that the CAT could not highlight.

The other main problem that we noticed with the actual test involved the sentence transformation questions. The computer program sometimes rejected answers that we considered perfectly acceptable. The reason for this is simple enough: sentence transformations can usually be completed in more than one way, and some of these are not always obvious to the question writer. If a candidate comes up with an answer not predicted by the computer program then no credit will be given. Computer programs are not able to exercise discretion.

The real issue here, of course, is the extent to which right answers are marked wrong. Any significant frequency has serious implications for the reliability of the test, and could be the main reason for the underestimation of candidates' ability. We were not able to keep a record of the aberrations that we observed; we could only report the existence of the problem to UCLES. Not surprisingly, they were already aware, and assured us that adjustments had been made to the subsequent version of the test, although all feedback on this sort of problem remained welcome. This constant need for piloting and debugging of open-ended computerised tests is probably to be expected (cf Henning et al 1990).

As regards the expected weaknesses of the CAT, it is not so easy to say whether experience proved them to be real. We have suggested that the perceived underestimation of many candidates' actual competence might be explained by the non-EAP nature of the test and/or the absence of an oral/aural component. However, there is also the point with regard to the latter that an appreciable number of candidates should have performed better than expected. This is because many students have better reading/writing skills than speaking/listening, and would escape having their overall score pulled down by a poor result on an oral/aural component. It is not immediately obvious, moreover, how much the non-communicative nature of the test contributed to any distortion of the results.

5. Conclusion

Having used the UCLES computer adaptive test for two consecutive years we are convinced of its value and could not countenance going back to traditional screening devices. Our concerns about the nature of the questions are alleviated by both UCLES' continuing development of the test (something we are proud now to be contributing to) and the effect of the test on our English Language Support programme. We reach more students, the students who we test seem happier (not entirely because of the CAT's shorter length, we hope), and other staff in the university have greater awareness of, and respect for, what we are doing.

References

Alderson J C (1990) 'Learner-centred testing through computers: institutional issues in individual assessment', in de Jong J H and D K Stevenson (eds) *Individualizing the Assessment of Language Abilities*, Clevedon: Multilingual Matters

Bachman L (1990) *Fundamental Considerations in Language Testing*, Oxford: Oxford University Press

Canale M (1986) 'The promise and threat of computerized adaptive measurement of reading comprehension', in Stansfield C W (ed) *Technology and Language Testing*, Washington DC: TESOL Publications

Carroll J B (1961) 'Fundamental considerations in testing for English language proficiency of foreign students', in Center for Applied Linguistics, *Testing the English Proficiency of Foreign Students*, Washington DC: Center for Applied Linguistics

Clapham C (1996) *Studies in Language Testing 4: The Development of IELTS*, Cambridge: Cambridge University Press

Cummins J (1979) 'Cognitive/academic language Proficiency, linguistic interdependence, the optimum age question and some other matters', *Working Papers on Bilingualism* 19, pp 197 – 205

Cummins J (1980a) 'The entry and exit fallacy in bilingual education', *NABE Journal* 4, pp 25 – 60.

Cummins J (1980b) 'Psychological assessment of immigrant children: logic or intuition', *Journal of Multilingual and Multicultural Development* 1, pp 97 – 111

Cummins J (1983) 'Academic achievement and language proficiency', in Oller J (ed) *Issues in Language Testing Research,* Rowley, Mass: Newbury House

Henning G, M Anbar, C Helm and S D'Arcy (1990) 'Computer-assisted testing of reading comprehension: comparisons among multiple-choice and open-ended scoring methods', in Douglas D and C Chapelle (eds) *A New Decade of Language Testing Research,* Alexandria, Va: TESOL Publications

Kreitzberg C B, M L Stocking and L Swanson (1978) 'Computerized adaptive testing: principles and direction', *Computers and Education* 2, pp 319 – 329

Tan S H (1990) 'The role of prior knowledge and language proficiency as predictors of reading comprehension among undergraduates', in de Jong J H and D K Stevenson (eds) *Individualizing the Assessment of Language Abilities,* Clevedon: Multilingual Matters

Tung P (1986) 'Computerized adaptive testing: implications for language test developers', in Stansfield C W (ed) *Technology and Language Testing,* Washington DC: TESOL Publications

Part Two:

Language Assessment in Academic Departments

Esther Daborn and Moira Calderwood

Collaborative Assessment of Written Reports: Electrical Engineering and EFL

1. Introduction

In any course, assessment is a key to measuring the success of an outcome for both the student and the teaching staff. On the one hand, assessment consists of a set of processes through which judgements are made about the learner's level of skills and knowledge (Nunan, 1990). At the same time, it is part of a cycle reflecting the type of input students receive, which in turn provides useful feedback through which the curriculum designer evaluates the course content and makes adjustments. It is with this diagnostic aspect of assessment that this paper is concerned.

The case in point is a collaborative project to improve undergraduate student writing between the department of Electronics and Electrical Engineering (EEE) and the English as a Foreign Language Unit (EFL) at Glasgow University. EEE is keen to produce articulate students, both from home and overseas, but perceives a problem with their communication skills in general, especially their ability to write coherent reports. For the purposes of the project, both EEE staff and EFL tutors assessed a written report. There were therefore two different audiences for the work, despite the normal assumption that any piece of written text has a specific purpose and audience in mind. Previous consideration of such a situation, in Wall et al's (1988) study, identified differences in priority, to which reference will be made.

A further problem with convergence of assessment criteria is that departmental staff seem to perceive English language as outside their domain. For many university departments it is a truism that most subject tutors check only for content, providing little feedback on organisation and style (Braine, 1989). Guidance is restricted to lists of section headings. The most common complaints are about grammar and spelling. In conversation with a science lecturer, the answer to the question, 'How did you learn to write a report?' was, 'Well, by seeing how others did it'. As Davies (1988) points out, the criteria for success are the norms of the people who control, either directly or indirectly, the different genres to which the students are exposed, namely textbooks, conference proceedings and journals. At the same time, these are also the criteria of the genres which the students are expected to produce, namely exam answers, laboratory reports, projects, literature reviews, theses, dissertations. There are two problems here. First, departments assume that learning to write can be achieved by noticing and synthesising style in the process of reading other materials. Second, all these genres have different purposes and therefore different characteristics.

In order to help students develop their writing skills, it seems that the best form of assessment of a course assignment includes feedback of a kind that will accentuate the formative and minimise the summative (Aren, 1996). It is the aim of this paper to show how this process of assessment and feedback can evolve and hopefully lead to developments in how language support is offered to students.

2. Background to the Study

2.1 The problem

As mentioned above, EEE perceive a problem with the communication skills of their undergraduate students. This is compounded by the fact that they have a third year group of 97 students of which more than half are from overseas. Of these, 38 are from Singapore where they have taken part of their degree and have come to the UK to complete it.

The task for the third year EEE undergraduates involves work on a team design project (TDP): to design, construct, test and demonstrate a specified electronic product over the academic year.

After the first week each team of six students is required to make a group oral presentation and submit an individual written report on (a) the group decisions on their approach to the design development and (b) the component they are responsible for developing.

The department's aim in this is to ascertain how the group is working together and to check that they are justifying their electrical design decisions. Most groups are a mix of home and overseas students. Thus, a further aim of the TDP is to integrate these students.

2.2 The EFL task

The department therefore asked us to:
a) evaluate the general language competence shown in all of the first written reports (2 pages), and in some oral presentations,
b) provide feedback, and
c) give support classes where necessary.

2.3 The EEE report

The first TDP report is a preliminary to a design, testing and evaluation report. As might be expected from the class handout, the task was fairly specific in electrical engineering terms, and prescriptive in content: to provide 'a summary of the overall system in your own words (1 page), details of the aspects for which you were responsible (1 page)' (Davies, 1996).

3. The Criteria for Assessment

We can construe the criteria for assessment in the EEE department from their feedback sheet (see Appendix) and the task guidelines, as follows:
a) the requirement to justify electrical design decisions,
b) the instructions in the course handout mentioned above,

c) the guidelines on report writing in the project handout (with a list of sections, and instructions to avoid jargon and complicated sentences – one idea per sentence).

The EFL assessment criteria were based on the formative feedback profile (Hamp-Lyons, 1986, reproduced in Hamp-Lyons and Heasley, 1994) (see Table 1). The criteria for assessment by the EEE Department and the EFL Unit respectively are given below in Table 1.

Table 1. EEE and EFL assessment criteria

EEE Criteria	EFL Criteria
Structure: introduction, body (subdivided if appropriate) and conclusions	**Communicative quality**: conveys the message clearly, causes the reader few difficulties
Material: appropriate content and level of detail; coherent, well-structured argument	**Ideas and Organisation**: effective arguments and supporting material
Presentation: general appearance of report; competent use of word processor	**Grammar and vocabulary:** wide range and fluent control of structure and vocabulary
Language: the report is easy to read and understand without excessive jargon and buzzwords	**Surface features**: handwriting/(typing), punctuation and spelling
Language: (mechanical aspects) spelling and grammar	

The EFL tutors inevitably had reservations about content. However, genre analysis as an approach to teaching writing has helped us to realise that any writing is situated in a social context. We can therefore expect two things: if it is well written, it should have the social context signals, and since all teaching at the university level should be training students to think critically, evidence of this should be apparent to the lay reader. This hopefully makes it less threatening for a non-specialist to read an engineering report.

Surprisingly, the marking is reported to have presented a problem for the EEE staff, who are not accustomed to using descriptive criteria to give feedback on a subjective scale. Assignments are usually right or wrong. Here they were asked to mark in five categories on a scale of 1 – 5.

If we compare how the two groups of criteria correlate, the table would appear as in Table 2 which follows.

Table 2. Correlation of EEE and EFL marking criteria

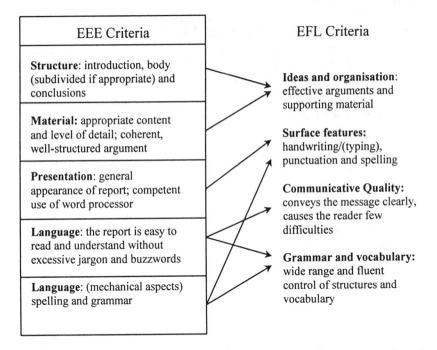

EEE Criteria	EFL Criteria
Structure: introduction, body (subdivided if appropriate) and conclusions	**Ideas and organisation**: effective arguments and supporting material
Material: appropriate content and level of detail; coherent, well-structured argument	**Surface features:** handwriting/(typing), punctuation and spelling
Presentation: general appearance of report; competent use of word processor	**Communicative Quality:** conveys the message clearly, causes the reader few difficulties
Language: the report is easy to read and understand without excessive jargon and buzzwords	**Grammar and vocabulary:** wide range and fluent control of structures and vocabulary
Language: (mechanical aspects) spelling and grammar	

The categories are shown in bold, with those of EEE on the left and EFL on the right. This listing shows the EEE priority in macro terms is Structure, that is, organisation, with Language in last place, whereas for EFL the global focus is on Communicative Quality with Surface Features in last place. Interestingly, though at the bottom of the list, Language for EEE is given two categories which EFL would describe as register and accuracy. There is an implicit assumption that spelling and grammar are 'mechanical', that is, just a matter of editing to achieve correctness.

It is clear from Table 1 that there is a mismatch between the two sets of criteria in terms of assessing content. The EEE department devotes an entire section to content, entitled 'Material', whereas the EFL criteria incorporate it as a subsection under the heading 'Ideas and organisation'.

The other mismatch here occurs where EEE puts grammar and spelling together as 'mechanical aspects' which combine to produce acceptable written English. Predictably, EFL separate them as representing different aspects of language competence. This shows the skew to non-native speakers which EEE do not share.

The comparison of the two groups of criteria shows similarities with the variation described in the paper by Wall et al (1988), mentioned above, in which writing tutors and a subject tutor compared points of view. The main conclusion was that the writing tutors looked at surface features and wished to address the problem of organisation by giving instruction on discourse signals. The subject tutor looked for content-supporting arguments and logical organisation. This is also supported by Weir (1988), who identified the priorities as relevance and adequacy of subject content, clarity of the message, and the arrangement and development of written work. For the subject tutor, although problems with the surface features were annoying, it was possible to understand the text. Nonetheless, the fact that the EEE Department's criteria include two sections relating to language should underline to the students the importance of communicating satisfactorily.

4. EFL Grading and Treatment

Five tutors marked the 97 scripts with the criteria above. We also allocated a grade using a 0 – 9 scale similar to the IELTS and ESU bands, but including half bands for finer discrimination. We then looked for patterns in the types of problems in order to determine appropriate divisions of the class and treatments for each group.

As far as range and control of grammatical structures and vocabulary were concerned, EFL markers found not only problems with NNS students, but also that some NS sadly lacked appropriateness of expression. They wrote as they spoke. Furthermore, it was noticeable that the overseas students (particularly those from Singapore) had a far better grasp of how to structure the report than their European and home student colleagues. As undergraduates, few home students have had any formal instruction in how to write reports. Some have used their wits and noticed what others do. Finally, the most common complaint in our marking, especially at the high levels, was with regard to spelling and punctuation. It would seem useful for all concerned that students be taught that to hand in material that has not been edited or checked is bad manners and likely to encounter censure from the audience.

Since the exigencies of time mean that we need to make students more responsible for their work in future, many of us agree that the EAP goal is to give formative feedback on organisation and logical flow, and concentrate only on language that affects meaning. Giving detailed feedback is an ideal solution, and Marshall (1991) usefully suggests a feedback form based on the genre criteria. However, in this case to fill in an individual form for each student on a computer template would have been too time consuming. Most students can transfer accessible instructions to their own work. A more pragmatic approach to writing looks at developing skills to manipulate information structure, for example, skills which aim to show the students the type of information which needs to be provided. Such tuition focuses not only on sentence level and discourse markers but also on information structure as part of teaching students how to negotiate meaning.

Based on the types of problems identified, the class was divided into three levels for different treatments, as shown in Table 3. They were:

a) those who would receive a handout giving advice on the information elements in the different sections of the report, suggestions for signposting the different sections and evaluations, and indications of level of formality,

b) those who would have a couple of sessions of class work to support the handout, and

c) those who needed more sentence level work as well as a global view of text structure and style.

Table 3. EFL grading and type of treatment

EFL band	Level	No of Students	Treatment
9.0	A	20% (19)	Handout
7 0 - 8.5	B	51% (50)	4 hours tuition plus handout
4.5 - 6.5	C	29% (28)	12 hours tuition plus handout

The reports at level A were, in general, good, well-shaped, and coherent, with section headings. The major problems were with editing. The students in group A received a handout (see Appendix), stressing the importance of editing written work, and with guidelines on structure, information elements, signposting and style. The reports at level B had problems with structure: no introduction, lack of section headings, and problems with style, such as lack of signposts, spoken style, poor linking words, or a limited range of sentence structures. Group B received 2 hours on structure and 2 hours on style plus the handout.

Reports at level C were all written by non-native speakers, including some home students, as will be seen from Figure 1. They were reasonably well organised, but generally difficult to read due to sentence level problems with grammar. Problems arose with singular/plural agreement, formation of the passive, and word choice. Those at the lower end of this group had limited control of grammar. Group C received 12 hours tuition focusing on the above.

5. The EEE Grading

The EEE department scored the reports on grades ranging from A to D. The general opinion of the staff was that the assignment was not well done. It lacked detail and design justification. This problem is to be expected as it is the first such overall design report the students have written. In the first year the task is to verify a design, in the second year they choose a component. So this assignment is asking for a new skill, and it must be remembered that these undergraduates are relatively unskilled writers. As Alexander (1996) noted, they lack the ability to construct whole texts as skilled writers do, and focus instead on surface features.

6. Comparison of EFL and EEE Grading

In order to consider the extent to which the differences in assessment criteria affected the grading outcome, we compared the two grades. We had access to EEE grades for 85 students. The scattergram in Figure 1 shows the distribution of students within the respective EEE grades and IELTS type bands, and the respective treatment levels.

The graph shows a predictable range in the clustering, from both points of view. There is a range of departmental scores reflecting academic ability, with the largest number scoring B. Similarly, within each EEE grade band there is a range of language ability. While most are predictable, there are a few unexpected results worthy of comment. One home student has good English (8.5) but wrote a virtually content free report (D). One bright Greek has both A for EEE and 8.5 for English. One Singapore student had an A despite a low English level (6). Several other of the Singapore students have scored high grades. They tend to be well organised and highly motivated which compensates in some degree for any language problems they have.

Esther Daborn and Moira Calderwood

Figure 1. Comparison of EFL bands and EEE grades, with treatment level

EEE Grade										
A				o		o	h	h h o	o	h h h h h
B			o	o oo o	o o	h	o oo o	h h	h h h h	h h h h h h h h
C		o o o	h o o	o o	o ooo o	h oo o	h	h h h o	h h	h h h h
D	h	o	o	o o	o	o ooo o	h o	h o o	h	
E										
EFL Band	4.5	5	5.5	6	6.5	7	7.5	8	8.5	9

Treatment
level   <------ Level C ------>   <---------- Level B --------->   ←---Level A---->

Key: h = home students, o = overseas students

From the EFL perspective, most of the overseas students can be said to have adequate IELTS/ESU equivalent levels for study. It is also clear that most of the home students score higher than 7.5. The exceptions are non-native speakers who include a) two students with a bilingual ESL background: children of first generation immigrants who have been through the Scottish education system, and b) a student from Scandinavia with Scotvec entry qualifications. Their status as home students means they are not eligible for free language support classes offered by the EFL Unit. These discrepancies show additional language variables influencing the correlation on EEE and EFL grading.

7. Discussion and Evaluation

The collaborative project described here obviously does not reflect the norm for all undergraduate courses. It is a particularly interesting case in that the large number of overseas students in the class meant the department asked for assistance, and in the process was able to deal indirectly with an additional problem of which there is a growing awareness in universities: namely with the communication skills of home students.

The correlation between EEE and EFL grades can only be said to provide food for thought. In discussion with the EEE department staff, we learned that they had done a correlation of first year maths exam marks with entry qualifications in maths, which showed a similar range of clusters. This is significant because the students' ability in maths and their use of English are of equal concern to the EEE Department. It is therefore necessary that we acknowledge other variables to account for the range of scores and lack of correlation.

There were several problems in the running of the project. One was with the attitude of some home students who found themselves outnumbered by overseas students in two of the level B classes, and felt resentful. This caused problems for teaching in that few came to the second class. Where there were more home than overseas students in the class, the home students were able to use the session to get what they wanted on their own terms.

The other main problem in the delivery of the project was time: the marking for tutors, the timetable and attendance for students. A major disadvantage was that the home students tended to look upon EFL classes as conflicting with the Engineering. Some of the weaker overseas students at level C were grateful for the classes, but needed to spend more time on class assignments and therefore had less time for coming to language classes. Some who had a high EEE grade could not see why they should come to language classes. At the other end of the scale, one or two students with good English were given low EEE grades. Is this a modified example of the Dr Fox hypothesis described by Andersen (1988), in which an actor gave a 'scientific' presentation to an educated lay audience and succeeded in fooling them? These students confused the EFL markers, but not those in

EEE. This suggests that genre-based approaches are not always foolproof in detecting content-free work.

In order to learn from this exercise, we asked students to evaluate the feedback they had received. We received completed forms from 43 of the 97 students, with more or less equal numbers from level A, B, and C students. Of greatest value seemed to be the handout, since it provided an overall view of report writing. Also, they appreciated the individual comments on their papers which both evaluated structure and clarity, and identified sentence level problems. Students at level C commented on the usefulness of input on sentence structure, tense, and punctuation. The overseas students identified a need for more input on speaking and oral presentations. The home students suggested a lecture on writing the final report: what to include and exclude, and guidance on the amount of technical information required. One even asked for a summary of grammatical rules in more detail than they had learned at school. This is not to say that all comments were 100% positive. Several students at level A felt they did not learn anything they did not know already. This is fine, since they obviously do not need the support. Nonetheless, the exercise has underlined the importance of feedback to the students, and their need for guidance of this kind.

The current plan for the next academic year is to integrate guidance on oral presentations and report writing in the second year, and to offer the direct entry students specific report writing tuition in week 0 of the third year. The Team Design Project handout will include an adapted copy of our handout and a copy of the marking criteria so that students have a better idea of what is expected. As Jenkins et al (1993) suggest, attention to writing skills needs to be more fully integrated into main academic programmes; that is, the subject specialists themselves should raise the profile of writing by providing guidelines, assessment criteria and feedback. This is also in line with recommendations from a fair amount of recent literature on EAP programmes in a variety of contexts ranging from the USA (Jenkins et al, 1993) to Zimbabwe and South Africa (Allison, 1996). It is helpful in that it allows account to be taken of the problems with language use identified not only in the work of overseas students but also in the work of those from the UK.

8. Conclusion

The main outcome of this collaboration has been to raise the profile of English language use in the EEE department with both staff and students, and to give both groups some tools to deal with the problem. The departmental staff agree about what constitutes good and bad writing. However, they lack the metalanguage to clarify what is missing and provide specific guidance on what to do for improvement.

Prevention is always better than cure. Clear guidance on what is required is the key to successful completion of any task. The value of the language tutors' contribution has been in boosting the confidence of those students with serious sentence level problems, and providing clear guidance on writing style for those whose problems were at a higher level. The recommendations from this exercise focus on integrating the language advice into mainstream teaching. This should be the goal of language support work: to encourage departments to be more self-sufficient in terms of developing writing skills.

References

Alexander O (1996) *Lost and Found in Skyville: A reader response to student writing*, MSc Dissertation, University of Edinburgh

Allison D (1996) 'Pragmatist discourse and English for academic purposes', *English for Specific Purposes* 15.2, pp 85 – 104

Andersen R (1988) 'Overwriting and other techniques for success with academic articles', in Robinson P (ed) *Academic Writing: Process and Product*, Oxford: Modern English Publications in association with the British Council

Aren D (1996) 'Assessment and feedback', *IATEFL Newsletter* No 133, p 8

Braine G (1989) 'Writing in science and technology: an analysis of assignments from ten undergraduate courses', *English for Specific Purposes* 11.1, pp 33 – 49

Davies F (1988) 'Designing a writing syllabus in English for academic purposes: process and product', in Robinson P (ed) *Academic Writing: Process and Product*, Oxford: Modern English Publications in association with the British Council

Davies J (1996) 'Team design project III', class handout, Department of Electronic and Electrical Engineering, University of Glasgow

Jenkins S, M K Jordan and P O Weiland (1993) 'The role of writing in graduate engineering education: a survey of faculty beliefs and practices', *English for Specific Purposes* 12.1, pp 51 – 68

Hamp-Lyons L and B Heasley (1994) *Study Writing*. Cambridge: Cambridge University Press

Marshall S (1991) 'A genre based approach to the teaching of report writing', *English for Specific Purposes* 10.1, pp 3 – 13

Nunan D (1990) 'Action research in the language classroom', in Richards J C and D Nunan (eds) *Second Language Teacher Education*, Cambridge: Cambridge University Press

Robinson P (ed) (1988) *Academic Writing: Process and Product*, Oxford: Modern English Publications in association with the British Council

Wall D, A Nickson, R R Jordan, J Allwright and D Houghton (1988) 'Developing student writing – a subject tutor and writing tutors compare points of view', in Robinson P (ed) *Academic Writing: Process and Product*, Oxford: Modern English Publications in association with the British Council

Weir C (1988) 'Academic writing – can we please all the people all the time?', in Robinson P (ed) *Academic Writing: Process and Product*, Oxford: Modern English Publications in association with the British Council, pp 17 – 34

Appendix

Handout on Report Writing for Team Design Project III Students

Introduction

The purpose of this handout is to explain our criteria for assessment of English language skills in the written report recently submitted as part of the Team Design Project III, and to offer or reinforce points you might find helpful in future report writing. This is intended to complement the points on report writing you were given in the class handout, and the feedback from the EFL Unit on your individual report. It will first outline the criteria of assessment we used, then summarise what a report is expected to contain, and finally comment on how you can help the reader.

Criteria for assessment

1. Communicative quality: is it easy to read?
2. Ideas and organisation: is the information appropriate and clearly organised?
3. Grammar and vocabulary: is there a good range of language used so that the meaning is clear and the text is not repetitive?
4. Surface features: is the punctuation and spelling accurate?

What do we expect to find in a report?

This section looks at the contents of the report structure, and presentation.

1   Structure

Your project handout tells you that a report structure should consist of title and authors, abstract/summary, table of contents, body, conclusion and references. You need to adjust this to suit the length of the report, but the question is: how does this help?

a) The title – tells the reader directly and at first glance what it is that you are discussing.
b) The abstract/summary and table of contents – gives the reader an overview of the report and a list of section headings so they can see the points included and decide which ones to look at.
c) The body – consists of the introduction and component sections.

    (i) The introduction should state the purpose of the report, show you are aware of the terms of reference, ie what is the subject and what is the purpose, state method(s) used and any limitations, and finally indicate how the report is structured. It is important to justify, or say why you are writing, and to give the reader a mind map of what is coming.

(ii) Component sections – should be organised under headings. This forces you to classify information and helps you remain relevant – in case you are likely to wander off the point.

d) The conclusion – starts by referring back to the purpose of the report, states the main points arising, draws conclusions, and possibly makes recommendations.

e) References and appendices: references list the material referred to in your work. Follow Departmental guidelines on format for presentation of references. Appendices provide additional material not included in the text.

2   Layout and presentation

Layout and presentation involves matters ranging from clear title and section headings to accurate spelling and punctuation. You must think of your reader. Presenting accurate text is equivalent to speaking clearly. Since you are not around to explain any problems to your reader, editing/checking your text is extremely important.

How can you help the reader?

Apart from the points raised above about structure, layout and presentation, the main tool you have is obviously the language. There are two main points to make: the first is about what we call 'signposts', the second about style.

1   Signposts

Apart from section headings, you can select language which gives your reader signposts to what you are trying to explain. Signposting helps the person read the text quickly by highlighting the main points and the logic of the argument/discussion. Some examples follow.

*   The first section of your report could start with
    'The aim of this report...' or 'The aim of this project...'
    and the second section
    'Within the group, my responsibility was to ...'
*   Within the first section the stages could be introduced with
    'The first stage is...', 'the second stage...', 'This section deals with...' etc
*   When you want to give an opinion or evaluate something you might signpost with 'The problem with this is...', 'What is significant about this is...', 'It is important to remember that...'
*   To show that you are drawing a conclusion, introduce the point with 'This means that..', 'The result shows that...', 'It is likely that...'

2   Style

Style means the tone of language you use to address the reader. There are three points to make: avoid repetition, avoid a narrative style, and avoid vague language.

i) Repeat only what is necessary, ie key words/technical terms. The reader has a memory. To flatter this, you can introduce your repeated point with words like 'As mentioned earlier...', 'As discussed above...'

Although it is acceptable to use 'I' or 'we' in a report, too many sentences with 'I' and 'we' become repetitive.
  Avoid: 'I had to...'
  Use: 'It was necessary to...'

ii) The reader does not wish to know about everything that happened, but rather your objective assessment of the situation.

  Avoid: 'First we discussed... then we decided...'
  Use: 'The first step was to discuss...' 'It was decided...'

iii) Be precise and be specific

  Avoid: 'There was a problem so we...'
  Use: 'A problem arose with... which meant it was necessary to...'

Conclusion and recommendations

Read over what you have written and check it against the guidelines. Pay particular ttention to punctuation and spelling.

Joan Cutting

Written Errors of International Students and English Native Speaker Students

1. Introduction

There is a growing concern in British universities about the poor literacy of home students. Recent studies show a preoccupation with students' spelling, apostrophes, and use of academic discourse (Lea, 1995; Wray, 1996). Ways of solving the problem are discussed at conferences, such as the 1997 'Writing Development in Higher Education' conference at the University of Wales, Aberystwyth. Some university lecturers have even voiced the opinion that home students do not write as well as top level international students.

Linguistic accuracy tends to be given greater importance by EAP lecturers in the assessment of the written work of non-native speaker of English (NNSE) students than it is by degree subject lecturers in the assessment of assignments of native speaker of English (NSE) students. This may have a washback effect on the attitude and performance of the students. NNSE students tend to take care in their writing, whereas NSE students, knowing that no credit will be given for linguistic accuracy, seem to attach less importance to it. Some NSE students appear to be unaware that clarity of written expression can affect the mark, in that it conveys their thoughts more effectively and subsequently can give an impression of a better command of the subject and issues involved in a piece of assessed work.

The study described in this paper tested the hypothesis that, in the University of Sunderland, NSE students use the language less accurately than top level NNSE exchange students on EAP modules. The paper looks in detail at the errors in written coursework of both groups of students and shows how they differ. This then leads on to a discussion of ways of addressing the problem of poor NSE literacy.

2. Method

The written assignments of 20 NSE students on a linguistics course and 20 international students on a level three (IELTS 6.5 entry) EAP course were compared in terms of errors of grammar, vocabulary, style, spelling and punctuation. The international students' assignments were 1,300 words long and on a free topic. The NSE ones were 2,000 words long and on any topic within the field of linguistics. The whole database was 66,000 words long.

The international subjects were German, Dutch, French, Italian, Spanish exchange students. They were aged about 22 and had done two years at university. The NSE students were British, mainly from north east England. They were aged about 19, being first year students.

The errors were counted and the percentage out of all words calculated. In the detailed analysis of each error type, two thirds of the number of NSE words were taken into account in order to maintain an equal number in both groups.

3. Results

3.1 General

Figure 1 shows that international students had many more problems with vocabulary than NSE students did, but that they had the same number of grammar errors as NSE students. NSE students, on the other hand, had worse spelling and punctuation than international students. Style was not such a problematic area as it might have been imagined for either group.

Figure 1. Error rates divided by type

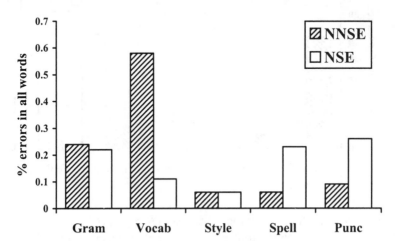

3.2 Grammar errors

In the grammatical analysis, the data dictated categories of tense and aspect, zero main verb, determiner, number agreement and discourse cohesion (parallel structures, reference and ellipsis: see below). As Figure 2 shows, whereas the international students' difficulties were principally with tense and aspect, the area that NSE students had problems with was number agreement and discourse cohesion.

Starting with the NNSE speakers, it can be seen that even these high level international students had considerable confusion as regards tense and aspect, for example,

Every season has its own festivities, through which religious rituals, legendary heroic deeds or the annual renewal of the cycles of nature ARE BEING celebrated.

In this example, the student uses progressive aspect when simple aspect is called for, as in 'cycles of nature are celebrated'. To a lesser extent NNSE students also showed confusion with regard to determiners.

Figure 2. Grammar Errors

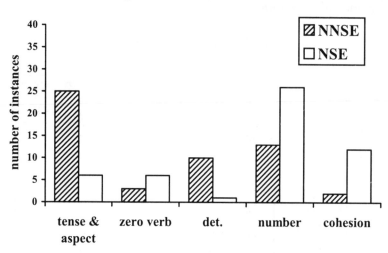

Unlike lower level international students who tend to have definite/indefinite confusion and over- or under-use articles, the top level international students have determiner errors such as,

> *The aim of the program is to provide facilities for education in*
> *AN European context,*

which is an example of overgeneralisation and evidence of an over-careful student being misled by the initial vowel. Their other main problem area was that of number agreement, as in,

> *THESE information is not really helpful,*

in which the lack of determiner-noun consistency maybe reflects pronunciation and could be a product of transfer from the mother tongue.

The NSE students, on the other hand, only occasionally made tense/aspect 'errors', when they used their non-standard varieties, as in,

> *I think that he MAY HAVE SAW the documentary as his perfect*
> *creation.*

This is most likely an example of regional variation as in 'could have went' and 'must have ate', typical of north east England and southern Scotland. Similarly, it was only occasionally that they produced sentences with zero main verb, as in,

Although he maintains his style while reading but returns to the vernacular using glottal stops when he becomes involved in discussion,

which is related to their punctuation problem of the full-stop and the lack of appreciation of what constitutes a sentence (see section 3.6). This example contains a subordinate clause following on from a main clause in the previous sentence. The giving of main clause status to a subordinate clause is not unusual with NSE students.

By far the biggest grammar problem for the NSE students was that of number agreement. Sometimes the explanation was that the final 's' is not pronounced in the writer's accent,

There are two WAY in which the data could be interpreted.

Usually, however, it appeared that they forgot how they had begun the sentence, as in,

All men may be referred to as Mr whether HE was married or not.

which might have been better expressed as 'All men may be referred to as Mr whether they are married or not.' The main reason for forgetting how the sentence began seems to be that the subject had been forgotten since it is far from the verb, or it had become separated from the verb by a subordinate clause, a prepositional phrase or an object. In the following two examples, the intervening nouns appear to have contaminated the verb. In,

The conclusion that I have came up with about the language use in the television documentaries WERE hard to establish.

the verb agrees with the nearby plural noun 'documentaries' in the prepositional phrase, rather than its singular subject 'conclusion'. In,

Advertisements have become a big part of popular culture, and IS now a part of everyday conversation along with film and television.

it agrees with the nearby singular 'culture' in the complement rather than its plural subject 'advertisements'.

The second largest area of NSE grammatical errors was that of the category of discourse cohesion, an umbrella category covering errors stemming from lack of sentence cohesion: inconsistency and ambiguity in clausal parallelism, reference, substitution and ellipsis. Sometimes the negative/affirmative parallelism went amiss,

The readability formula does not give me any personal feedback, AND NO idea weather (sic) the text will be comprehensible.

Here, it might have been clearer to say, 'The readability formula does not give me any personal feedback, or any idea whether the text will be comprehensible'; thus each half of the sentence would have followed the pattern 'negative verb + any'.

Sometimes there was ambiguity because of two or more possible presupposed items in the preceding text to which a pronoun could conceivably refer, as in,

The children were informed that they would be recorded for a couple of weeks, until they have (sic) become accustomed to the observer and the tape-recorders. Then THEY were subtly switched on when required.

Here, 'they' could, in theory, have referred to the tape-recorders or the children, and indeed the initial impression may be that it is cohesive with 'The children' since they are the subject of the previous sentence. There were also instances of ambiguity because of participial clauses with too many possible subjects, agents or objects, as in,

Miller and Swift believe that women lose their identity entirely when referred to as part of her husbands property BY LUMPING their relationship under one name, that of the mans.

Here, it is unclear who is doing the 'lumping' – women or society in general – and it is unclear what they are 'lumping'. This example also carries a problem of style, and the choice of inappropriate informal vocabulary. There are several ways of repairing the sentence; one would be to re-phrase it as 'Miller and Swift believe that women lose their identity entirely when they are referred to as part of their husband's property, and their relationship comes under one name, that of the man'.

Sometimes ambiguity was also brought about by both reference and ellipsis, as in,

Halliday explains that in most forms of written text the flow of language is different to that of spoken language, in the way that spoken language is fragmented and written language is not, EXCEPT IT IS in newspapers.

This is ambiguous because it is unclear what 'it' refers to and what exactly is elided in 'is'. Presumably the 'it' refers to 'written language' and 'is' means 'is fragmented', but uncertainty of reference arises because the confusion of the three verb 'to be's in the preceding text is compounded by the string of noun phrases 'written text', 'the flow of language', 'spoken language' (twice) and 'written language'.

3.3 Vocabulary errors

Vocabulary errors were mainly a concern of the international students (see Figure 1). Many of the NNSE vocabulary errors were a matter of mother tongue transfer,

> *These are made of flour, eggs, oil and GLOBULES of coloured ANIS.*

On other occasions, it seemed that the students had derived words from ones that they already knew, and thus overgeneralised as in,

> *He also spends a considerable part of his time in pubs to improve his DARTING skills.*

in which the student seems to be extending her knowledge of collocations such as 'footballing skills' and 'language learning skills', maybe because she had heard the word 'darting' in a context when it was the participle from the quite separate verb 'to dart'. Sometimes the errors appeared to occur as a result of wrong choice of word from the dictionary, as in,

> *Various HINTS are SPREAD OUT and a number of persons are suspected before the true crime is found out.*

whose meaning is not entirely clear, as a result. It might have meant 'clues are followed' or 'traps are laid'. Often, international students made an error of collocation,

> *Keith is ABSOLUTELY fond of watching TV.*

Whereas 'absolutely crazy about' or 'absolutely delighted' are generally acceptable, NSE speakers might prefer 'fond' to collocate with 'really' or 'very'.

NSE students had very few problems with vocabulary. Those that occurred appeared to reflect a desire to sound academic and formal. The students made a wrong choice of low frequency words, as in,

> *The very nature of my title has CONTRIVED that these opinions have been UNDERTAKEN.*

in which simple, high frequency ones would have been acceptable, for example 'The very nature of my title has made me express these opinions' or 'The very nature of my title has led me to express these opinions'.

The other sort of NSE vocabulary error was the malapropism, as in,

> *I have to step away from the readability formula and look closer at reader COMPRESSION*

in which the intended word must have been 'comprehension'.

3.4 Style errors

Style is a matter of taste, and conventions change. Style was considered inappropriate in the present study if it contained colloquial vocabulary, vague language (general words and the generic 'you') and spoken abbreviations. This was the smallest category of error; out of all the style errors, the use of colloquial vocabulary was the most frequent type (see Figure 3).

International students used more colloquial vocabulary than NSE students. This suggests that international students with fluent spoken English enjoy displaying their native-speaker-like command of everyday English. They used a more personal tone than is conventional in most academic prose,

> *I SUPPOSE people are rather unaware of the current situation.*

when the more impersonal 'It would appear that people are unaware of...' would have been more acceptable.

The NSE students did not make so many errors in terms of formality. When errors occurred, they tended to cluster, as if once the student had started writing informally, it was difficult to break out of it,

> *YOU have to buy the product it's so good but reason ADS, WELL, they obviously reason with YOU.*

Here, the formal context demanded impersonal and unabbreviated prose as in 'Customers are encouraged to buy the product because it

Figure 3. Style Errors

is so good but 'reason' advertisements reason with customers, as the name suggests'. NSE students used slightly more vague language than international students, possibly because this is part of the in-group code used by NSEs when speaking to other student members of the same discourse community (Cutting, 1999),

> *By the 1960s, THINGS were GETTING REALLY sophisticated.*

Here the semantically empty general noun 'things' would have been better replaced with 'mechanisms of promotion' or 'the products', and the meaning of the non-contentful general verb 'getting' more elegantly expressed with 'becoming'.

3.5 Spelling errors

The NSE students had many more spelling errors than their international counterparts. Figure 4 shows that whereas the few NNSE students' errors were mostly in nouns, the NSE ones were in adjectives, a category which for the purposes of this analysis includes the possessive determiners 'its' and 'their'. These possessives are not in the determiner category of 'gram' because the error is not a question of the wrong choice of determiner but of the wrong spelling of the right choice of determiner.

Figure 4. Spelling Errors

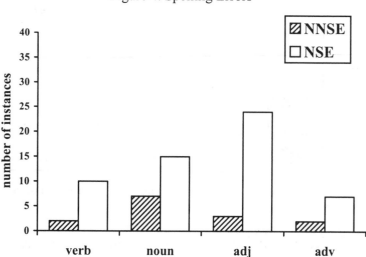

Occasionally the international students misspelt a word, as a result of transfer or pronunciation,

> *Former exchange students should give their TELEPHON numbers to students who wish to know more about the program.*

International students tend to avoid words that they are unsure of, or check first in the dictionary.

In contrast, NSE misspellings were frequent,

> *It is important to keep the question simple, and AVOIDE the DANGERIOUS ROUT of INCORPERATING TO many variables.*

being a classic example. Here, although 'to' may have been a typing error, it occurs often enough in this context for it to be interpreted as a spelling error. Another example is the well-known 'a lot',

> *ALOT of chanting also uses taboo words.*

NSE spelling showed a confusion between pairs of similar words,

> *We can see how the media has an AFFECT on society.*

There were 21 instances of 'it's'/'its' and 'their'/'there' confusion, for example,

> *I will talk about the background of American English, IT'S*
> *spelling, pronunciation and different usages of words.*

and,

> *People who choose THERE own text are more likely to find the*
> *material more satisfactory.*

Some NSE students did not seem familiar with basic rules of spelling changes,

> *Readability is a very broad subject covering hundreds of areas*
> *with differing THEORYS.*

3.6 Punctuation errors

Punctuation errors were again more a concern of the NSE than of the international students. Whereas the international students occasionally misused the comma, many NSE students seemed not to know where to put full-stops, and the use of apostrophes was generally unsystematic (see Figure 5).

Some international students put commas between the subject and the verb, as in 'Most people, live in small houses in the country', or between the verb and the immediately following object, as in,

> *Talking to them, I found out, that everybody made different*
> *experiences in organising their study here.*

This may occur because of the hesitation of NNSE students searching for words, or it may be a transfer of mother tongue punctuation conventions.

The NSE students' work showed a lack of sentence structure. Not only were there sentences lacking a main clause (see section 3.2), there were also numerous instances of several sentences run into one.

Figure 5. Punctuation Errors

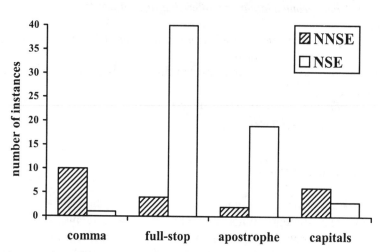

Sometimes the sentences were not separated by any punctuation,

> *The more complex a book is in terms of sentence structure the harder it is to comprehend active verbs are easier to read than passive verbs.*

which should presumably have been 'The more complex a book is in terms of sentence structure the harder it is to comprehend. Active verbs are easier to read than passive verbs.' The danger here is that the reader may understand 'The more complex a book is in terms of sentence structure the harder it is to comprehend that active verbs are easier to read than passive verbs'. Sometimes the full-stop was replaced by a comma, as in,

> *The reflective documentary is concerned with the making of the documentary alone, the film-maker is often present and the microphone is often seen, the Cook report is made mainly in this way.*

in which 'The Cook report' should have started a new sentence, and perhaps 'The film-maker is often present' could have started one before it. Often the comma had weight in that it introduced explanations or examples,

> *Bauer's evidence for supporting the theory that a standard must change is historical, he looks at scripts from both the 10th Century and the 14th century.*

Here, the comma might be substituting for a full-stop or a colon, which would have made the relationship between the two parts more explicit.

In some cases, the absence of full-stop was partly compensated for by the presence of a new sentence marker in the form of a conjunction, adverbial or discourse marker, with a comma before,

The noise level is higher when the children are unsupervised, AS WELL AS the sound of everyday speech there are sounds of singing, screaming etc.

or with a comma after,

The assignment did not involve testing people in different classes like middle class or upper class as Labov's did THEREFORE, the situation for the recording was changed.

or no comma,

The Guardian is much more difficult to comprehend than the Sun this criteria that has been used to measure this conclusion has in my my (sic) been a success HOWEVER other measures could have been incoraprated (sic) that would have provided more informed results.

Comprehension could suffer if the reader related the wrong parts of the sentence and had to re-read it.

The misuse of the apostrophe is a feature of everyday life. It was frequently omitted,

The Cook REPORTS opening sequence is limited.

Occasionally a noun was made plural when it should have been possessive,

The women's use of expletives has been restricted by SOCIETIES perception that swearing is not part of 'ladylike' behaviour.

Often an apostrophe was added to a singular noun making it look genitive when a plural with 's' was needed,

The explicit story, RECONSTRUCTION'S and the dramatic language commentary add major drama.

Another major problem of the NSE students was paragraphing. This was not analysed in the study. Impressionistic observation showed paragraphs often containing what should have been two or three paragraphs and occasionally stretching for a whole page.

4. Discussion

4.1 Causes of error

In this analysis of written assessments, the errors could have been graded and weighted, but it is not evident which category of error is the most important. Grammar and punctuation seem to be the most suitable candidates for heavy weighting in that they can most seriously affect comprehension and affect the final mark for the assessment.

It may be that lecturers feel that NSE writing is worse because they expect better English, and they perceive the misspellings and lack of apostrophe to be a result of carelessness or poor education. They know that there are some NSE students who write well. There is considerable variability in the NSE group.

This is not the case with international students, who are less likely to write in perfect English, and of whom readers may be more tolerant, expecting the occasional verb tense or vocabulary error. There was less variability within this group because the students had been placed in the top class by means of a written grammar test. They were exchange students: they had all been in university for two years and were familiar with the academic written genre in both their language and English.

International students are aware of their language problems. They have volunteered to come to the EAP class to improve their accuracy and formal academic writing skills. They pay attention to their language because in EAP assessment most of their marks are given for the form of their writing, content being secondary.

4.2 Ways of addressing the problem

It is likely that NSE students would benefit from having their language awareness developed. They seem to be handing in their first draft, possibly written late and in a hurry. Students should be given the general advice to make time for spell-checking, editing and re-drafting. The advice would carry more weight if a small proportion of the mark for written work across the university were given for the students' ability to handle the language.

However, for lecturers to give marks for grammar, vocabulary, style, spelling and punctuation, their own awareness needs to be raised. Lecturers need to be shown that their inability to comprehend their students' writing has clear linguistic causes. Lea advocates 'explicit identification by academic staff of the ways in which knowledge is expected to be ordered and processed in the written form within their own subject areas' (1995: 71), but it is not certain that non-language-specialist staff are qualified to give guidance.

In the University of Sunderland, an Articulacy and Literacy Commission was set up to look into ways of solving the NSE writing problem. In induction week, all students and lecturers are already issued with guidelines containing rules of spelling and punctuation, to strengthen the underlying language competence. One proposal of the Commission is to add rules about number agreement and discourse cohesion to these guidelines. Students could also be referred to work sheets on specific problem areas in the university's Learning Development Service, which has self-study materials and gives tuition on study skills and overall assignment structure. Ideally, these problem area work sheets should be computerised.

The Commission welcomed the establishing of an in-sessional remedial course especially for NSE, called WAPENS (Writing for Academic Purposes for English Native Speakers). The present study has shown that it is not useful to put NSE students in EAP classes designed for international students, as happens in some universities. Their errors and needs are different and such a solution could be humiliating for the NSE students. Some universities, such as Kent, Middlesex, Wales Lampeter, and Westminster, run courses to help their NSE students.

Sunderland's WAPENS is a 10-credit-bearing one-semester level-one module which has been running since 1997. It caters only for students referred by their Heads of School because of their poor written expression. The course consists of twelve weeks of three hours a week, one hour being for learning rules and examining anonymous case studies, and two hours for individual attention to focus on each student's problems in their own assignments.

5. Conclusion

It is hoped that this paper may guide EAP lecturers. It suggests that
top level NNSE students had difficulty with tense and aspect, but that
their main problem was vocabulary, errors being caused by mother
tongue transfer, target language overgeneralisation, wrong choice of
word from the dictionary, and unusual collocation.

It is also hoped that this paper may guide EAP lecturers who
have been asked to set up a support service for their NSE students.
NSE writers do indeed have less linguistic accuracy than top level
international students. Their difficulty is not just one of the surface
features of spelling and apostrophes, however; it is also one of whole
stretches of incomprehensible text. This study showed that
grammatically, their biggest problems were, firstly, with number
agreement, with subjects being 'separated' from the verb by
intervening subordinate clauses, prepositional phrases or objects.
Secondly, problems occurred with discourse cohesion, with ambiguity
arising because of two or more preceding presupposed items to which
a pronoun could refer. They also had more punctuation errors than
NNSE students, with their full-stops being replaced by commas, or by
conjunctions, adverbials or discourse markers with a comma before,
after or missing.

University lecturers may offer those students who will not go on
to further study or who may not continue to read extensively after
university their last chance to improve their literacy. As Wray says,
'Those who do not have access to an adequate range of varieties of
written English are at a disadvantage in the employment market'
(1996: 96).

References

Clark R and R Ivanic (1991) 'Consciousness-raising about the writing process', in James C and P Garrett (eds) *Language Awareness in the Classroom*, London: Longman

Cutting J (1999) 'The grammar of the in-group code', *Applied Linguistics* 20.2, pp 179 – 202

Lea M (1995) "I thought I could write until I came here': student writing in higher education', in Graddol D and S Thomas (eds) *Language in a Changing Europe*, Clevedon: British Association for Applied Linguistics in association with Multilingual Matters

Wray A (1996) 'The occurrence of 'occurance' (and 'alot' of other things 'aswell'): patterns of errors in undergraduate English', in Blue G M and R F Mitchell (eds) *Language and Education*, Clevedon: British Association for Applied Linguistics in association with Multilingual Matters

Part Three:

The Requirements of Different Academic
Institutions and Departments

Julie Hartill

Assessing Postgraduates in the Real World

1. Introduction

The aim of this paper is to address a fundamental issue in EAP, namely assessment, which arose from reporting on a university-wide study of departmental contexts with specific relation to postgraduates at the University of Essex between 1995 and 1996. We all have a conceptualisation of what EAP is; what an EAP syllabus contains or should contain. I would like to question what these premises are based on. As universities and colleges recruit more and more international students and EAP continues to expand, there is a risk that EAP and study skills courses are becoming formulaic and that EAP teachers are becoming complacent, assured in the knowledge that, for example, the assessment tasks for which postgraduate students need to be prepared are: giving a seminar paper, writing a dissertation and producing a number of shorter essays or lab reports. My own experience of a range of preparatory, pre-sessional and in-sessional courses supports this, as does the developing body of received knowledge on which EAP is based. But is this a realistic representation of what awaits students once they become integrated into their subject departments? What are the expectations of colleagues in departments once the students are actually there? And what is the role of the EAP tutor in clarifying these expectations for international students or at least making expectations more explicit? I would like to question the underlying assumptions relating to these aspects of EAP based on the evidence of the empirical findings of one strand of a descriptive research project. First, I will give a brief outline of the project itself and how it was conducted before moving on to discuss my findings related to assessment and assessment tasks.

2. The Project

This research project aims to compile as detailed a picture as possible of subject department contexts and to this end involved representatives of each department in the University. Data were collected by means of structured interviews to ensure a 100% response rate. The questions which were asked were devised in consultation with colleagues in the EFL Unit at Essex so that the information elicited was relevant to their needs. Graduate Directors in each department were interviewed and, where taught Masters schemes within a department differed greatly, individual scheme directors were also interviewed. Each Graduate Director received a draft of the write up for their department and was asked to comment on or amend the information so that it was an accurate portrayal of teaching and assessment in that department. Once this stage was complete and all information had been validated by departments, the data were compiled to make an internal report available to all staff in the Unit and abstracted into a computer database. By distilling findings into database format, we have been able to record departmental contexts in a manner which can be easily updated. In terms of using the data, a database enables scan searches to be carried out and facilitates comparisons between departments.

3. Findings

The findings of this research are at the same time encouraging and unsettling. A number of aspects of EAP are confirmed by the data collected. However, the data also reveal some important variations and even contradictions. I have grouped the key findings relating to assessment under two main headings: identifying and defining assessment tasks and clarifying expectations and marking practices/policies. Then I will put forward findings relating to trends in assessment.

4. Identifying and Defining Assessment Tasks

4.1 Terminology and task types

From the outset, one of the issues this research seeks to highlight is the danger of over-generalisation. This exists even at the level of terminology used to define assessment tasks. Although this study is based in a single, small and relatively 'compact' institution, there is, I have discovered, no shared classification for assessment tasks. If we think of parallels in research into teaching contexts, such as seminars, this is not surprising. We know that a seminar in one department may be an individual presenting a paper and a group discussion of a set text in another, yet it is unlikely that we apply the same reasoning to the nature and types of assessment tasks set by departments.

For example, I know what I mean by dissertation, but is this necessarily the same as my students' schema for a dissertation? In most departments a dissertation is the description and analysis of a substantial piece of original research and is submitted at the end of the course. In Sports Science, however, students write two 'dissertations', 7,000 – 8,000 word essays, in the first two terms and end the course with a project. In fact, Science programmes tend to end with a research project, while Social Science and Humanities students complete their degrees with a dissertation. In other departments, the equivalent of the Sports Science dissertations can be a 'research paper' (for example, Law) or possibly a 'term paper' (for example, Economics). To complicate matters further, in a fourth department (AFM) the term paper is a 3,000 word essay on a core subject. All this shows that as EAP teachers we need to be aware of these differences and make our definitions of these terms clear to students with the proviso that they may have different meanings in their own subject area.

4.2 Course work assignments

Since the mid-1980s there has been a shift in academic writing from a product focus to a more process-centred approach highlighted in the collection of papers from the 1985 BALEAP conference *Academic Writing: Process and product* (Robinson, 1988). Intuitively, the process approach seems particularly relevant to the needs of students on taught postgraduate courses (postgraduate instructional students, henceforth PGI students), who have to write assessed course work assignments plus a longer project. The data confirm that this is the area where EAP received wisdom is most accurate. Even here, though, there are one or two exceptions. One department (Psychology) has no assessed course work requirement. Assessment is by means of exams, computer practical and dissertation.

The length and number of course work assignments varies considerably with few discernible patterns. Essays range from 2,500 to 6,000 words. In statistics-based subjects (Economics, AFM) there is a small number of course assignments and then optional term papers can replace up to 50% of the marks available for an examination. The least complex assessment patterns are for the Arts (for example, Art History, History, Language and Linguistics and Literature) which require one essay per module/course, although the number of modules varies as does the word requirement. There are of course variations between schemes as well as between departments.

4.3 The importance of examinations

Probably the most important finding of this project for the EFL Unit, and certainly one of the most surprising, is the number of formal examinations that PGIs at Essex have to sit. Only 6 out of 17 departments have no sit down examinations, preferring a greater number of assessed essays and a longer dissertation. These are all Humanities or Social Science courses. The remainder allocate approximately 12–16 hours to testing, which means that some students, for example those in Electronic Engineering and Psychology, will sit as many as eight 2 hour papers during their degree. Fewer examinations does not necessarily mean fewer hours of testing: Mathematics students only have two papers, but each one lasts 6 hours. So, although process writing, encouraging drafting, writing and re-writing based on teacher feedback are important skills for non-native speaker (NNS) PGIs to practise, there is also firm evidence that the majority of PGI students need to be able to produce the equivalent of a coherent and accurate first draft under pressure (cf Ballard and Clanchy 1991:65).

4.4 A survey of examination questions and question words

Writing as product remains a key skill for students of all disciplines. In addition to numerical tests and data analysis, all 'hard science' (Physics, Biology) courses include at least one essay paper. Only the Mathematics department does not set essay-style examination papers, and only four departments use short answer questions (Computing, Electronic Systems Engineering (ESE), Mathematics and Sports Science). Four departments (Accountancy Finance and Management (AFM), Law, Physics and Sports Science) include a number of examination questions with a problem-solving focus. All of this serves to emphasise the importance of examination writing. Only one department (Sports Science) was keen to stress that there was a deliberate progression in testing techniques moving from multiple choice questions to essay questions as the course progressed and intentionally using a range of testing techniques to account for learner differences and preferences.

 An informal survey of question words at the interview stage revealed that essay question prompts across the disciplines often require discursive essay answers or answers to a question beginning 'how far'/'to what extent'. Two tutors also suggested 'outline'. Obviously, this needs to be investigated further by examining a large sample of past papers from across the disciplines (cf Horowitz, 1986) but it has serious implications for what Jordan (1997: 165) terms a rhetorical-functional approach to the teaching of academic writing as product.

4.5 Other assessment tasks

There are two assessment modes which occur less frequently and as a result are not yet catered for by EAP courses. The first is the take home paper. There are comparatively few formal take home papers across the disciplines, with just two departments (Physics and Law) acknowledging the usefulness of this mode of assessment. The Law department is actively moving towards take home examinations because it has realised that even the best non-native speaker (NNS) students, who outperform native speakers (NS) on assignments, fall down under the constraints of examination conditions. Because examinations test control of language and form as much as subject matter, Law has found that NNS students very rarely achieve distinctions at MA level, and it is felt that this does not always reflect either their ability or the quality of their work generally. Other departments may begin to follow suit.

Second, group projects crop up occasionally as non-assessed course requirements, but only two departments implement group projects as a formal means of PGI assessment. Individuals in several other departments expressed interest in collaborative assessment tasks but cited the problems of setting authentic tasks with authentic outcomes and the difficulty of allocating marks to individuals as the major obstacles to their introduction. The two areas which have introduced collaborative assessed projects are Computing and Electronics, where group output is the norm in industry and the projects are partly a response to this. The question for EAP is how can we, or even should we, prepare international students for these assessment contexts?

I would also like briefly to consider presentations, of which it seems the opposite is true. They are one of the staple components of EAP and study skills courses, yet the data show that they feature rarely as a means of assessment in departments. Only three departments formally assess presentations as part of the course requirement during the academic year, even at PGI level. Masters scheme tutors expect rather than compel their students to participate in presentations and give papers. Based on the anecdotal evidence of my in-sessional group, international students tend to be more concerned about how to participate in large group discussion than the formal presentation of papers. In only one case (Philosophy) is a presentation a developmental task. A paper which has been presented can be written up as an essay for assessment, which seems to me to be an authentic academic task.

5. Clarifying Expectations and Marking Practices/Policies

These are the kind of data that are most difficult to obtain, as they are subjective and tend to vary between and within disciplines. Most participants in this study were quite candid in discussing the differing expectations in course work and examinations. Expectations in examinations are not as high as those for assessed course work. Ballard and Clanchy (1991: 65) describe an examination script as 'fundamentally a rough first draft' and, although this was not expressed in quite these terms, I found nothing to contradict this view. According to the data gathered, the take home paper fits in somewhere between the two, with the time constraint lifted to some degree and greater depth and more detail expected than for a sit down examination answer.

A number of departments evaluate course work according to what could be termed 'communicative effectiveness'. This is particularly true of Science subjects, where technical and scientific competence are rated above academic literacy. Few departments assess work on the quality of the language used to formulate and express ideas (cf O'Brien's 1988 findings). The extent to which linguistic accuracy, or inaccuracy, influences the outcome of a piece of work is left very much to the individual tutor's discretion with comparatively few departments including a marking policy beyond the breakdown of marks in their documentation. My most recent data suggest that even departments which have traditionally insisted on high standards of written expression are having to relax these standards or put in place measures to ensure that they are maintained.

The Literature department, with a high language entry requirement which is applied rigorously, is currently formulating an official language policy, including a log of approved proof readers to be held by the departmental office. It is one of only two departments to address this issue formally. The other (Sociology) employs a Student Support Officer whose role includes organising a resource centre for all students and operating a volunteer proof reading service for international students. As a result the department has raised its expectations regarding presentation, content and accuracy of written work at all levels.

6. Assessment Trends

From the interviews with graduate directors, it seems that gradually departments are becoming aware of the need to initiate all new students, and new international students in particular, into the academic environment. At present two departments (AFM and Literature) have a non-assessed formative assignment with a third (Government) considering the introduction of one. However, formative assignments have a dual purpose. They also give the department the chance to see what their new students can do, although the students are not told this explicitly. The formative assignment in one department was described as optional but any non-native speaker (NNS) students who did not attempt it were referred to the first progress committee. If we as EAP teachers have access to this information we can advise students about what to expect and what will be expected of them.

In addition to the growing interest in formative assignments, there are other indications that awareness and attention to pedagogy are increasing. Economics students are set fortnightly tasks, which are marked but do not count towards their final assessment. While I suspect that this is to show evidence of monitoring students' work and progress for teaching quality assessment and quality assurance, the students obviously benefit from regular practice, contact with tutors and feedback on their work. Both Sports Science and Biology are keenly aware of progression in tasks. For instance, Sports Science students have three assessed presentations throughout the year, beginning with a 5 to 10 minute presentation of their research proposal, followed by a 15 minute synopsis of completed dissertations and an oral examination on their final project. Since this department was founded in 1995, it is tempting to surmise that this developmental approach to assessment (which also carries through into teaching) is an indication that new departments are offering new courses which are more firmly rooted in pedagogy. However, this is not borne out by the description of the other major new course in 1996, run by the second newest department, Psychology, which as I have already mentioned, relies on examinations, a computer practical and a research project to assess its students. To summarise, then, there is a growing awareness of patterns of teaching and learning, but this does not yet permeate the whole institution.

7. Implications

I would now like to discuss in more detail the implications of these findings for EAP by considering whether they confirm or raise questions about issues relating to assessment.

7.1 A common core or subject specific approach?

A recurring issue in EAP is whether courses should focus on common core language and study skills or whether they should be aimed at specific subjects or subject groups (cf Blue's 1988 distinction between EGAP and ESAP). A common core approach is more frequently advocated and the data confirm that unless a group is totally homogeneous then a subject specific approach is impossible. Furthermore, grouping students according to what we perceive to be related disciplines does not guarantee that they require the same skills for success. There is no guarantee that they will be expected to perform the same or similar tasks or be assessed in the same ways. An alternative solution to the common core – subject specific dichotomy would be to use a databank to identify and analyse academic tasks so that similarities across disciplines could be established. For some of their study time, students could then be grouped according to the tasks they need to be able to perform - an echo of Johns' (1988) call for the identification of generalisable academic skills through analysis of genre across disciplines.

7.2 Relevance of English language provision

It is generally assumed that the hows and whats of a syllabus have to be relevant to students' needs. In terms of the relevance of EAP courses to assessment modes in departments, the data confirm the usefulness of the short EAP library research assignment such as pre-sessional projects, where students write an essay of about 2,000 words relating to an issue or topic in their field. However, they reveal that, in the case of Essex at least, present provision for examination preparation could be expanded, given the importance of examinations as a mode of assessment. This has in fact happened this year. A third area, which is neglected in EAP generally, is input for writing longer essays and projects. At present, the only support we offer for dissertation/project writing is one to one in-sessional writing tutorials. Since all students have to write at least one longer assignment on a piece of original research, there is scope for the development of research-oriented writing classes. Because of the conventions of different disciplines this would ideally be a multidisciplinary undertaking, offering training in generic research and writing skills with tutorial support from both language and subject specialists. More targeted provision could focus on the research essay or dissertation/project as a student-produced genre in a particular subject area, or practice in qualitative research methods such as ethnographic techniques could be practised early in the academic year as a 'way in' to academic culture (cf Johns, 1988: 57).

7.3 Writing as process and product

There needs to be a balance between writing as process and product. How this balance is to be achieved is less clear. The data suggest that preparatory courses need to focus primarily, but not exclusively, on process writing. On in-sessional programmes, where most students are constantly engaged in writing shorter assignments in their departments, there is a need to practise writing for examinations. This suggests that a more product-oriented approach is suitable for in-session EAP classes. However, as I have just indicated, this also needs to be supplemented with specific training for writing up research.

7.4 Broadening EAP assessment

The data also indicate that there is scope for broadening the range of assessment tasks on EAP courses to reflect departmental assessment requirements such as group tasks, mid-length assignments written over several days, written problem-solving tasks and timed essays.

7.5 Marking and language policy

As marking becomes an issue for subject specialists this could spill over into EAP. Traditional emphasis on grammatical accuracy is clearly beginning to be relaxed in some departments and the indications are that this trend will continue. It is possible to foresee a time when students will be more preoccupied with content and structure than language, with ramifications for EAP teachers, who cannot be specialists in every subject. If this is the case, EAP practitioners may need to work more closely with tutors in departments and may have to carve a new role for themselves, perhaps acting in an advisory capacity. In 1975, *The Bullock Report* recommended that all teachers should assume responsibility for the teaching of language, yet these recommendations had little impact on higher education. Now, subject departments are beginning to consider implementing their own language support strategies as a pragmatic response to wider social changes and shifts in educational management and policy.

7.6 Overt and covert expectations

A thread which runs through both the findings of this project and its implications is the importance of identifying and making explicit expectations at all levels. Success in higher education depends partly on a student's ability to decode attitudes and expectations and recognise norms. On preparatory EAP courses, students want to gain as much information about their future departments as possible and look to course tutors to advise them. EAP specialists therefore need to be well-informed and up to date with departmental practices and expectations. It is particularly important that temporary tutors on summer courses have access to comprehensive and accurate information.

Students need to be aware that expectations will vary between, and even sometimes within, departments and that they will not necessarily be told directly what is expected of them. International students must be encouraged to adopt a pro-active approach to establishing expectations, and EAP specialists must continue to gather information which enables them to make explicit the cultural and academic norms of both an institution and its departments.

7.7 Monitoring and responding to change

In the past, change in Higher Education has been slow. During the Nineties, the rate of change has been increasing. The institution seems to have begun to adapt to its students. For example, in recent years NNS students have been permitted to take a general (that is, non-specific) bilingual dictionary into examinations and read-only electronic dictionaries are now permitted too. This, combined with the external influences of initiatives such as teaching quality assessment, means that greater diversity in both teaching and testing will continue to be introduced. EAP teachers will need to keep up with these developments, requiring continued large-scale research supplemented by detailed study of individual contexts.

8. Conclusion

This investigation of postgraduate assessment in subject departments reveals that there are significant differences between the picture of assessment EAP practitioners may hold and what happens in reality. There is a tendency for EAP to overgeneralise about the kinds of assessment tasks and the criteria which are used for marking. The range of assessment tasks in subject departments is varied, with examinations constituting a more common means of assessment at postgraduate level than might generally be acknowledged by EAP practitioners. The interpretation of marking criteria by individual tutors tends to depend on personal attitudes and preferences, although there are indications that some standardisation is occurring at least at a departmental level.

The data discussed here represent a single institution and there will no doubt be differences between university contexts. Further studies are needed to extend EAP practitioners' understanding of assessment patterns across disciplines and institutions and generate generalizations about the assessment tasks that NNS postgraduate students need to be able to complete to ensure academic success. This in turn will enable EAP practitioners to continue to raise NNS students' awareness about the existence of such differences, train students to identify them and consult relevant data when designing courses and materials to prepare students for the assessment tasks they will meet as part of their subject study.

References

Ballard B and J Clanchy (1991) *Teaching Students from Overseas: A brief guide for lecturers and supervisors*, Melbourne: Longman Cheshire

Blue G (1988) 'Individualising academic writing tuition', in Robinson P (ed) *Academic Writing: Process and product*, Oxford: Modern English Publications in association with the British Council

Bullock A (1975) *A Language for Life (The Bullock Report)*, London: HMSO

Horowitz D (1986) 'Essay examination prompts and the teaching of academic writing', *English for Specific Purposes* 5.2, pp 107 – 120

Johns A M (1988) 'The discourse communities dilemma: identifying transferable skills for the academic milieu', *English for Specific Purposes* 7.1, pp 55 – 60

Jordan R R (1997) *English for Academic Purposes: A guide book and resource for teachers*, Cambridge: Cambridge University Press

O'Brien T (1988) 'Writing for continuous assessment or examinations – a comparison of style', in Robinson P (ed) *Academic Writing: Process and product*, Oxford: Modern English Publications in association with the British Council

Robinson P (ed) (1988) *Academic Writing: Process and Product*, Oxford: Modern English Publications in association with the British Council

Acknowledgements

Thanks are due to colleagues in subject departments who participated in the research project.

Rita Green

Life after the Pre-Sessional Course: How Students Fare in their Departments

The overall aim of this study was to ascertain how accurate the end of pre-sessional assessment procedures used at the Centre for Applied Language Studies (CALS), at the University of Reading, were in predicting students' ability to cope linguistically with university courses, and whether in the light of these findings any changes might need to be made to these procedures. Approximately 21% of the students at the University of Reading come from outside the UK and most do not have English as their mother tongue. The In-sessional English Language Support Programme (IESP), which was established to help such students, provides support in the form of English for Academic Purposes in all four skills. In addition, students can make appointments for tutorials on a one-to-one or small group basis.

The first two sections of this paper describe the procedure and the research instrument used in this study, whilst the third section discusses the various findings. In the final section of the paper, a number of conclusions are drawn up.

1. Procedure

In stage one of the research, questionnaires were sent to ex-pre-sessional students who were three months into their university courses, and to their academic tutors. In part one of the questionnaire, academic tutors were asked to assess their students in all four skills as well as general ability; students were similarly requested to provide self-assessment grades. In part two of the questionnaire, both groups were asked to indicate which factor(s), out of a list of 13 based on an adapted version of the questionnaire used by Tonkyn et al (1993) helped, hindered, and/or were of importance to academic performance.

In stage two, the data from the returned questionnaires concerning language assessment and performance factors were analysed. The returned questionnaires comprised 59 from academic tutors, representing 18 departments and 48% of those sent, and 58 from ex-pre-sessional students, representing 47% of those sent. Of these returned questionnaires, 32 were matching pairs; in other words, both the student and their academic tutor had each returned the questionnaire. These data were also compared with the grades given by the pre-sessional teachers on their students at the end of the pre-sessional course.

In stage three, interviews were carried out with a total of 24 academic tutors as a follow-up to the questionnaires and in stage four, three case studies are reported on. In stage five, a follow-up search was carried out to ascertain the academic outcome of the ex-pre-sessional students. In the light of these findings, it was decided that a similar search could usefully be made on the previous year's ex-pre-sessional students so as to be able to look at such data over two years. The data concerning passes and fails were then analysed in conjunction with final pre-sessional report grades, pre-sessional entry scores, and final pre-sessional test scores.

2. Research Instrument

As mentioned above the research instrument comprised two questionnaires: one directed at academic tutors, the other at ex-pre-sessional students (see figures 1 and 2).

Figure 1. Extracts from questionnaires sent to academic tutors
and ex-pre-sessional students

---

a)   Language assessment

  i) Instructions to academic tutors:

Please rate the English language ability of the student named above
with regard to his/her ability to cope with his/her academic course at
the PRESENT TIME. You should rate each student both in terms of
their general ability in English and their individual language skills.

  ii) Instructions to ex-pre-sessional students:

How would you describe your level of proficiency in English? Please
rate your English language ability both in terms of your general
ability and your individual language skills. Please note that although
this form is very similar in format to the one you were given at the end
of the pre-sessional course, we are interested in your assessment of
your ability NOW, and not what it was in September.

Ability Rating	Description		Individual Language Skills			
			List	Speak	Read	Write
☐	Shows native speaker ability		☐	☐	☐	☐
	(5 other levels)					
☐	Shows very little ability in English and is well below a satisfactory level		☐	☐	☐	☐

It will be noted from Figure 1 that the first part of the
questionnaire concentrated on language assessment. The final report
form comprised a total of seven descriptors which summarised the
candidates' abilities in terms of their command of the language, and
how this may facilitate or handicap them in their chosen studies. At
the lower levels, the descriptors also indicated to what degree the

overall standard of the students' abilities was felt to be insufficient for tertiary study through an English-language medium. The instructions for academic tutors and ex-pre-sessional students were very similar, and the descriptors used in the scale were identical to the ones used in the final pre-sessional report form thus making direct comparisons possible. Academic tutors were asked to indicate which of the descriptors best described the language ability of their students, whilst students were asked to grade themselves.

In part two of the questionnaire, which looked at performance factors, the instructions for both academic tutors and ex-pre-sessional students were practically identical, and the list of factors was exactly the same. The list comprised: communication (oral/written), diligence, knowledge of subject, ability to use resources, relationship with fellow students, relationship with teaching staff, personal situation, degree of intellectual curiosity, ability to think critically, ability to think in English, and personality factors.

Figure 2. Performance factors

i)   Instructions to academic tutors:
Which of the following factors have helped or hindered this student's academic performance? Please put X in those boxes you feel relevant. In addition, please indicate the factor(s) which, in your opinion, are the most important.

ii)   Instructions to ex-pre-sessional students:
Which of the following factors have helped or hindered (caused problems with) your academic performance? Please put X in those boxes you feel relevant. In addition, please indicate the factors which, in your opinion, are the most important.

	HELPED	*HINDERED*	*MOST IMPORTANT FACTOR(S)*
Communication skills			
a) oral			
b) written			

(+ 10 other factors ↓)

Nearly half the questionnaires sent to academic tutors and ex-pre-sessional students were returned. The information generated by these questionnaires was then fed into the database on the ex-pre-sessional students using the Statistical Package for Social Sciences (SPSS). At this point in the study, the database contained the students' biodata, their entry levels (IELTS/TOEFL) to the pre-sessional courses if available, the pre-sessional teachers' grades, their final report/test scores, the academic tutors' grades, the students' self-assessment grades, and the performance factors selected by the academic tutors and students.

3. Stages of the Investigation

3.1 Stage 1: Pre-sessional grading

A number of experienced and well-qualified teachers are employed at CALS every summer as pre-sessional teachers. During the period of this research, 18 teachers completed a total of 346 end-of-course forms which were then submitted to the course directors.

The final pre-sessional report used by CALS is based on an internal 9–point scale (as briefly outlined in Figure 1) and provides an indication of the student's ability in all four skills as well as general ability. Grades are given by the pre-sessional teachers based on continuous assessment and class participation, whilst the final pre-sessional test provides supplementary information for use in borderline cases and as a measure of how students perform under examination conditions. Based on these sources of information, the pre-sessional course directors make their final decisions concerning each student's ability.

In many cases two, and in some cases, three teachers submitted grades on the same student on one or more skills. This made it possible for comparisons of grades given to the same students, to be made across teachers. The results are displayed in Table 1 below:

Table 1. Agreements and disagreements between pre-sessional teachers
on pre-sessional students

Agreements					
	Gen	**List**	**Spk**	**Rdg**	**Wtg**
totals	41	34	39	18	16

Disagreements					
Grade	**Gen**	**List**	**Spk**	**Rdg**	**Wtg**
0.5	32	27	46	13	20
1	28	30	31	13	10
1.5	14	12	17	2	4
2	2	5	4	3	1
2.5	1				
totals	77	74	98	31	35

The results showed that there were a total number of 148
agreements between teachers and 315 disagreements. However, it
should be noted that 44% of these disagreements differed by only half
a point on the internal 9 – point scale, thus leaving 177 differences of
opinion ranging from 1 to 2 grades with just one case of a 2.5
disagreement.

Even though there are differences of opinion between the
teachers, it should be remembered that it is the course director who
makes the final decision with regard to the report forms which are
issued, and that this decision will be based on all the information to
hand – 1, 2 or 3 teachers' opinions as well as the results of the final
pre-sessional test. To some extent, the fact that such triangulation
takes place should help to ensure that fewer inaccuracies result than
might be the case where only one measure of a student's ability is
available. Clearly though, even with experienced and qualified
teachers, these statistics show the importance of maintaining
standardisation and training in assessment procedures.

3.2 Stage 2: Questionnaire study

In this stage of the research, the data resulting from the 32 matching questionnaires (academic tutors and students) were compared with those from the final pre-sessional report and test. A summary of the findings is displayed in Table 2.

Table 2. Comparison of ratings by academic tutors, ex-pre-sessional students, final pre-sessional report and final pre-sessional test

	significant correlations (n = range of 26 to 32)
Academic tutors vs final pre-sessional report	general** speaking** listening** writing**
Academic tutors vs final pre-sessional test[†]	general** listening** writing**
Academic tutors vs students' self-assessment	general * speaking *
Students' self-assessment vs final pre-sessional report	speaking** reading*
Students' self-assessment vs. final pre-sessional test [†]	reading*

† no spoken component in the pre-sessional final test
* sig at .05, ** sig at .01

The findings show that there is a significant correlation at the .01 level between the academic tutors' judgement of their students and the grades awarded on the final report at the end of the pre-sessional course in general ability, speaking, listening and writing; only in reading is the correlation not significant. This might perhaps be partly explained by the fact that during interviews (see stage 3 below), tutors revealed that that they had some difficulty in assessing reading.

The students' estimates correlated less well, with only speaking and reading producing moderate though significant correlations with the final report (.46** and .42** respectively). An analysis of the data concerning listening showed that half the students gave themselves higher grades. This could have been due to a natural improvement in this skill through longer residence in UK, during which the students had become more accustomed to listening to native speakers. In writing, half the students gave themselves lower grades. This might be partly explained by the difference in the type of tasks students face in the department in comparison with those on the pre-sessional course.

This stage also included an analysis of the factors affecting academic performance and Table 3 shows a summary of those factors mentioned most by ex-pre-sessional students and academic tutors.

Table 3. Factors mentioned most by ex-pre-sessional students and academic tutors as affecting academic performance

		HIGHEST NUMBER OF MENTIONS (n = range 18 – 39)	
H **E** **L** **P**	ex pre-s students	• relationship with fellow students • relationship with teaching staff • knowledge of subject	[39] [39] [39]
E **D**	academic tutors	• diligence • degree of intellectual curiosity • relationship with fellow students	[38] [31] [31]
H **I** **N** **D**	ex pre-s students	• oral skills • ability to think in English	[18] [18]
E **R** **E** **D**	academic tutors	• oral skills • written skills	[19] [18]
I **M** **P** **O**	ex pre-s students	• knowledge of subject • ability to think critically	[23] [19]
R **T** **A** **N** **T**	academic tutors	• written skills • ability to think critically • intellectual curiosity	[21] [19] [19]

It may be noted that both academic tutors and students emphasised non-linguistic factors as being of help as opposed to linguistic ones, whilst in terms of factors hindering performance, linguistic factors received most mentions from both academic tutors and students. With regard to importance, students placed emphasis on non-linguistic factors, in particular on the knowledge of their academic subject rather than linguistic factors, which confirms Grundy's (1993) findings. Academic tutors, on the other hand, selected both linguistic and non-linguistic factors. Of the 21 academic tutors (representing 10 departments) who selected written skills, 15 also chose *ability to think critically*.

3.3 Stage 3: Interview study

A number of interviews were carried out with academic members of staff in twelve departments. Not perhaps surprisingly, the results revealed that they found it easier to give general impressions of students than comments on individual skills but most agreed that writing skills needed most attention. They felt that students' speaking and listening abilities naturally improved the longer they remained in an English speaking environment, despite the fact that many students do not mix a great deal with native speakers and are often disappointed at the slow speed of their spoken development. Most of those interviewed found it difficult to comment on reading skills but observed that many students appear to spend too much time on texts, which they blamed on their inadequate language ability.

Another finding which surfaced during the interviews was the difficulty of distinguishing between problems stemming from language, and those related to culture and content. Often non-native speakers have all their problems blamed on language but many academic tutors stress that native speakers also have problems with writing. Some preliminary efforts have been made to try to tease out these overlapping elements (see Stage 4: Case Studies below) by distinguishing those unacceptable elements which a native speaker might produce from those which only non-native speakers produce. In addition, an analysis of which 'types' of English are perceived as being acceptable is being undertaken.

Another area which was commented upon by tutors is flow, the moving from one statement in a text to another, suggesting that students often require help with establishing a clear connection of ideas in a way that is acceptable to those reading and marking their work. They commented that the style of a particular piece of writing must be consistent and must take into account both the message and the reader.

With regard to test scores, discussions showed that scores of 6.5 or 7.0 on IELTS or the Pre-sessional course were taken to be the minimum by most faculties, though some tutors said they allowed lower scores in certain circumstances, and some EU students entered without pre-testing. A few tutors mentioned that occasionally it appeared that some NNS students with higher scores struggle while others with scores below 6.5 seem to have no problems. Some tutors also felt that for PhD students doing research even a score of 5.0 might suffice, but that for MSc's where there were many lectures and essays, the 6.5 should be adhered to, though not all MSc's are heavily lecture/essay-based. Finally, a few comments appeared to suggest that TOEFL scores were less useful than IELTS, TEEP or Pre-sessional ones.

3.4 Stage 4: Case studies

A number of case studies were drawn up based on the various sources of information available: course report grades and comments, test results, the academic department's opinions and in-sessional data on the student. Three of these studies are reported on in this section.

The first concerns a Belarussian student who was enrolled for an MSc in Economics. Both her course report and her test results suggested that her linguistic ability was sufficient to cope with an academic course. She was described as 'A very competent student. An active participant, and able to express herself well over a range of tasks.' Her academic department, however, felt her level of written English was insufficient, which led her to attend in-sessional courses throughout her MSc studies. Although her English did improve during the year and she did obtain her MSc, the department continued to criticise her written academic English.

The second study, a Jordanian student studying for an MA in International Issues, also received good results in her course reports and tests. The student did not register for the in-sessional course until the following February as she felt that her English was good enough. She attended only two in-sessional tutorials even though she acknowledged that her written work needed more attention, the main criticism of her work according to her tutor being that 'the use of English ... is a problem throughout the essay. By this I do not mean that your English is poor or unintelligible but it is too colloquial and the phraseology is poor.'

The third case study involved a student from Mozambique who was enrolled for a Diploma in Rural Development. Her course report gave her a 6.5 though her test results were somewhat weaker – averaging 4.75 across reading, listening and writing. Despite being asked to attend the in-sessional course by her department, the student attended only three out of six classes and contributed little. Although she returned later in the Lent and Summer terms for further tutorials, her written work was still perceived as being around 5 by the in-sessional staff.

Although only three cases have been reported on here, some tentative conclusions may be drawn. Firstly, achieving the required minimum English language scores for university entrance does not guarantee trouble-free, academic study. Several students with high scores found that their work was often not acceptable in their departments. Secondly, the case studies would seem to suggest that the relationship between the type of written work which students carry out on the pre-sessional course and/or before they attend the university, and that which they are expected to produce in the department may benefit from further scrutiny. Thirdly, where the course report and test results differ markedly (as in the third case they do by nearly 2 points), care must be taken to flag such cases for particular attention by the receiving department.

3.5 Stage 5: Academic outcomes

The final stage of this study entailed analysing data concerning the ex-pre-sessional students of the current and the previous years. A summary of the academic outcomes for those students studying for masters degrees are displayed below:

Table 4. MA/MSc degree results of ex-pre-sessional students
over two years

MA/MSc degrees	Attempt	This year (TY)		Previous year (PY)	
		n	%	n	%
Pass	1st	68	82.9	57	90.5
Pass	2nd	9†	11.0	3	4.76
Fail	1st	3	3.66	3	4.76
Fail	2nd	2	2.44	-----	------
TOTALS		82	100%	63	100%

† includes some students re-sitting from previous sessions

These findings show that in both years, approximately 94% of these students were successful, and that only 5% to 6% failed. The latter came from three out of the five faculties, namely, the Faculty of Agriculture & Food, the Faculty of Letters & Social Sciences and the Faculty of Science. Table 5 below illustrates the details concerning these various sub-groups.

The final pre-sessional reports for the pass sub-groups for these two years reveal means of 6.75 and 6.91 for the masters' degrees. For the same years, the fail/second attempt sub-group has means which range from 6.5 to 6.75 – not markedly different. Entry scores of the two sets of groups also appear similar though perhaps the TOEFL scores for those students passing at first attempt is slightly higher than for those who failed/passed at the second attempt (542 – 549 all passes, 548 – 552 masters' degrees, compared with 513 – 543 for the fail/second attempt groups).

Table 5. Data concerning the ex-pre-sessional students, pass
and fail sub-groups (extract)

	n	*final pre-s report**		*pre-s entry score***	
		range	*mean*	*range*	*mean*
TY – failed 1st attempt	3	6.5	6.5	540 5	540 5
PY – failed 1ˢᵗ attempt	3	6.5	6.5	503-523 5.5	513 5.5
TY – passed 2ⁿᵈ attempt	9	6.0 - 7.0	6.72	523-563 5.0 - 6.0	543 5.6
PY – passed 2ⁿᵈ attempt	3	6.5	6.5	507-523 6	515 6
TY – failed final attempt	2	6.5 - 7.0	6.75	5 - 6.5	5.75
PY – failed final attempt	0	----------	-------	--------	-------
TY – passes – 1st attempt (Masters)	68	5.0 - 7.5 n=68	6.75	483-613 4.5 - 7.0 n=57	552 5.85
PY – passes – 1st attempt (Masters)	57	6.0 - 9.0 n=56	6.91	495-580 4.5 - 7.0 n=47	548 6.06

* based on an internal 9 – point scale   ** IELTS/TOEFL

In other words the information provided by the final pre-sessional report alone does not appear to be sufficient to signal future academic problems which would appear to support the findings of the case studies (see stage 4 above).

4. Conclusions

Several conclusions may be drawn from this study into the accuracy of the end of pre-sessional assessment procedures in predicting students' ability to cope linguistically with university courses. Firstly, even with well-qualified and experienced pre-sessional teachers, it is important that standardisation procedures and training in carrying out assessments on pre-sessional students be maintained, in order to promote accurate measures of the students' linguistic abilities (Table 1).

Secondly, there was a significant relationship between the academic tutors' assessment of their students and the final pre-sessional report in speaking, listening, writing, and general ability at the .01 level (Table 2).

Thirdly, academic tutors felt non-linguistic factors helped their students' academic performance, that linguistic factors hindered, and both played an important part in their academic performance. Students agreed to some extent though they prioritised knowledge of their academic subject over the importance of linguistic factors (written skills were ranked fourth) in contrast with their academic tutors who ranked written skills first (Table 3).

Fourthly, a comparison of the final university results attained by those who had academic problems, and those who did not, did not reveal any marked difference when compared with final pre-sessional report scores (Tables 4 and 5).

Finally, of the 57 students who took masters' degrees in the two years studied, only eight failed, in other words approximately 5 – 6%. Even assuming that these students failed due to linguistic reasons, and not due to a combination of factors, this picture would seem to confirm that the assessment procedures being carried out at the end of the pre-sessional course are predicting students' ability to cope fairly accurately and the data from academic tutors, and final university results would seem to support this.

Feedback from the students and their departments would seem to suggest a need to look more carefully and critically at what is being taught. Already, several major changes have been made to the in-sessional classes at Reading as a result of this feedback whilst the suite of EAP books used in the pre-sessional course is currently under review.

References

Blue G M (ed) (1993) *Language, Learning and Success: Studying through English,* Modern English Publications in association with The British Council

Grundy P (1993) 'Student and supervisor perceptions of the role of English in academic success', in Blue G M (ed) *Language, Learning and Success: Studying through English,* Modern English Publications in association with The British Council

Tonkyn A, C Locke, P Robinson and C Furneaux (1993) 'The EAP teacher: prophet of doom or eternal optimist? – EAP teachers' predictions of students' success', in Blue G M (ed) *Language, Learning and Success: Studying through English,* Modern English Publications in association with The British Council

Acknowledgement

I would like to acknowledge the contribution of Andy Seymour, University of Reading, with whom Stage 3 (the interview study) was carried out, and who produced the case study notes discussed in Stage 4 of the investigation.

Lynn Errey

Stacking the Decks: What does it Take to Satisfy Academic Readers' Requirements?

1. Introduction

The role of EAP teaching in British universities today is a complex one. Through research and good practice, EAP tutors endeavour to fit course design and teaching around the perceived and specific needs of students. Simultaneously, there is an expectation that EAP instruction should reconcile these needs with the requirements of the academic institution, particularly in regard to writing for academic purposes. As Ballard (1993) baldly puts it, most students' academic problems come down to writing, not just writing in itself but writing within the 'strange' constraints of academic culture. This means writing in a way which fits the specific expectations of different lecturers working within different fields.

How far EAP instruction should push students to meet the demands of the academic discourse community has at times been a political issue (Benesch, 1994; Ivanic, 1992; Pennycook, 1989). Nevertheless, it is inescapable that EAP students should be taught to consider and predict the academic expectations and values of the lecturers who are going to mark their essays, if they are to establish a 'shared sets of communicative purposes' (Swales 1990: 46). To this end, EAP tutors need to analyse the requirements of academic lecturers, and to understand where expectations are shared or not shared amongst students and lecturers. Otherwise EAP instruction and feedback remain theoretical and general, based on idealised reactions to idealised essays, rather than pragmatic and authentic, based on the work students actually produce, and how it is assessed.

Pragmatically speaking, it is easier said than done to talk about what academic readers really expect from a 'good enough' essay (Tonkyn et al, 1993). It is difficult to speak authoritatively about academic readership when so little is known about how lecturers react or respond to the essays submitted to them, in particular essays written by students from another language and culture. Giving 'authentic' EAP feedback on students' academic writing seems of doubtful use, without some idea of the real criteria by which EAP students' writing is read by other readers. For instance, Santos' study (1988) suggests that rhetorical structure and content in academic writing are more important to lecturers than accurate grammar. But if this is true in theory, can we really say to what degree departures from linguistic and genre norms in an NNS essay will skew a reader's judgement? Can we say what factors, in a less than perfect NNS essay, would make that essay acceptable, or 'good enough'? If a basic tenet of good communication is meeting the expectations of the intended reader, do we know how far unintentional rule-breaking will be tolerated in the playing out of student/reader expectations of task? These are questions which merit closer study.

Various approaches have been taken to researching academic readers' requirements and expectations in regard to student writing across the curriculum. Such studies are valuable, but nevertheless have presented a number of limitations. Firstly, analyses of academic task types and rubrics (Braine, 1989; Casanave and Hubbard, 1992; Horowitz, 1986; Jenkins et al, 1993) have clarified the kinds of tasks students are expected to do. However, it is also well documented that many international students have difficulty 'reading' the implicit expectations embedded in the rubrics of tasks they are set (Ballard, 1992; Campbell, 1990; Houghton, 1984). Also, lecturers do not always communicate their requirements as explicitly as they think they do (Allison, 1996; Howe, 1993; Johns, 1991). In other words, task instructions may hide a number of non-explicit expectations which can themselves lead to confusion.

Secondly, many survey questionnaires, usually based on the Bridgeman and Carlson model (1983), have sought to rank the importance which lecturers give to various factors in academic writing. This is done both to find out what factors will be most and least rewarded in assessment, and which should be most prioritised in teaching EAP. However, asking lecturers in the abstract what they most rank in student writing gives us at best an overgeneralised or idealised idea of their academic values. Such surveys do not necessarily give us a usable or even accurate picture of what exactly lecturers react to when assessing the less than ideal texts of 'apprentice' undergraduate writers (Cohen and Cavalcanti, 1990), or how much their reactions govern their assessment. Another difficulty is that ranking survey methods do not always make clear how far concepts such as 'content', 'development of ideas' or 'appropriate style' have been pre-defined, to ensure that in fact lecturers are all talking about the same thing in academic writing. Jenkins et al, (1993) demonstrate how lack of shared concepts in terminology can lead to 'vague' data.

Potential mismatches in concept are diminished in studies using ethnographic methods based on interviews with lecturers, such as those conducted by Ballard and Clanchy (1991) and Johns (1991), and are used to probe faculty perceptions of NNS writing difficulties. Data arising from such interviews have been invaluable for providing insights into reader-writer relationships in the student essay genre, and revealing how lecturers perceive their students' writing processes as well as their written product. But these studies too are limited in being general and post-experiential. They do not tell us much about the lecturers' reading or assessment processes as they read less-than-perfect student texts, nor about how much they juggle, tolerate or penalise perceived difficulties in their overall assessment decisions.

A number of studies have focused specifically on lecturer reactions to language error in NNS writing (Carlisle and McKenna, 1991; Janopoulos, 1992; Santos, 1988; Vann et al, 1991). However, such studies have usually been based on generalised, non-academic writing. As such they cannot necessarily predicate parallel reader reactions to subject-specific writing where content is important to that reader's field. In other words, where a lecturer is focussing on authentic discipline-specific content in an essay, we do not know how far language error interference makes a difference to a reader's overall judgement. Studies such as Ballard (1993), Campbell (1990) and Johns (1991) suggest that even small language errors, which do not obscure meaning, can still bias a lecturer's overall judgement. It seems that even if in principle lecturers may claim to focus on content rather than on language, they risk misinterpreting NNS language surface errors as an overall lack of ability in task comprehension or related writing skills.

In practice, experienced EAP tutors may rely on their own personal academic experience to advise students what lecturers might look for in an ideal essay, and may verify this with lecturers in various disciplines. However, it seems there is scope in research for clarifying what really happens between academic readers and NNS writers in the assessment process. Where the textual quality of an essay risks being problematic, as in essays written by non-native speakers, an observation of the lecturer's reading process itself may clarify what combination of factors constitutes the difference between a 'good enough' essay, and a fail.

2. The Study

An action-research study was undertaken at Oxford Brookes University to explore what lecturers from different disciplines require in essays written for them. The aim was to gain phenomenological insight into what these lecturers reacted to as they assessed essays written for them by first year NNS undergraduate students. The objective was to gain a better insight into how lecturers themselves analysed the essay tasks that they set, and to evaluate how far the lecturers' reactions to students' writing could inform EAP course design and feedback at the institution. The study specifically investigated which factors in an essay script provoked the most salient reactions from lecturers, and how far perceived language problems skewed lecturers' final grading of the essay they were reading.

Data for the study were gathered by using the introspective verbal report method. This involved asking readers to voice aloud their immediate impressions and reactions to a text as they engaged in the act of reading. The verbal reports were recorded, transcribed and coded, firstly to determine how frequently various factors were mentioned in each essay, secondly to ascertain whether each factor (for example, content, use of sources, or language) was mentioned in a neutral, positive or negative way.

3. Introspective Verbal Method

The method of introspective verbal report has been used with some success in the last decade, in studies such as Vaughan (1991) and Milanovic et al, (1993) to check inter-rater reliability of reader reaction, and by Cohen and Cavalcanti (1990) to check quality of consistency in rater feedback. The use of the introspective verbal report method has been positive: it has been found to yield richer data than simple post-reading recall; actual recordings of reader reactions provide more accurate data than post-reading reconstruction; and direct access to reader reaction avoids potential misunderstandings based on imprecise terminology. The rationale for using introspective verbal report method in this study was twofold. Firstly, to investigate the degree to which data gathered by this method might add to or support quantitative findings from previous survey studies. And secondly, to provide a rich body of ethnographic data which would be useful 'case study' material for direct classroom application.

4. Methodology

Five lecturers from different departments (Sociology, Law, Hotel Management, Business and Computing) were approached to volunteer for the study, since these represented the departments most favoured by NNS students following EAP programmes at Oxford Brookes. Each lecturer was given the rubric of an essay he or she had set for first year students and were asked to record on audiotape what they would expect to see in an essay written for that rubric. As an immediate follow-up, the lecturers were given an essay written for them by an NNS first year undergraduate in response to that same rubric. The lecturers were asked, while reading and evaluating the essay by their normal criteria, to give a running verbal report of their impressions. It was emphasised that their responses should reflect as normally as possible their habitual thought processes when assessing an essay, and that they should not edit out any repetitions, backtracking, hesitations or silences while reading. A post-reading questionnaire was also applied to check readers' post-reading perceptions of their general and habitual marking behaviour against their reactions while reading the NNS essay scripts.

The essay scripts selected for the study were controlled for several criteria. Firstly they had to have been written by students with the same first language background and with the same period of exposure to teaching at the university. Sample scripts were taken from first year Hong Kong Chinese students, who were also undertaking an EAP course. Hong Kong Chinese represent the largest L1 group doing EAP courses at Oxford Brookes. The scripts selected were of essays these students had written as part of their discipline-specific assessed coursework, for various lecturers, at the end of nine weeks of instruction at the university.

The scripts were controlled for overall writing competence in three ways: firstly, the sample was limited to writing from students who had a mean rating of four on a seven band scale of overall writing competence in holistically marked EAP assignments. Secondly, this band was cross-checked against students' English language level on entry to the university. Thirdly, scripts that satisfied these criteria were read holistically by two different EAP tutors to identify the five best matched scripts in terms of overall comprehensibility and acceptability, using Santos' definitions (1988). Although all of the scripts were typed, none appeared to have been put through a spellchecker facility.

The data from the audio-taped verbal reports of lecturers' reading of the essay scripts was fully transcribed, and encoded using a coding scheme of factors likely to arise in the reading of an academic essay. The coding scheme was adapted from an earlier coding scheme designed for the analysis of reader-responses to non-academic writing (Milanovic and Saville, 1994).

5. Results

5. 1 Lecturers' specifications for response to an essay rubric

Lecturers had first specified what they would ideally expect to see in an essay written on a given rubric. The data recorded from these specifications were analysed to ascertain how often lecturers had specified factors such as content, organisation, use of sources, language and so on. Unsurprisingly, most references were to *content*. It was found that, in regard to *content,* no lecturer specified a discrete 'list' of content items which could be checked off as part of the 'right' answer. Instead, there was speculation as to the various kinds of content students might develop within the given scope of a particular task and how the student might interpret that scope. In other words, *content* involved student choices, not just *what* to write about it, but *how* to develop it.

Lecturers' comments on organisation, on the other hand, were much more prescriptive: every reader specified a definite structure to the essay, and overall coherence in the use of sources. Each reader specified a clear introduction which would define key terms, define the parameters of the question, and outline the steps through which the discussion would develop. For the main body of the text, lecturers required that students should create a conceptual framework for the topic, followed by an exploration of theoretical issues and from this point, a focus on the problem in hand. Understanding of the problem was to be demonstrated, followed by a reasoned argument giving an interpretation of data and how the writer had come to a given conclusion. Description was not sufficient but needed to be balanced by analysis. Thus there was an encouraging correspondence between what we know from studies in genre analysis, and how the lecturers anticipated students selecting and organising ideas in their given fields.

The most significant aspect of lecturer specifications, however, appeared to be their discussion of pre-writing strategies that students would need before fulfilling the essay task. These strategies were described as integral to the execution of the essay task. In other words, students needed method knowledge as well as subject knowledge before writing. Examples of strategic knowledge required (and assumed) of students were: to have an extensive familiarity with literature search methods from multiple sources; to show an ability to discriminate between greater and lesser authorities in the reading; to exploit a familiarity with the local geographical and commercial environments; and to have an ability to seek out and conduct face-to-face interviews with members of the local business community.

It was taken as axiomatic that essay prompts, and any written guidelines provided on essay layout, content, or rules against plagiarism would have been fully assimilated before writing. It was not questioned whether the range of culture-specific and locale-specific strategies considered necessary for task fulfilment would have been acquired by students who had been in the institution (and in some cases, in the country) for only nine weeks.

With regard to language use, only the Law lecturer specified a degree of competence in use of language. Language was mentioned as being part of a 'good legal package', and it was suggested that clear language was an essential component of a good essay on Law: in his words, one would not consider 'a non-numerate mathematician'.

5.2 Readers' reactions to essay scripts

Following the recording of lecturers' specifications on a theoretical essay, their reactions to the reading of an authentic NNS essay were recorded and transcribed. The transcripts were coded for the frequency with which various essay factors were mentioned, and for whether such mentions were positive or negative. Table 1 demonstrates that the larger part of most lecturers' comments as they read were negative; that is, they tended to comment more when there was a perceived problem with the text than in the absence of a problem.

Table 1. Values attached to total comments per reader

Subject	Total No. of comments	Negative	Positive	Neutral
Sociology	75	67	5	3
Law	229	204	19	6
HM	63	34	27	2
Business	89	84	3	2
Computing	132	118	11	3

If most of the lecturers' comments on all factors were negative, then where there was positive comment it was almost invariably in regard to the student's *content* knowledge, as is illustrated in Table 2. This suggests that the lecturers read for, and attended as much as possible to content, only stopping to notice other factors where they arose as problematic.

Table 2. Breakdown of positive comments per reader

Factors	Sociology	Law	HM	Business	Computing
Format			1		
Coherence			1		1
Organisation		1	1		2
Punctuation		1			
Legibility	1				
Paragraphing			1		
Addressing topic			1		
Reading	1				
Use of sources			1		1
Content	2	17	18	3	7
Fulfilling task	1		3		

In order to determine the overall picture of what lecturers most commented on across all essays, the total number of factors mentioned were normalised and ranked for overall frequency, in order to determine which factors had gained the most attention across readers.

On first impression, the ranking order which emerged from the lecturers' comments, as shown in Table 3, appears to compare well with rankings from previous studies of what lecturers say they most look for in an essay. We can also see that the factors appear to fall into loose natural groupings. That is, *content* and *use of sources* emerge as having attracted the most attention, with other factors, including those related to language quality, coming behind.

Table 3. Overall ranking order of grouped factors across readers

Rank order	Factor	% freq	Rank order	Factor	% freq
1	content	20.6	13	layout	2.4
2	use of sources	13.0	14	punctuation	2.2
3	coherence	7.7	15	understanding of reading	1.6
4	organisation	7.0	16	appropriate register	1.4
5	addresses topic	6.2	17	appropriate expression	1.4
6	pre-writing strategies	5.5	18	accurate vocabulary	1.2
7	development of ideas	4.9	19	essential vocabulary	1.1
8	completion of task	4.9	20	length	1.1
9	general ling. accuracy	4.7	21	paragraphing	0.8
10	grammatical accuracy	4.4	22	L1 interference	0.6
11	fluency/style	3.8	23	legibility	0.4
12	spelling	3.0	24	cohesion	0.1

There is, however, an important difference to note between the ranked list of factors in Table 3 and the ranked criteria reported from questionnaire-based studies. Whereas studies using general survey methods reflect lecturers' *projection*, or *retrospection* as to what they think should be most attended to in academic writing, the ranking order arising from the method used in this study reflects reader *reaction* to various factors as they arose in the reading of actual imperfect essay scripts. Thus, we see not only what is noticed most by lecturers, but what they perceive as most problematic in a particular essay. The ranking order in Table 3 reflects not hypothetical *desirables,* but rather perceived strengths and weaknesses of the student writers. Analysis of lecturer reactions makes it possible to see whether a factor at any given point in the text is being praised or criticised, with an opportunity to see what surrounding textual factors might have contributed to the lecturer having a positive or negative reaction to a particular factor.

An interesting outcome of using the introspective verbal report method was the way that the most commonly mentioned factors could be analysed for positive and negative reaction. As Table 3 shows, *content* and *use of sources* received the most comments. However, they were not entirely similar in the values attached to them by lecturers. *Content* was the only factor to have a significantly 'double face', attracting the most comments, but with a mixed value reaction. Lecturers noted some positive aspects of text content (around 8%) as well as negative aspects (approximately 12%) out of the normalised total of around 20% of comments made on *content. Use of sources,* on the other hand, which attracted a normalised frequency of 13% of lecturer comments, attracted predominantly negative reactions, as indeed did all other factors mentioned.

In other words, most commented-on problems in these student texts were not perceived as having to do with *content* itself, but much more with the textual delivery of information. In fact, in his questionnaire the Law reader indicated that he marked an essay for what content he could find, and then took off marks for poor expression. In these five scripts the 'core' problems, according to the ranking table, appeared mainly to be poor manipulation of content (usually information missed out, left undefined or insufficiently contextualised); inadequate use of sources; poor overall coherence and poor textual organisation. Inadequate pre-writing strategies were also seen as an important problem. The main problems identified with these factors are described below.

5.3 Lecturer comments on content

Positive comments were often a mere affirmative 'yes' or 'good' in relation to propositions, facts or claims given in the text. Often there was a kind of 'clawback' effect, with the lecturer reacting positively to content but adding a negative comment on a less successful writing factor, (for example, *a useful question but it might have been better structured ... Fine, got the idea there but it's very badly expressed ...quite a bit of detail there, but I'm not happy with the way it's laid out)*. Criticisms in regard to content arose from over-condensed or missing information, information given without context or definition of key terms, or claims with insufficient back-up evidence. At many points the lecturers expressed irritation with the writer's assumption that the reader, as expert, was omniscient, and that statements did not need full explanation.

5.4 Lecturer comment on use of sources

Comments covered a wide range of perceived problems, from poor mechanics of citation, inaccuracies of spelling or punctuation in the bibliography, through non-acknowledgement of sources and plagiarism, to sources being reproduced without sufficient analysis. It was surprising that even minor surface errors in citation led some lecturers to suspect that students had skimped on research or had used a crammer. It was also revealing that some lecturers tolerated a degree of apparent plagiarism as part of the writer's academic 'apprenticeship' whilst others took a very severe punitive attitude to this misuse of sources.

5.5 Lecturer comment on overall coherence

Coherence as a factor became salient in two ways, reflecting what Carrel (1982) would call formal and schematic coherence. Lack of formal coherence was mentioned, minimally, when lecturers wished to signal that a student's ideas were accessible in spite of poor language usage. In these cases the language did not usually affect coherence or understanding of content.

More comments were based on content-incoherence; that is the content given was not a problem in itself, but might be difficult to follow if the writer moved from one point to another without indicating that there was a shift in focus. This was linked to poor *development of ideas.* Poor coherence was remarked on when information was given in the wrong place, for example new information in a conclusion. This was linked to poor *organisation.* Confused headings and layout also made it difficult for a lecturer to follow the development of content. This was linked to poor paragraph *layout.* Lack of explicit reference to argument when content information was being given led to an assumption that the writer had no idea what he or she was saying. This was linked to poor *fulfilment of task.* Some lecturers made explicit reference to poor coherence being linked to the writer being a non-native speaker.

5.6 Lecturer comment on organisation

Some positive comments were elicited, mainly in regard to a logical structure and the presence of an introduction and conclusion. Poor organisation was commented on where the writer had not made explicit connections between content items to create a coherent argument. In this case, the lecturers tended to ascribe the problem to the writer's poor planning rather than lack of clarity over task specifications. Information which was irrelevant or inappropriate to the section of the essay being read was also seen as lack of organisation.

5.7 Lecturer comment on pre-writing strategic knowledge

It is difficult to impose a narrow definition on the kinds of strategic knowledge that were required by the lecturers. Each lecturer expressed an assumption that certain kinds of knowledge were implicitly understood by students, although the students' essays demonstrated that that assumption had not necessarily been well-founded. Lecturers, assuming that students shared with them certain kinds of general knowledge about academic writing, did not specify these in task instructions, but reacted to them in the students' writing where they saw them flouted.

A disquieting finding was that there appeared to be some mismatches between what these lecturers assumed about their students' knowledge, and what the student in fact did know. At times this was not serious; for example, one lecturer expressed irritation at the over-personal style used, involving excessive use of the first person singular in the essay. The lecturer chose not to downgrade on this, but said that they would on a later occasion. More serious mismatches were in the layout required. One lecturer was critical of lack of headings in his essay, while admitting that he did not explicitly ask for these; nevertheless, he chose to downgrade the essay for weak organisation, including lack of headings. Another lecturer was critical of the fact that his script did not conform to a certain structure, and downgraded for this, whilst not appearing to realise that the student was closely following the structure of a model essay given in a handout as part of course documentation. There appeared to be some mismatches between lecturers' assumptions of what students would know about gaining access to local, field based and non-library based information for an essay, and the reality of the students' experience. In addition, no lecturer questioned whether there might be any problem with their essay instructions where these were not followed.

6. Correspondence Between Introspective Verbal Reports And Post-Reading Questionnaires

It was found that every lecturer was consistent in attending to those factors in the NNS essays that they had specifically highlighted in their pre-reading discussion of essay rubrics. What *did* differ for some was the degree of attention to language issues; three of the five lecturers had virtually ignored language related factors in their pre-reading specifications but had marked reactions to grammar and style in the NNS essay scripts. Only the business lecturer was consistent in virtually ignoring language error throughout while on the other hand the Law lecturer was consistent in his focus on language issues throughout.

An interesting finding was that some lecturers had perceived themselves as less tolerant than their actual marking behaviour indicated, whilst others perceived themselves as more tolerant than they appeared to be for this particular study. Only the Law reader appeared consistently to mark as he said he did. The final assessment judgements for each reader are summed up below:

6.1 Law

This lecturer made subject specific requirements for layout of essay and for precise use of language. The essay was passed with a B on the basis of content knowledge then downgraded to a C because of misuse of vocabulary, poor paragraphing and layout inappropriate to the genre.

6.2 Business

Language errors were deliberately ignored, but failure to define key terms of vocabulary was penalised. The lecturer looked for attempts at analytic thought and analysis, and failed the student on this basis: for this lecturer, not enough thought had been given to how theoretical knowledge could be applied to practical situations; that is, there was insufficient exemplification. As the student had not fully developed the part of the task asking for critical evaluation of a case study, the lecturer failed the essay, assuming that not enough attention had been paid to the task instructions, which were very long and detailed.

6.3 Sociology

Although this reader described himself as making allowances for NNS writers, there was a general lack of tolerance of language inaccuracies in the script; the lecturer felt that students exhibiting problems at language level usually had problems at every level. The lecturer was hostile to the student's essay layout, without headings, and to inaccuracies in the spelling of bibliography entries, assuming missing dates and spelling mistakes to be evidence of cribbing and plagiarism. Although the lecturer ascribed the failure of the essay to poor organisation and weak development of ideas, it was clear that poor mechanics of citation had a major impact on the reader's summative assessment.

6.4 Hotel Management

The essay was passed on the basis of its grasp of key ideas and good organisation. Problems of language were tolerated, as was some evidence of plagiarism, since the positive qualities were felt to outweigh these weaknesses, and tolerance was expressed of the 'first essay' learner status. The reader did state that an accumulation of more than two or three textual problems unrelated to content, such as poor citation of sources or poor sentence structure, would lead to an overall downgrading.

6.5 Computing

The essay was passed on the basis of content knowledge, even though one section of the task had not been attempted. Poor organisation, quality of language and failure to explain graphic data had a moderate impact on the final judgement. Although the lecturer was tolerant of language weaknesses and some plagiarism, he stated that he would not accept these at postgraduate level.

6.6 Summary of lecturers' intended and actual marking

To sum up, lecturers were consistent in marking for content, but in regard to language error, showed a range of consistency in their marking behaviour. So-called mechanics of writing, small points of style and punctuation and aspects of layout appeared in some cases to have a marked effect on assessment. First impressions especially appeared to count for a great deal.

7. Conclusions

Although this study, being ethnographic in nature, has obvious limitations in terms of exactly replicable data for other lecturers or other institutions, it does, however, provide invaluable insight into the way some of the academic readers of our EAP students' work interact with essays. Where lecturers focus exclusively on content, for EAP specialists this feature vies for attention with problems in the construction of the text. This study confirmed certain kinds of difficulties for NNS student writers.

Firstly, students may not be able, even with hard work, to have in place the required pre-writing strategies needed to fulfil certain kinds of academic task, what Hamp-Lyons has termed 'the product before' (1988), even though their lecturers assumed these strategies to be unproblematic.

Secondly, there appears to be a 'gap' in proper pre-writing training for task preparation, as opposed to text production, which students will not necessarily get from their subject specific tutors. Students clearly need help and practice in implementing knowledge from field and library-based sources into text, and in learning to read their work critically for optimal clarity in the text. All the student writers in this study had difficulties with the 'product before', partly through inexperience, but also, disturbingly, through lack of explicit knowledge about what their readers required. These lecturers specified a number of strategies which students would need, not just to create a better product but to fulfil the task *at all*. It is disquieting that in specifying such strategies the lecturers did not trouble to verify whether these were within the range of achievement for all their students, particularly non-native speakers, given the short time such students had been in the university. And because of this mismatch in perceptions, some lecturers attributed problems to their students' neglect of or inattention to instructions, rather than to their own possible failure to make instructions clear and explicit.

8. Implications for EAP

The implications for EAP teaching are firstly, that it is essential for students to think about their intended readers if they are to do well. This is endorsed by findings from previous studies (Clark, 1992; Houghton, 1984; Johns, 1991). To this end, we should create formal opportunities for our students to contact their academic tutors as part of their EAP coursework, both to increase student confidence but also to establish proactive rather than remedial reasons for conferencing with their faculty tutors.

Secondly, while the EAP classroom should be a safe place for NNS students to explore their language and text-making processes, it must also serve as a microcosm and as a step-off to the wider academic community. This should involve students undertaking tasks which are not only as intellectually and linguistically challenging as those they will meet elsewhere in the university, but tasks which are also designed to develop pre-writing strategies for managing the larger academic environment. This would involve practising the usual range of text-focused writing skills, but also a wide range of pre-writing information gathering and information-using skills.

Thirdly, this study suggests, encouragingly, that many of the problems experienced by apprentice NNS writers are already being addressed in general EAP instruction using what is known as the process-writing approach. The writing issues which are covered even in non-content specific EAP courses would seem to be highly relevant to what lecturers perceived as student writing problems in these essays. But more work may need to be done on exploring the pre-writing processes of information search and reading, and less emphasis on personal experience as is sometimes the way in writing classes even at university level.

Fourthly, EAP tutors need to be clear and critical in their feedback on writing, including attention to small local errors which may have important implications for the reader. Above all, students must be encouraged to develop the necessary rigour of reading their own essays and learn to become autonomous in anticipating the criticism of their tutors.

References

Allison D (1996) 'Pragmatic discourse and English for specific purposes', *English for Specific Purposes* 15.2, pp 85 – 103

Ballard B and J Clanchy (1991) 'Assessment by misperception: cultural influences and intellectual traditions', in Hamp-Lyons L (ed) *Assessing Second Language Writing in Academic Contexts*, Norwood, N J: Ablex

Ballard B (1992) 'Teaching international students: a new dimension in problem solving', in *Quality in Education: An Academic Perspective*, University of Southern Queensland

Ballard B (1993) 'Supervising students from overseas: a question of attitudes', in Cullen D (ed) *Quality in PhD Education*, CEDAM, ANU

Benesch S (1994) 'ESL, ideology and the politics of pragmatism', *TESOL Quarterly* 27. 4, pp 705 – 717

Braine G (1989) 'Writing in science and technology: an analysis of assignments from ten undergraduate courses', *English for Specific Purposes* 8.1, pp 3 – 15

Bridgeman B and S Carlson (1983) *Survey of academic writing tasks required of graduate and undergraduate foreign students*, Research Report No 15, Princeton, NJ: Educational Testing Service

Campbell C (1990) 'Writing with others' words: using background reading texts in academic compositions', in Kroll B (ed) *Second Language Writing: Research insights for the classroom*, Cambridge: Cambridge University Press

Carlisle R and E McKenna (1991) 'Placement of ESL/EFL undergraduate writers in college-level writing programs', in Hamp-Lyons L (ed) *Assessing Second Language Writing in Academic Contexts*, Norwood, N J: Ablex

Carrel P (1982) 'Cohesion is not coherence', *TESOL Quarterly* 16, pp 479 – 488

Casanave C and P Hubbard (1992) 'The writing assignments and writing problems of doctoral students: faculty perceptions, pedagogical issues and needed research', *English for Specific Purposes* 11, pp 33 – 49

Clark R (1992) 'Principles and practice of critical language awareness in the classroom', in Fairclough N (ed) *Critical Language Awareness*, London: Longman

Cohen A and M Cavalcanti (1990) 'Feedback on compositions: teacher and student verbal reports', in Kroll B (ed) *Second Language Writing: Research insights for the classrooom*, Cambridge: Cambridge University Press

Dudley-Evans T (1988) 'Recent developments in ESP: the trend to greater specialisation', in Tickoo M (ed) *ESP: The state of the art*, Anthology Series 21, Singapore: SEAMEO Regional Language Centre

Hamp-Lyons L (1988) 'The product before: task-related influences on the writer', in Robinson P (ed) *Academic Writing: Process and product*, Modern English Publications in association with The British Council

Hamp-Lyons L (ed) (1991) *Assessing Second Language Writing in Academic Contexts*, Norwood, N J: Ablex

Horowitz D (1986) 'What professors actually require: academic tasks for the EFL classroom', *TESOL Quarterly* 21, pp 327 – 349

Houghton D (1984) 'Overseas students writing essays in English: learning the rules of the game', in James G (ed) *The ESP Classroom*, Exeter Linguistic Series, Exeter: University of Exeter

Howe P (1993) 'Planning a pre-sessional course in English for academic legal purposes', in Blue G (ed) *Language, Learning and Success: Studying through English*, Modern English Publications in association with The British Council

Ivanic R (1992) 'Who's who in the academy?', in Fairclough N (ed) *Critical Language Awareness*, London: Longman

Janopoulos M (1992) 'University faculty tolerance of NS and NNS writing errors: a comparison' *Journal of Second Language Writing* 1.2, pp 109 – 121

Jenkins S, M Jordan and P Weiland (1993) 'The role of writing in graduate engineering education: a survey of faculty beliefs and practices', *English for Specific Purposes* 12, pp 51 – 67

Johns A (1991) 'Faculty assessment of ESL student literacy skills: implications for writing assessment', in Hamp-Lyons L (ed) *Assessing Second Language Writing in Academic Contexts*, Norwood, N J: Ablex

Milanovic M, N Saville and S Shuhong (1993) *A Study of the Decision-making Behaviour of Composition Markers*, Unpublished manuscript, Language Testing Research Colloquium, Cambridge: UCLES

Milanovic M and N Saville (1994) *An Investigation of Marking Strategies Using Verbal Protocols*, Unpublished manuscript, Language Testing Research Colloquium, Cambridge: UCLES

Pennycook A (1989) 'The concept of method, interested knowledge and the politics of language teaching', *TESOL Quarterly* 23, pp 589 – 618

Robinson P (ed) (1988) *Academic Writing: Process and Product*, Modern English Publications in association with The British Council

Santos T (1988) 'Professors' reactions to the academic writing of non-native speaking students', *TESOL Quarterly* 22, pp 69 – 90

Santos T (1992) 'Ideology in composition: L1 and ESL', *Journal of Second Language Writing* 1, pp 1 – 15

Swales J (1990) *Genre Analysis: English in academic and research settings*, Cambridge: Cambridge University Press

Tonkyn A, C Locke, P Robinson and C Furneaux (1993) 'The EAP teacher: prophet of doom or eternal optimist? EAP teachers' predictions of student success', in Blue G (ed) *Language, Learning and Success: Studying through English,* Modern English Publications in association with The British Council

Vann R, F Lorenz and D Meyer (1991) 'Error gravity: faculty response to errors in the written discourse of non-native speakers of English', in Hamp-Lyons L (ed) *Assessing Second Language Writing in Academic Contexts,* Norwood, N J: Ablex

Vaughan C (1991) 'Holistic assessment: what goes on in the rater's mind?', in Hamp-Lyons L (ed) *Assessing Second Language Writing in Academic Contexts,* Norwood, N J: Ablex

Gill Meldrum

I Know I have to be Critical, but How?

1. Introduction

One of the important criteria for giving high marks in assessed written assignments and dissertations, especially for postgraduate degrees, is a critical approach to the literature. This applies most clearly in the arts and social sciences, although it can also sometimes apply in literature review projects for science or engineering Masters degrees. Critical evaluation is one of four main marking categories for MA ELT assignments at Nottingham. The descriptors for the upper range of marks demand that '…The work includes reference to a substantial range of sources, and this material is used critically…'. However, EAP teachers are aware that international students often have difficulty with being critical in terms of the way criticality is perceived in the Anglo-American academic community. Richards and Skelton (1991) concluded in their study of MSc TESP students that 'overseas students evaluate less, and evaluate less critically' than home students. This lack seemed, in part, to have contributed towards the lower marks of the overseas students at Aston. Departmental tutors who refer students to our Nottingham Centre for help repeatedly report lack of critical evaluation as a contributory factor to failure or low achievement in assignments. These reports suggest that higher marks can be achieved, in social science, management studies, politics, philosophy, and education, as well as in applied linguistics, if students can be helped to adapt to the central role criticism plays within the academic culture.

To a large extent, critical skills begin before or at the reading stage of any arts or social sciences assignment, and involve examining arguments for flaws, examining research literature for what is missing, and weighing the reported arguments and ideas of others. Most EAP programmes attempt in various ways to help students develop critical skills and, perhaps more radically, the Lancaster group have advocated the Critical Language Awareness approach to reading and thinking (Allwright et al, 1996; Clark and Ivanic, 1991). Clark and Ivanic, (1991) and Clark, (1991, 1992) have also described how they go about consciousness-raising for critical writing, using Critical Language Awareness, with politics students.

One common reason for international students' problems with criticality is a different educational background and culture, which often leads to lack of confidence in operating within the British academic culture. What is it acceptable to criticise and what is taboo? A second, connected reason is a lack of confidence in using the language. What is a polite criticism and what is rude? Richards and Skelton (1991) believed that confidence played a very important role in both the quantity and quality of critical evaluations, and that it was mainly the native speakers in their study who were confident, and the international students who were unconfident.

We clearly need to continue to develop students' critical approach to ideas in reading and writing. I argue in this paper that, in addition, we can increase their confidence through awareness raising of and practice in adapting the language and strategies of criticism. I base my ideas on a study I recently carried out on the politeness of criticism in applied linguistics 'controversy' articles, an overtly critical genre which contains strong and forthright, as well as more muted, criticism. In this paper, I outline some relevant aspects of the study, focussing on the seriousness of particular criticisms in the academic community and briefly comparing the occurrence of politeness strategies identified by Myers (1989) in molecular biology research articles with those I found in the applied linguistics (AL) controversy articles, giving some examples of the kind of language and strategies used in the latter. Then, I explain how I have made use of the concept of 'face' and both Myers' and my own study in helping pre-sessional students to tackle the problem of being critical in the English language. The focus is on only one aspect of using critical language – that of criticising the work of other writers – one of the most difficult things for many international students to do.

2. Outline of Aspects of the Politeness Study

In my study into the politeness of criticism in 10 applied linguistics 'controversy' articles, I adapted Brown and Levinson's politeness framework to take account of how politeness operates within the contextual features of extended written discourse. Much of my adaptation was based on Myers' (1989) study of science research articles. The adaptation clearly indicated a need for some departures from Brown and Levinson's essentially speech act framework of politeness (1987) and is recorded elsewhere (Meldrum, 1994). In this section I outline some aspects of the study relevant to my teaching of critical language.

Criticism is a double-edged sword. The notion of exposing one's academic work to the critical scrutiny of one's peers or superiors is deeply ingrained in the Anglo-American philosophy. However, in spite of the ideological necessity to criticise in the interests of the community as a whole, tension is created and face/reputation is threatened when one writer criticises the work of another.

In terms of the two genres mentioned in the politeness study, the purpose of a research article is to make claims and hopefully have them accepted. It would be counterproductive under such circumstances to risk causing severe loss of face to other members of the academic community. In contrast, the purpose of the controversy article is largely to present a critical argument, so that threats to the face of the criticised academics are unavoidable.

Regarding relations within the discourse communities in the study, applied linguistics is much younger than the scientific community and has strong links with the teaching and other professions. It therefore tends to use more interpersonal language, and, I suggest, has configurations of power and distance which are less formal, in print, than those described by Myers for molecular biology, though writers still need to defer to the discipline as a whole (Meldrum, 1994; cf Myers, 1989).

2.1 The seriousness of particular criticisms

One aim of the study was to explore the range, or extremes, of ways in which criticism is carried out within the academic community. The threat to face/reputation of any criticism is likely to be heavily influenced by the 'rank' of the criticism (Brown and Levinson, 1987). The rank of a criticism is its value as a quality to the particular community. For example, a quality such as 'scholarly rigour' is highly valued by the academic community but less so by a street gang. Criticising scholarly rigour in the academic community therefore risks a greater threat to reputation than, say, criticising punctuation. To gauge how seriously particular criticisms were considered to threaten face, I recorded those which were actually made in the AL controversy articles. I then noted which particular criticisms in the initial attacking articles were reacted to by the writer of the responding article in the controversy. The strength of the reaction was also noted.

I found at least 16 types of values which were both attacked and defended in the 10 articles of study (see Appendix for a summary). These were then categorised as high or low ranking criticisms, depending on the reaction provoked in the defending articles. The study indicated, as one might expect, that an attack on the relevance of the research was taken very seriously (high ranking), whereas for a criticism about the clarity of the writing, little notice was taken (low ranking).

While Myers stated that the high ranking criticisms, such as accusations of unscholarly approach, were almost never carried out explicitly in molecular biology, they were frequently explicit in the AL controversy articles, and vigorously defended by the person criticised. Whether explicit or implicit, these values reflect the criteria which academics have long applied to their own (and each others') work and to the work of their students.

2.2 Face and the Brown and Levinson politeness macrostrategies in AL texts

The concept of 'face', which has now been mentioned several times, is familiar to those of us who work in EAP. I do not propose to discuss the universality of face. From the Anglo-American point of view face has been described by Goffman (1972) and Brown and Levinson (1987) as emotionally invested, bound up with emotions such as embarrassment, pride, honour and shame. I also view it as being connected with public image and reputation. Brown and Levinson claim that we have positive face wants (bound up with the desire to be approved of and valued) and negative face wants (bound up with the need for independence of decision and the right not to be imposed upon). The latter notion of face is disputed by Matsumoto (1989) and Gu (1990) for Japan and China respectively, but it does seem to be relevant within the British academic community, where the definitions originated. Since criticism in academic writing can potentially threaten both to damage public approval of a researcher and to impede her/his further work, I take it that criticism can threaten either positive or negative face, and so will not further elaborate on these distinctions.

We cannot avoid threatening face, even if our criticisms are intended to be constructive. Therefore, according to Brown and Levinson, we have five politeness macrostrategies at our disposal to deal with the tensions and risk of aggression that arise if face is ignored. Brown and Levinson claim that we rationally choose our strategies according to the level of risk to ourselves and others in terms of face. These macrostrategies are (with slight adaptation) known as: bald criticism, positive politeness, negative politeness, going off record and finally, avoiding the criticism.

2.2.1 Direct and unambiguous criticism

The first and most risky macrostrategy is to criticise baldly, without any mitigation at all, so as to be as direct and unambiguous as possible. One would expect that this would be very risky with high ranking criticisms. Bald criticisms of any kind were indeed rare in Myers' science research articles, and were never used with high ranking criticisms. In the AL controversy texts, however, bald criticisms were very common, even with high ranking criticisms. A searing example of a bald criticism (high ranking: lack of scholarly approach/rigour) is:

To use the word 'insightful' to describe the decision of the first researchers in the field (Naiman, Frohlich, Stern and Tedesco 1978; Tucker, Hamayan, and Genesee 1976) to use the EFT and the FI/D construct renders the word meaningless. *They omitted to carry out the necessary exhaustive investigation of either the test or the construct and in doing so created an illusory impression of a soundly-based hypothesis.* (Sheen, 1993: 99) (my italics)

The lexis is negative, the criticism is made directly at the researchers, and there is no other form of mitigation.

2.2.2 Positive politeness

If the risk of face loss is considered too high to criticise baldly, the second, less risky macrostrategy of positive politeness can be used. It 'gives' face to the other, by emphasising what the two writers have in common. Thus, it is often termed 'solidarity' politeness. The use of solidarity politeness strategies to mitigate criticism was very common in both Myers science research data and the AL controversy texts.

Examples of positive politeness microstrategies include: claiming in group membership, using humour, using modifiers such as 'unfortunately' to show that you value the intentions of the person you criticise or using a limited range of emotional responses such as disappointment at the failure of an attempt. Frequently noted were the use of 'gifts' of praise/credit/compliments before or after the criticism, pointing out common ground before or after the criticism; and the strategic use of pronouns (such as 'we') to stress solidarity as the criticism is made. The manipulation of naming and pronouns is especially interesting in the following example of pointing out common ground:

The theories we construct to explain L2 acquisition and the methodologies we use to test or derive them are CONTEXT DEPENDENT. They depend, in particular, on the researcher's purpose. IT IS HERE THAT GREGG AND I PART COMPANY. For while I have been primarily concerned with educational questions, *GREGG* is preoccupied with linguistic issues. (Ellis, 1990: 385)

In the following criticism (of inadequate explanatory power of a framework) Hulstijn (1990: 42) first gives the gift of credit:

> *The Analysis/Control framework seems especially designed to account for individual differences in performance on metalinguistic tasks, in terms of two constructs (Analysis and Control).* The framework does not seem to be designed to account for the acquisition of primary linguistic skills in the first place. Hence, each time it is invoked to do so, the Analysis and Control dimensions are stretched to their explanatory limits (and sometimes beyond), giving the explanations a forced air.

Giving reasons for a criticism (in the following example a criticism of erroneous interpretation) can, of course, be explained in several ways apart from as a politeness strategy. Nevertheless, explaining this strategy as a means of disarming potential attack on face can provide a fresh perspective for students:

> Hulstijn's interpretation of our data is ruled out *by methodological factors in our research. In all our studies, we compare across tasks only those structures which we have held constant.* (Bialystok, 1990: 49)

2.2.3 Negative politeness

In higher risk situations, the even safer macrostrategy of negative politeness can be used. Negative politeness addresses negative face by indicating the desire not to impose upon or offend the reader. It is often known as 'deference' politeness, as it may manifest itself as formality, deference, restraint and respect. Particularly common is hedging the illocutionary force of the criticism so as to give the reader a feeling of not being coerced.

Criticisms mitigated by negative (deference) strategies were very common in both Myers' science and the AL articles, though there was less use of hedging in the AL controversy articles. However, in both sets of texts, impersonal constructions, such as passives and inanimate grammatical subjects, were prevalent.

In both articles, *it is argued* that *there is serious confusion in the communicative view of these matters.*

and

If *one* reads through the standard books and articles on the communicative teaching of English, *one finds assertions about* language use and language learning falling like leaves in autumn; facts, on the other hand, *tend to be* remarkably thin on the ground. Along with its many virtues, *the Communicative Approach* unfortunately has most of the typical vices of an intellectual revolution: *it* overgeneralises valid but limited insights until they become virtually meaningless; *it* misrepresents the currents of thought *it* has replaced; *it* is often characterized by serious intellectual confusion; *it* is choked with jargon. (Swan, 1985: 2)

The second Swan example seems to be a very strong criticism and highlights an interesting point. When viewed within a stretch of discourse like this, the fact that the last five clauses have inanimate subjects does not seem sufficient to mitigate the strength of the criticism. The strength seems to derive rather from the negative, sometimes emotive, lexis, and the fact that there is an accumulation of one criticism after another. The latter was a common phenomenon in the data and one which I called 'discourse aggravation' – the opposite of politeness mitigation.

All three of the above macrostrategies are known as 'going on record'. That is, it is clear to the reader (and could be corroborated by other readers) that the intention behind the act was unambiguously to make a criticism.

2.2.4 Going off record

The fourth macrostrategy, that of going off record, is usually the option chosen when the risk to one's own face (perhaps because of the strength of the criticism) is perceived as very high indeed. An off-record criticism allows both the reader and the writer a 'way out', by being ambiguous, so that the writer cannot be said unequivocally to have intended to carry out the criticism. Examples are rhetorical questions, implicature, metaphor and irony.

Off-record strategies were rare in Myers' science research texts. Off-record *devices* abound in the AL controversy articles, but the very frequent use of such devices in close proximity, or through juxtaposition with other criticisms often seemed to bring them on record. That is, they unambiguously seemed to represent a criticism. For example:

> One of the incontrovertible facts of language use, whether L1 or L2, is that it varies. It varies across members of a speech community (I say tomayto, you say tomahto); it varies for the output of any given acquirer of a language, whether over time (I say tomayto, I used to say tomahto) or at any given time (I say tomayto but I also say tomahto). The fact is incontrovertible; *is it interesting?* Or rather, *since nothing human is alien to us, etc, and there's no disputing etc – is this fact of importance in constructing a theory of second language acquisition? Is it a fact to be dealt with by a theory, or is it simply that least valued of objects in scientific enquiry, a mere fact?* Do we extend our investigation to the question of who says potayto and who says potahto, or do we call the whole thing off?* (Gregg, 1990: 364)

Here, the protracted use of the song allusion is combined with no fewer than six rhetorical questions and, in lines 5 – 7, the presupposition that Gregg's readers are so tired of the counter-arguments that it is quite unnecessary for him to repeat them. The overall effect, agreed by seven readers, is mocking, and constitutes an unambiguously on-record criticism. There were, however, also many cases in the AL texts where the criticism remained off-record.

2.2.5 Avoidance of criticism

The fifth macrostrategy, if the risk is too great, is to avoid the criticism completely. This was not investigated in the study, being impossible to identify without consulting the writer of the article or recourse to the original writer's notes.

2.2.6 Avoidance of personal criticism

Nevertheless, in addition to the five Brown and Levinson macrostrategies, Myers found that direct criticism of persons in microbiology and other science research texts was extremely rare, 'almost inadmissible'. Thus, a politeness sub-strategy in academic writing could be considered to be avoiding direct criticism of persons. In the AL controversy texts, however, direct criticism of persons was extremely common. This may be seen as another form of discourse aggravation:

> *G and S* [Griffiths and Sheen] fail to appraise any results of FI/D studies at all! (Chapelle, 1992: 378 – 379)

In the AL controversy texts, it was even quite common to criticise people for personal qualities:

> *Swan, by ignorance or design*, fails to acknowledge the fact. (Widdowson, 1985: 161)

so that a second politeness sub-strategy for academic writing might be avoiding criticism of personal qualities.

The tone of the controversy texts was in some cases both personal and mocking, something which seven (AL based) readers mostly found to be unacceptable. A strong mocking style of rhetoric then suggests a third source of discourse aggravation in academic texts.

2.3 Conclusions

Criticism seems to be present in both science and AL texts but the range from cautiously polite to high risk and verging on the rude has been observed to be very wide. The level of risk taken in the AL controversy texts was considerably higher than that described by Myers in the science research texts which may reflect differences in the discourse community as well as genre specific differences. It would be interesting to compare AL controversy tests with a similar genre in another discipline.

At least sixteen academic values, when commented on as being deficient, were perceived to threaten face. These values, such as scholarly rigour, are the foundation of academic criteria for assessing the work of peers, of one's 'betters' and the work of students. They are therefore an academic imperative which overrides the problem of threatening face.

Since face still has to be addressed, however, four Brown and Levinson politeness macrostrategies were observed to be operating, even in the extremely critical AL genre, to mitigate the threats. What is of note in terms of range of criticism is that in the AL texts there were bald and off-record criticisms which were virtually absent from microbiology and other science texts examined by Myers. In several cases, the off-record criticisms were judged by readers to come on record because of the sheer number of them, very close together.

What I called discourse aggravation (remarks perceived to be rude or unacceptable by readers) also seemed to be a feature of AL controversy texts. The extreme nature of the AL controversy texts, when compared with Myers' microbiology research texts suggested three sources of discourse aggravation: accumulation of several criticisms one after another, direct criticism of people and their personal qualities not normally considered relevant in academic papers, and a strongly mocking rhetorical style. Since such aggravation was a common feature of the AL controversy texts, avoiding such aggravation could be said to constitute further politeness strategies.

The (AL) readers' tolerance for all kinds of criticism which avoided the personal and mocking, however, was high. Presumably such tolerance in the face of extreme criticism reflects the academic imperative within arts and social sciences to take a critical approach. The notion of acceptability (what constitutes acceptable criticism and what constitutes rudeness) is an important one that seems likely to vary between academic communities and between genres as well as between different power configurations, and it merits further investigation. Acceptability in all three areas is an important issue when it comes to encouraging students to criticise.

3. Implications for Teaching

The controversy texts revealed highly provocative criticisms that might generally be regarded within the academic community as unacceptable or risky for students to emulate. This in turn suggests that, while we want our students to be critical, avoidance or mitigation of some of the controversy discourse aggravation techniques constitutes a politer form of criticism. Materials preparation can then become a matter of studying existing linguistic resources which allow criticisms of similar values or rank to be made in politer terms. These should aim to be acceptable to the particular discourse community, particular genre or particular power configuration. By examining the more extreme end of academic criticism, we gain insight into what is rude and what is acceptable. I believe it emboldens timorous students to first see the extent to which criticism can become aggravated in the hands of well established academics and secondly to practise looking for linguistic techniques which would express the same criticism in a politer way, working backwards from rude to polite. Students who have previously lacked confidence to express *any* critical opinion (other than positive) thus tend to raise their idea of what is acceptable.

EAP teachers strive to explain the academic criteria of assessment and their underlying values to new members of the academic community but often find students have difficulty in taking them on board because of their abstract nature. It may help if they see reactions to such criticisms in print. For teaching purposes, I have since expanded and modified the list in the Appendix. I discuss this list with students as criteria they may be able to use when evaluating what they read and making critical comment. We also discuss the criteria as means by which students can both assess and be assessed. Many international students find they are emboldened to see that such qualities *need* to be scrutinised for the good of the community, and that writers *are* often explicitly criticised on these grounds in some disciplines and genres, even though the criticisms can threaten face/reputation. It also helps students to know which criticisms are considered high ranking, so that they can consider what is a very serious criticism, requiring to be approached with cautious politeness strategies, and what is a less serious criticism and therefore able to be approached more boldly.

The interpersonal concept of face is useful in teaching academic writing to international students. It is usually familiar and can set up useful cultural discussions in itself. However, students do not need to know the ins and outs of Brown and Levinson's theory of positive and negative face and resulting positive and negative politeness strategies. Simply, the concept of protecting one's own face and maintaining that of others in order to 'disarm' attack is a useful explanatory factor in British academic writing. In the light of this concept, I encourage students to air their reasons for discomfort in being 'critical' in the British sense. It helps them to learn that there are several identifiable strategies at their disposal (that is, not only hedging) for expressing criticism politely. This encourages them to practise using these strategies to soften strong existing criticisms such as some of those illustrated above. They experiment with the language and strategies they feel comfortable using. Looking at examples of strong criticism as well as more muted criticism has helped make them aware of the range of academic criticisms and helped to open up their options for expression. We discuss the idea that different genres and power configurations can affect linguistic appropriateness and then try to decide what this means in terms of students' own written assignments. While research articles aim to make claims and controversy articles aim to present critical argument, the students' assessed assignments constitute a third genre which often requires both argument and some claim making. I encourage them to investigate how criticism is usually carried out within their own discipline. Social science students, for example are often expected to be boldly critical.

An example follows of how I have adapted teaching ideas from the controversy study. The lesson is based on Unit 4 in *Reading Skills for the Social Sciences* (Haarman et al, 1988). The passage is a review by Olga Semenova, of Schapiro's book *1917: The Russian Revolution*. The review, like the controversy texts, is forthright in its critical comment, containing both positive and negative evaluation. It is not a genre that the students will have to produce in the near future, but it has the twin advantages of being reasonably accessible to most students and of being only one page long. I use it with advanced pre-sessional as well as in-sessional students in the arts and social sciences. The pre-sessional students at this stage are already reading in their own subject area for their projects and so have had some exposure to academic books and articles in their own discipline with which to compare the passage. Ideally they are in a broadly subject specific group but it is also possible to teach a group of mixed disciplines within the arts and social sciences.

The book already contains an excellent lead in, an activity in which the students are asked to read the first sentence of each paragraph (which expresses critical opinions) and decide if it presents an opinion on a scale from very favourable to very unfavourable. Students are asked to underline the language in these sentences which supports their interpretation. Usually, by this time the students are incredulous at the strength of some of the criticisms. We examine what makes them strong, looking, for example, at emotive words like 'hate' in '*He hates the Bolsheviks*' and the personal nature of the criticism '*Schapiro was old and rigid*'. We discuss whether there are likely to be contexts within the students' future discourse community in which there might be a good reason for discussing a writer's age and personal qualities (as there might well be, for example in literature) and whether the students think it is relevant in the context of this passage. We look at the effect of accumulated criticisms such as '*Schapiro's thesis is prejudiced, one-sided and out-dated*', and work through the criticisms in this way.

However, we also look at whether the strong criticisms have been mitigated in any way and experiment to see if they could have been stronger. The students often have fun at this point, suggesting all sorts of ways of making the criticisms outrageously strong. This is useful, enabling us to start thinking about the circumstances under which different strengths of criticisms could be used. We consider, for example, the difference between '*Schapiro* is prejudiced, one-sided and outdated' (personal subject) and '*SCHAPIRO'S THESIS is prejudiced, one-sided and out-dated*' (inanimate subject). Students usually conclude that the latter is more academically relevant in this context, and that the criticism has in fact been mitigated by a politeness strategy to some extent.

We look at the list of highly valued qualities or common criteria for academic evaluation (See Appendix) and try to decide which values are being critiqued in this passage. For example, [lack of] 'objectivity' is clearly being criticised through the accusation of being '*one-sided*'. '[In]competence' in interpretation' is another ground for criticism, in the sentence '*His interpretation of the Russian Revolution is crude and unashamedly biased*'. Looking at the list we think about which (rank of) criticisms may threaten face more seriously than others and therefore which ones may need to be approached more cautiously and be more muted.

After going through the text in this way, there are usually mixed feelings in the group as to whether the students themselves would feel comfortable using strong negative criticism. At this point I give them a handout illustrating a selection of (positive and negative politeness) strategies that might be useful in mitigating the critical comments. A suggested hedging strategy (negative politeness) for example is:

                seems (to be)
Use   *appears (to be)*   with an inanimate subject
                tends to (be)

For example: *Schapiro's attitudes tend to be* rigid.

Rather than: Schapiro was rigid.

The handout shows how students can still express their opinion, but do it in a 'polite' way, using hedges and other politeness strategies to protect face. I emphasise that these are not *all* the strategies at their disposal, but that we will continue to look for more in subsequent lessons, and that it is important for students to search the literature in their own subject areas for these and collect a bank of other means of politely (or impolitely!) criticising.

We also consider how the strength of the language used indicates the extent of the criticiser's conviction and commitment to her/his opinion. We discuss the fact that it is highly valued in many disciplines to have strong convictions, though the means of expressing them may be milder or stronger in different discourse communities (the scientists tending to express them more mildly, the social scientists more strongly). We then go on to consider the very strong academic need to save face (both one's own and that of the person being criticised), by not only stating one's own convictions but also supporting them with evidence.

Finally, I ask each student to study, from their own point of view, a list of critical comments extracted from the text, and decide if they would feel comfortable using this language, both according to their own feelings and according to their expectations of the discipline they will soon be entering. If they do not think they would be comfortable with the language they should either soften or strengthen it, using some of the language and strategies we have discussed in the handout. Although these are sentences that we have already discussed, at this point the students have to take stock, and judge them in relation to their own situation.

There are, of course, problems with the fact these are not the students' own opinions, and that therefore they cannot judge the strength of their commitment to them. I try to tackle this later, by asking students to write a critical appraisal of a provocative passage that they read in class.

As an important concluding activity, the students assess the extent to which Semenova uses evidence to support her criticisms in the *Russian Revolution* text. This focuses them on the perhaps overridingly important strategy of providing evidence for their criticism, and on the need to assess the evidence, when reading texts in their own subject, with critical eyes.

4. Conclusion

The research study outlined in part above was an exploratory study. There are of course several areas requiring further investigation. The applications of the study are towards the criticism of other writers and their work, rather than the critical approach of comparing and contrasting machines or methods which tends to be more common in engineering or science articles.

However, I feel the materials arising from the study have been helpful to both my pre-sessional and in-sessional students. Because we assess our students at the end of their pre-sessional course on their critical approach, and because they are further assessed on it in their departments, I believe we have an obligation to teach them not only how to think critically, but also how to manipulate the language and strategies available to them. If we raise their awareness of politeness resources through discussion and practice, they can gain in confidence.

Motivation and excitement are the two key aspects I see emerging from students in classes such as the one outlined above. A fresh interpersonal perspective such as that concerned with face can help students find the 'I' in academic writing that Ivanic and Simpson (1992) feel is so important. It can increase students' feeling of personal involvement and commitment to their writing. Finally, awareness of the strength of criticism they are expressing can motivate students to take responsibility for their criticism, and set down the evidence on which it is based.

References

Allwright J, R Clark and A Marshall-Lee (1996) 'Developing a critical approach to study', in Hewings M and T Dudley-Evans (eds) *Evaluation and Course Design in EAP*, Hemel Hempstead: Prentice Hall Macmillan in association with The British Council

Bialystok E (1990) 'The dangers of dichotomy: a reply to Hulstijn', *Applied Linguistics* 11.1, pp 46 – 51

Brown P and S C Levinson (1987) *Politeness: Some universals in language usage*, Cambridge: Cambridge University Press

Chappelle C A (1992) 'Disembedding 'Disembedded figures in the landscape ...': an appraisal of Griffiths and Sheen's 'Reappraisal of L2 research on field dependence/independence", *Applied Linguistics* 13.1, pp 375 – 384

Clark R (1991) 'Developing practices of resistance: critical reading for students of politics', in Graddol D, L Thompson and M Byram (eds) *Language and Culture*, Clevedon: British Association for Applied Linguistics in association with Multilingual Matters

Clark R (1992) 'Principles and practice of CLA in the classroom', in Fairclough N (ed) *Critical Language Awareness*, Harlow: Longman

Clark R, C Constantinou, A Cottey and O C Yeoh (1990) 'Rights and obligations in student writing', in Clark R, N Fairclough, R Ivanic,

N McLeod, J Thomas and P Meara (eds) *Language and Power*, London: CILT

Clark R and R Ivanic (1991) 'Consciousness-raising about the writing process', in James C and P Garrett (eds) *Language Awareness in the Classroom*, Harlow: Longman

Ellis R (1990) 'A respose to Gregg', *Applied Linguistics* 11.4, pp 384 – 391

Goffman E (1972) *Interaction Ritual*, London: Penguin

Gregg K R (1990) 'The variable competence model of second language acquisition, and why it isn't', *Applied Linguistics* 11.4, pp 364 – 383

Gu Y (1990) 'Politeness phenomena in modern Chinese', *Journal of Pragmatics* 14.2, pp 237 – 257

Haarman L, P Leech and J Murray (1988) *Reading Skills for the Social Sciences*, Oxford: Oxford University Press

Hulstijn J (1990) ' A comparison between the information-processing and the analysis/control approaches to language learning', *Applied Linguistics* 11.1, pp 30 – 45

Ivanic R and J Simpson (1992) 'Who's who in academic writing?', in Fairclough N (ed) *Critical Language Awareness*, Harlow: Longman

Matsumoto Y (1989) 'Politeness and conversational universals – observations from Japanese, *Multilingua* 8.2–3, pp 207 – 221

Meldrum G (1994) *The Politeness of Criticism in Applied Linguistics Articles: Readership and aspects of aggravation*, unpublished MA dissertation, University of Sheffield

Myers G (1989) 'Pragmatics of politeness in scientific articles', *Applied Linguistics* 10.1, pp 1 – 35

Naiman N, M Frohlich, H Stern and A Tedesco (1978) *The Good Language Learner*, (Research in Education Series No. 7) Toronto, Ontario: The Ontario Institute for Studies in Education

Richards K and J Skelton (1991) 'How critical can you get?', in Adams P, B Heaton and P Howarth (eds) *Socio-Cultural Issues in English for Academic Purposes*, Modern English Publications in association with The British Council

Sheen R (1993) 'A rebuttal to Chappelle's response to Griffiths and Sheen', *Applied Linguistics* 14.1, pp 98 – 100

Swan M (1985) 'A critical look at the communicative approach (1)', *Applied Linguistics* 39.1, pp 2 –12

Tucker G R, E Hamayan and F H Genesee (1976) 'Affective, cognitive and social factors in second language acquisition', *The Canadian Modern Language Review* 32, pp 214 – 216

Widdowson H G (1985) 'Against dogma: a reply to Michael Swan', *ELT Journal* 39.3, pp 158 – 161

Appendix
Highly Valued Qualities to which Face /Reputation is Attached in the Applied Linguistics Community

In 10 controversy articles, comments which very strongly indicated deficiencies in these qualities were perceived as threatening face.

HIGH RANKING	LOWER RANKING
Scholarly approach/rigour	Rhetorical competence
Methodological competence	Clarity of reporting
Intellectual competence and reasoning powers	Explicitness of stance
Competence in interpretation of data and drawing of conclusions	Conformity to politeness standards of community
Worthy research (valuable, relevant, central to discipline)	Conformity to presentation conventions of community
Objectivity	Originality (in written approach)
Openness to new paradigms	
Critical, evaluative approach	
Accurate representation of others' work	
Honest reporting of own work	

Part Four:

Non-Traditional Forms of Assessment

Katie Gray

Assessment in EAP: Moving away from Traditional Models

1. Exploring the Paradigm Shift

In all areas of the education system in the UK there seems to be a move away from a testing and examination culture to an assessment culture. In all areas too there are issues of accountability and comparability in tension with issues of improving student learning.

Ros Mitchell, in her plenary at the ELT Journal 50th anniversary symposium in 1996, looked at the tension between models of teachers' professionalism in the national and the international context. She highlighted the ironical fact that the competency based model wished on teachers by the National Curriculum emphasises effective outcomes, and so implies both a move away from the learning process in favour of lockstep targets and a teacher centred transmission of knowledge model, while the reflective practice model is ridiculed (and she pointed to the right wing attack on pupil centred learning in Phillips, 1996). Yet, despite the small research base and its application mainly in Western Europe these are theories developed through practice, with the learners and teachers jointly constructing learning experiences, which are attractive and convincing. They are to be found in new approaches to teacher education in this country (which inevitably go back to 1978 and Vigotsky's zone of proximal development – the gap between unaided performance and potential under guidance).

Indeed in teacher education, both mainstream and in EFL, the idea of reflective practice is firmly established. In the world of TEFL the work of Richards and Lockhart (1994), Edge (1992) and Underhill (1992) is well known. Less well known perhaps is the idea of individual action plans (IAP's), where student teachers are asked to identify, through an audit of their skills, qualities and strengths, areas for development and achievable targets. The IAP process, in common with many reflective approaches to personal development, involves a continuous loop which moves from a *reviewing* stage, to a *reflecting* stage, to a *planning* stage to an *achieving* stage and on again. It requires too a sense of commitment and conviction from the student teacher and support and encouragement from the teacher educator in order to ensure that the experience is a positive one.

There are of course political reasons too for student centredness and in many institutions resource based learning is a necessity which can usefully build on all the ideas of learner autonomy, and focus on the learner that are current. Thames Valley University has recently documented the virtue its team has made out of reduced contact hours (Clark et al, 1996): students have been given tasks, based on resources available in the learning centre, to work on in groups, and in the process have learnt both to collaborate and to become independent thinkers. The politics of funding also lies behind the focus on transferable skills in so many vocational courses.

It is worth thinking of using such ideas in the EAP context, not least because we need to prepare our students to cope with the changing demands of Higher Education in the UK. In the EAP field Waters and Waters (1992) have already identified the need for deep learning and have suggested ways of developing the *study competence* necessary to the acquisition of successful study skills. Figure 1 illustrates the fundamental abilities which underlie the aspects of studying typically focused on by EAP materials.

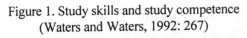

Figure 1. Study skills and study competence
(Waters and Waters, 1992: 267)

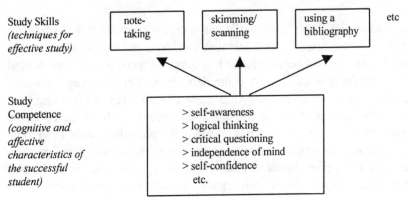

The oppositions between formative, criterion referenced assessment, and summative, norm referenced ones are familiar. In this new paradigm we want to know how well our students are doing, as well as how many have reached certain standards (as described by grades, IELTS scores and so on). So what are we to assess? learning? performance? competence? attainment? achievement? progress?

Now that we do not simply want to check that a body of knowledge has been transferred from teacher to student, now that we know that knowledge construction is more complex, now that we aim to produce students who can learn in many domains, we need to follow a fitness for purpose model. This requires us to involve our students in the assessment process, by making the purpose of assessment, the criteria of assessment and the outcomes of assessment explicit to students. With this information they should be better able to make use of the information we give them in so many areas, from the grades awarded to summary comments. In this way we can create a 'trickle up' effect as the information thus gained affects decision making in the classroom and then upwards. Gipps (1994) examines closely this growth view of learning, within mainstream education. She gives a clear and useful account of the way that our developing understanding of cognition and learning leads us to want to map assessment directly on to the processes we wish to develop.

2. Student Centred Assessment

As Gibbs (1995) points out it is common for innovation in assessment to lag behind teaching and learning methods, and the development of appropriate assessment methods has often followed a long way behind the introduction of student centred courses. Yet, the way in which assessment operates probably has more effect on student learning than any other aspect of course design. The learner must be involved in the assessment process in a number of ways: the procedures used need to be explicit and transparent, often negotiated with the learner; there must be a clear distinction between assessment tasks, aims and methods; and feedback must focus on both knowledge construction and metacognition.

2.1 The essay

The essay still occupies a central place in many academic courses. It is not surprising that it is still a favourite vehicle for assessment as it can be used as feedback to students on their progress or part of the grading process for the final qualification, thus allowing the flexibility to move between process and product, formative and summative assessment. It clearly has a place in the EAP classroom, even if in other educational sectors the staff student ratio makes marking drafts and even final versions for all students problematic. There are many models for the way in which tutor and learner can interact through the writing process. Keh (1990), for example, writes of a three part model for feedback, all focusing on higher order concerns before lower order concerns, and all student centred. This model includes peer feedback, where students gain a wider sense of audience. It includes conferences between the teacher as reader and the students as writers; this can be done at any stage of the writing process and is clearly beneficial to both oral and written work. And finally it involves written comments, where the teacher reacts as a reader, as a writing teacher concerned with confusion and breaks in logic, and as a grammarian.

Despite the fact that the essay can be used in so many productive ways, the issue of standards is often not fully explored, leading to accusations of falling standards. Tutors need to explore their preconceptions first, in order to allow for proper negotiating with students. A simple version of a familiar exercise involves asking tutors to work together to grade two essays chosen to illustrate a 'good' and a 'bad' essay; the discussion should focus on the strengths and weaknesses of each essay, suggestions for improvement and a grade (Brown et al, 1994: 7 – 8, have excellent worksheets for this exercise). Predictably there will be a lively discussion, centring on the need to clarify what was expected. The question of what standard very quickly becomes the question of whose standards? Teacher centred values will focus on the relevance to the question set, the characteristics of good essay writing and so on. Student centred assessment will have different values: originality, personal relevance and so on. So these will have to be made explicit to students and other teachers. If we believe that it is students who make student centred methods work, then students have to be brought into the game. One solution is to ask students to brainstorm their list of criteria for peer assessment of essays and presentations, and also to establish the relative weight to be accorded to each criterion. This will undoubtedly influence the tutors' approach to assessment too. Another way to get students and tutors to negotiate on the question of standards is to use a version of the self assessment form taken from Race (1995), and which is included in the Appendix.

2.2 Alternatives to the essay

Though one of the most common assessment tasks, the essay is only one of a growing array of possible options for assessment. Some of the better known alternatives are unseen written exams, pre-disclosed exams, dissertations, presentations, essay plans, reviews, journal articles, lab reports, case studies, fieldwork, literary searches, photographs, audiotapes, videotapes, interviews, posters, records of achievements, projects, portfolios, group work, diaries. In order to make such tasks student centred, they have to be matched to self assessment techniques and methods, which also come in a bewildering array. Harris and McCann (1994: 66 – 67) have a useful photocopiable list.

For the purposes of this paper I will concentrate on the last four task types on my list: projects, group work, portfolios, and diaries, as they overlap in terms of the methods and issues of assessment involved.

2.3 Projects

Projects, probably the most common way of assessing undergraduate as well as pre-sessional students' coursework, can be seen as a student centred version of an essay or a dissertation, specially when students are allowed to determine the choice of topic, to find the resources, to negotiate the length. As with many other student centred methods, there is a conflict between the way a project would run to maximise learning (emphasis on process) and the way it needs to be managed in order to assess it properly (emphasis on product). The problem of proof of authorship, or plagiarism, comes in here: if the emphasis is on the work undertaken then portfolios of drafts and logs will show this well; if the emphasis is on product then a *viva* or a project exam will enable understanding of content to be checked.

2.4 Group work: in spoken or written medium

One of the reasons for using group work is to save resources, as it can be more economical to set up, supervise and mark than individually undertaken work. Of course it should also develop team skills and other transferable skills, and it enables students to be involved in more complex and more open-ended learning tasks than they could manage on their own; it is also a good way of fostering informal peer tutoring and peer feedback.

The main problem here is in the assessment procedure: how to allocate grades to individuals fairly. While tutors may be in the best position to judge the quality of the product of group work, the group may be in the best position to judge the relative contributions of its members, and individuals in the group are well placed to assess their own contribution to the effectiveness of the whole project. In some systems the tutor gives the project a grade which is multiplied by the number of students in the group; the students then assess each other's contributions and allocate marks to individuals. In other systems the tutors assesses the product, allocating the same grade to each student, while the students assess each others' group work skills. The Thames Valley University study reports interestingly on student reactions to such systems.

In the electronic context, group tasks and group support and group discussion can operate through computer mediated conferencing and e-mail. The Institute of Education at London University runs a Certificate in On-line Education and Training. This is an experiential course with a first module on collaborative learning. Despite the often vaunted advantages of such a medium in the literature – democratic in the sense that there can be no issues of status and that it gives women and non native speakers an equal voice and equal turns – in fact, no doubt in part due to the fact that participation on the course is ungraded (assessment is through a good old fashioned end of course essay sent by mail) there is a great deal of 'lurking'. Students read the messages that are posted by the uninhibited few. Then a conference is opened on 'lurking' and students seem to prefer analysing their reactions to doing the group tasks. The tutor has the problem of setting up the discussion tasks and then pulling together the results of the interaction, in order to satisfy everyone. The Open University, whose PGCE has a computer mediated conferencing element, restricts this to inter-student support and discussion of tasks, in some ways making the most of the medium and letting the students work out among themselves their study problems. As Gibbs (1995) suggests, sometimes the key to making student centred assessment work with inadequate resources is to stop trying to obtain marks from it. Certainly in all student centred methods each additional layer of student centredness and flexibility brings with it additional problems.

2.5 Portfolios

Portfolios, as a common method of continuous assessment, come in various forms: collections of finished assessments, best work, vehicles for reflection on learning, evidence of process, evidence of achievement of competencies and standards. Students need to understand what they are for; otherwise the task will not generate desired and appropriate learning activity. Students often produce quantity rather than quality in these circumstances. One of the advantages of portfolios to the overworked tutor is that they can be graded by sampling.

2.6 Diaries

Learning diaries are a useful tool for self reflection and metacognitive thinking and because they are rarely used for summative assessment purposes there is a lack of consensus on the ground rules. Yet, they are used in an assessment of the learning process; so it is useful to establish writing conventions. For instance, are there categories of writing or topics which are expressly included or excluded? Should there be reflections on reading as well as on experience? Should all personal reflection about the tutor and other students be excluded? Who will see it? How long should it be? Is the writing saved up until a final assessment or is it reviewed as the course progresses? The values associated with diaries, logs and journals often clash with those of conventional courses, and the tutor needs to be clear about whether these study behaviours are to spread to other areas of work.

3. From Reflection and Self-Assessment to Perceptions of Progress

Assessing skills, competencies, abilities and capabilities, instead of only knowledge, is one of the major changes currently taking place in higher education (and the professions). This is a change involving fundamental reconceptualisations of the purpose of higher education and the design of curricula. The focus is moved from aims to learning through the assessment process itself: to some extent in the EAP context this is already in place, when we acknowledge and give weight to skill components of existing courses or assignments, for example the oral communication skills involved in a seminar presentation. In this way, new elements and emphases can be introduced into otherwise content-dominated courses, and evidence can be produced for profiles or records of achievement which document individual students' capacities rather than only a degree classification. For this particular emphasis to work, feedback needs to be central. This brings us back to perceptions of progress, achievable targets and tangible outcomes, and the old distinction between formative and summative assessment, and in the EAP context, to cultural orientation.

In many countries learning is still regarded as the digestion of a body of knowledge, with the acquisition of knowledge and facts prioritised over the acquisition of performance skills. Many learners equate progress with increased accuracy, and indeed progress checks in coursebooks are often only checks of the language learnt. Waters and Waters (1995: 194 – 200) on the other hand provide a final comprehensive checklist of seven pages, under such headings as organisational and self-awareness skills, thinking skills, information-locating skills, skills for coping with extended use of English, discussion skills, research skills, all referring back to the appropriate sections of the book. The following are just the first few items of a 30-item breakdown for academic skills.

Figure 2. Skills Assessment Checklist
(Waters and Waters, 1995: 198)

Skill	I can do this well	OK, but I need more practice	I can't do this	I don't need to do this	Ref Unit: section task
6. Academic writing skills					
a) I can construct a bibliography					4:4.5-6
b) I have a positive attitude towards writing					8:1.3-4
c) I can determine the constraints on writing					8:2.1-4
d) I can narrow (focus) the topic					8:2 (all)
e) I can read and question to focus and expand my ideas					8:2.3
f) I can organise my ideas to develop the topic					8:3.1-3

Because we know that self-assessment can increase awareness in terms of communicative objectives, performance and thinking about to how to learn, the process must be engaged with from the start, so that students have a record of their own performance and can review it periodically. Harris and McCann (1994: 80) helpfully visualise just such a process:

Figure 3. Reviewing progress (Harris and McCann, 1994: 80)

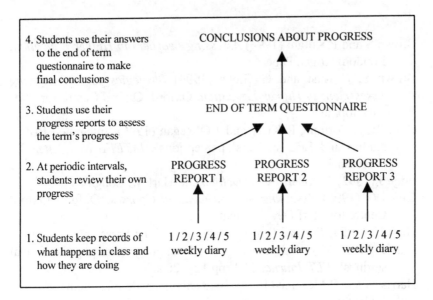

4. Students use their answers to the end of term questionnaire to make final conclusions — CONCLUSIONS ABOUT PROGRESS

3. Students use their progress reports to assess the term's progress — END OF TERM QUESTIONNAIRE

2. At periodic intervals, students review their own progress — PROGRESS REPORT 1   PROGRESS REPORT 2   PROGRESS REPORT 3

1. Students keep records of what happens in class and how they are doing — 1 / 2 / 3 / 4 / 5 weekly diary   1 / 2 / 3 / 4 / 5 weekly diary   1 / 2 / 3 / 4 / 5 weekly diary

4. Conclusion

This article began by exploring examples of reflective practice and went on to evaluate ways of involving the learners in their learning and in the assessment of their learning. Finally, ideas for showing progress were examined. Deep learning and metacognition cannot be achieved without reflection, and in the loop going from evaluating our strengths and weaknesses to setting targets and achieving them, it is important to keep the emphasis a positive one.

References

Brown S and P Knight (1994) *Assessing Learners in Higher Education*, London: Kogan Page

Brown S, C Rust and G Gibbs (1994) *Strategies for Diversifying Assessment in Higher Education*, Oxford: Oxford Centre for Staff Development

Clark R, A Fortune, R Kiely and J O'Regan (1996) 'Integrated British studies and EFL students' perceptions', *IATEFL Newsletter* 13, November

Edge J (1992) *Co-operative Development*, Harlow: Longman

Gibbs G (1995) *Assessing Student Centred Courses*, Oxford: Oxford Centre for Staff Development

Gipps C (1994) *Beyond Testing*, Brighton: Falmer Press

Harris M (1997) 'Self-assessment of language learning in formal settings', *ELT Journal* 51.1, pp 12 – 20

Harris M and P McCann (1994) *Assessment*, London: Heinemann

Keh C (1990) 'Feedback in the writing process', *ELT Journal* 44.4, pp 294 – 304

Phillips M (1996) *All Must Have Prizes*, London: Little Brown

Race P (1995) *Who Learns Wins*, London: Penguin/ BBC Books

Richards J and C Lockhart (1994) *Reflective Teaching in Second Language Classrooms*, Cambridge: Cambridge University Press

Underhill A (1992) 'The role of groups in developing teacher self-awareness', *ELT Journal* 46.1, pp 71 – 80

Vigotsky L (1978) *Mind in Society: The development of higher psychological processes*, Cambridge, MA: Harvard University Press

Waters A and M Waters (1992) 'Study skills and study competence: getting the priorities right', *ELT Journal* 46.3, pp 264 – 273

Waters A and M Waters (1995) *Study Tasks in English*, Cambridge: Cambridge University Press

Appendix

Self-assessment Form

Please complete your part of each of the questions below as objectively as you can, and hand this form in with your assignment. The aims of this self-assessment are:
- To give you an opportunity to reflect on the work you are about to hand in;
- To give you further feedback on your work, and on your own assessment of your work.

This form will not be looked at until after your work has been assessed, and your comments on this form will not affect your assessment..

Your name: Date:

Title of Assignment:

Tutor's name: Date of marking:

1. What do you honestly consider will be a fair score or grade for the work you are handing in?

   Your estimate: Tutor's score/grade:

   Tutor's comments on agreement between your self-assessment and the tutor assessment or grades.

2. What do you thank was the thing you did best in the assignment?

   Tutor's reply on the above:

3. If you had the chance to do the assignment again from scratch, how (if at all) might you decide to go about it differently?

   Tutor's reply to your second thoughts:

4. What did you find the hardest aspect of this assignment?

   Tutor's comment on how you actually did on this aspect:

Alicia Cresswell

The Role of Portfolios in the Assessment of Student Writing on an EAP Course

1. Introduction

Few practitioners would argue against the view that teaching and assessment should be guided by compatible underlying principles. Yet in practice there is often a mismatch between the two. Nowhere is this more evident than in the teaching of writing. Research into the composing process and its pedagogical applications (see, for example, Flower, 1979, 1994; Flower and Hayes, 1981; Zamel, 1983) has had a huge impact on what goes on in the writing class. Students work on pre-writing activities, plan and draft their work, seek feedback from teachers and peers and revise the emerging text. The atmosphere is supportive and collaboration is actively encouraged. When it comes to formal assessment, however, the rules of the game often change radically. Students sit silently at their desks and engage in the solitary task of writing a timed impromptu essay. The focus is now firmly on the product and there is hardly any time for planning and revision: writing under test conditions requires different skills and strategies from those practised in class.

Another discrepancy between teaching and assessment gives further cause for concern. In class, students work on a variety of writing tasks, thus familiarising themselves with the requirements of different genres or text types and writing on a number of different topics. Timed essay tests, on the other hand, typically consist of one or two tasks. The fact that judgements about writing ability are made on such a restricted sample of writing raises doubts about the reliability of the proficiency measure. Research has shown, for example, that writing task and subject matter knowledge have an impact on students' written production (see Peyton et al, 1990; Tedick, 1990). Results based on a very narrow sample of writing are more likely to be influenced by these two variables. White (1995) argues that although timed essay tests may have *scoring* reliability, which can be achieved through the development of rigorous grading criteria and regular standardisation, overall *test* reliability is low because a single measure cannot accurately establish writing competence.

The timed essay test is of course not without advantages. It is easy to administer and relatively uncomplicated to mark; more importantly, it provides a useful tool for the placement of incoming students when no other measures of writing ability are available. But in language programmes where the development of writing skills is of paramount importance, as is the case with most EAP courses, the sole use of this type of test for assessment purposes seems unnecessarily reductionist.

In the last decade portfolio assessment has gained increasing popularity as an alternative to the traditional timed-essay test, particularly in the USA, where it is widely used in undergraduate composition programmes (see Belanoff and Dickson, 1991; Hamp-Lyons and Condon, 1993; White, 1994). This paper describes a project investigating the feasibility of portfolio assessment for the writing component of a year's course in English for Academic Purposes at the University of Newcastle upon Tyne.

2. Background

A writing portfolio is a compilation of student work submitted in fulfilment of a course requirement. Most portfolios consist of a set number of texts and many include multiple drafts and a self-assessment task. Portfolio assessment appeals to teachers who are committed to process pedagogy because, as Belanoff and Dickson (1991: xx) put it,

...(it) builds a textured, multi-layered, focused measure of the writing ability students can demonstrate when given time to revise papers, and portfolio assessment alone can map the process students go through as they write.

There are different models of portfolio assessment and different methods of grading the portfolios. Class portfolios involve no-one other than a group of students and their teacher, who sets the criteria for the portfolio and marks the work. When used for large-scale assessment across a programme or institution, portfolios are usually marked by a team of trained readers who are not familiar with the students' work, although in some cases the work is marked by both the reader and the class teacher. Large-scale portfolio assessment aims to ensure consistency of standards across the programme or institution, but to-date very little is known about the reliability of scoring procedures as the literature on the subject consists mainly of practitioners' reports which, although informative, are not based on the findings of empirical research (see Hamp-Lyons and Condon, 1993, however, for a notable exception).

A number of common themes run through the literature on portfolio assessment. Most practitioners agree that the introduction of portfolio-based programmes has brought about benefits beyond improved assessment practices. Portfolios can have an impact on curriculum and teacher evaluation (Larson, 1991) and can help to increase interaction between teachers, readers and programme organisers, thus leading to shared knowledge and consensus on important issues of instruction (Belanoff and Elbow, 1991; Condon and Hamp-Lyons, 1991). Most importantly, they are excellent tools for student empowerment (Wauters, 1991), the development of metacognition (Mills-Court and Rae Armiran, 1991) and self-evaluation (Tierney et al, 1991). However, there are a number of difficulties, particularly in the implementation of large-scale portfolio assessment (Condon and Hamp-Lyons, 1991; Anson and Brown, 1991), and it is recognised that this approach to assessment generates heavy workloads for both teachers and readers. Planning is crucial, as is a flexible approach and willingness to experiment (Condon and Hamp-Lyons, 1991).

3. Portfolio-Based Writing Assessment in an EAP Programme: A Pilot Study

Growing dissatisfaction with the use of timed essay tests for the assessment of writing in our full-time EAP programme prompted the search for an alternative which would permit a more integrated approach to teaching and assessment. Such an approach would require a method of assessment capable of reflecting the complexity and recursiveness of the writing process and the range of tasks students perform in the writing class. Although this assessment would not necessarily exclude testing, it would eliminate final grades which rely solely on a timed essay test as this is not only a poor reflection of what goes on in the writing class but is often perceived as unfair by students. Finally, there was an expectation that a closer correspondence between teaching and assessment would have a beneficial effect on learning.

These expectations clearly pointed in the direction of portfolio-based assessment. But immediate implementation was out of the question since the existing literature on the subject made no secret of the difficulties involved in establishing a successful large-scale portfolio assessment programme (see, for example, Condon and Hamp-Lyons, 1991; Anson and Brown, 1991). Acknowledging that assessment, particularly for a course with a gatekeeping function, is too important an issue to risk ineffective or unreliable procedures, we decided to conduct a pilot project in order to explore the feasibility of portfolio assessment in the context of a full-time EAP course and identify problem areas in advance.

The project took place over a ten-week term, from January to March 1997. Twenty-two students of different nationalities and two experienced EAP teachers participated in the project. All students except one, who arrived in January 1997, had entered the course in October 1996. They had taken the IELTS test before admission and had achieved scores ranging from 5.0 to 6.5. The students were divided into two groups, each taught by one of the participating teachers. At the time of the pilot project the students were working at what can roughly be described as the upper-intermediate and advanced levels.

The pilot project set out to answer three questions:

1. Is portfolio assessment feasible in the context of a year's course in English for Academic Purposes?
2. If so, how can the portfolios be assessed?
3. Can this approach to assessment enhance learning?

3.1 Portfolio requirements

The selection of tasks for the pilot portfolio was accomplished without introducing any substantive changes to the curriculum or the course requirements. By the time the project started, the students had already completed a term's work based on rhetorical functions such as definition and exemplification, comparison and contrast, cause and effect and description and interpretation of graphic and numerical data. The syllabus for the second term focuses on descriptive and argumentative essay writing but also includes revision tasks and practice in the composition of problem-solution-evaluation texts. Reading-to-write tasks feature prominently among the pre-writing activities. Students are expected to synthesise information from different sources and display some degree of critical thinking. They are also taught how to refer to the sources they have read, both in the text itself and in the bibliography.

The course already carried a submission requirement of 80% of all classwork and homework, so the only innovation introduced to accommodate the pilot project was the submission of a collection of coursework assignments in portfolio format at the end of term.

Briefing notes distributed at the beginning of term informed students which tasks would be included in the portfolio. These were:

1. One descriptive essay
2. One argumentative essay
3. One timed in-class essay
4. One problem-solution-evaluation essay

All tasks required some reading and the timed in-class essay, on the topic of gender and career choices, also involved the interpretation of tabular data, thus providing an opportunity to revise language learnt in the first term. The in-class essay was the only single-draft task: it was introduced to give students the experience of writing under timed conditions on a topic that they had researched and discussed in class. In this respect, it was different from the impromptu essay tests normally used in the formal assessment of writing, and probably more akin to an academic subject written examination. Another reason for the inclusion of a timed in-class essay was to obtain a piece of writing indisputably authored by the student. Obtaining this type of evidence seemed important since the issue of text ownership was perceived as a potential source of difficulties in the assessment of writing portfolios.

In terms of the day-to-day management of teaching and learning, normal classroom practices remained unchanged. Students brainstormed ideas, planned and drafted their work, received feedback from their teacher and peers, and acted on that feedback to improve their work. In the last week of term, students compiled their portfolios and, prior to submission, completed an in-class self-assessment task.

4. Assessing the Portfolios

This section explores the issues raised by the first two questions the pilot project set out to answer: (1) Is portfolio assessment feasible in the context of a year's course in English for Academic Purposes? and (2) If so, how can portfolios be assessed? It also briefly describes the correlation between the marks given to the portfolios and the results of the standard end-of-term test that the students participating in the project were also required to take for comparative purposes.

Feasibility was deemed to be contingent on two factors. The first one was the effective management of the practicalities of portfolio administration, specially marking. This is not a trivial issue as the number and range of writing tasks in a portfolio make far greater demands on markers than the traditional timed essay test. The second factor was evidence that assessment standards would not be compromised by doubts about the authorship of the work in the portfolio. It soon became clear that these issues could not be considered without reference to the manner in which the portfolios would be assessed. In other words, the first two questions the project aimed to investigate had to be considered jointly.

Apart from a slight increase in the amount of record-keeping, the day-to-day administration of the portfolios caused no problems worth noting here. But as anticipated, the management of marking proved more complex, particularly because double-marking seemed necessary, or at least highly desirable, in order to ensure scoring reliability. This meant that the teachers involved in the project faced a substantial increase in the amount of marking they were required to do.

The demands that this approach to assessment would make on teachers/markers raised some interesting but difficult questions. Should markers read all drafts of multi-draft tasks or only the final draft? If markers read all drafts, how could good revision processes be rewarded? Would markers faced with several multi-draft assignments do justice to the process orientation of the portfolio? According to Hamp-Lyons (1996), there is little evidence that proof of the application of writing processses is rewarded by portfolio graders. This is probably an indication of the difficulties involved in marking multi-draft portfolios in a systematic manner, both in terms of the amount of time needed and the criteria to be used. Looking at the problem from a different perspective, however, it can be argued that final-draft marking of multi-draft portfolios may reward effective revision processes indirectly, as these are likely to result in a better product than would otherwise be the case and thus attract correspondingly higher marks. Adopting this point of view, we concluded that there was little point in choosing the more administratively complex multi-draft marking approach, although, for self-assessment purposes, it was desirable to include all drafts in the portfolio.

Another decision to be taken was whether to mark the portfolios holistically or grade individual pieces and average the results. The literature on the subject pointed to a potential pitfall of the former method: Hamp-Lyons and Condon (1993) found that readers in their programme made decisions about grades very early in the marking process, often assigning grades to portfolios after reading a single piece of writing. Although marker training and frequent standardisation can probably keep this problem to a minimum, this was nevertheless a useful warning of the difficulties that may arise if markers'workloads are not carefully managed. On a similar note, the teachers participating in the project expressed concern that the holistic method would lead to the accumulation of marking at the end of term, when other duties such as progress report writing make heavy demands on teachers' time. Since one of the markers, the class teacher, would have to read each piece of writing as soon as it was completed in order to provide feedback to students, it was decided that it would be preferable for the first marker at least to grade each piece at this stage.

The issue of text ownership, which we identified in the early stages of the project as a potential source of difficulty, did not in fact present any major problems. Teachers were asked to avoid direct correction when giving feedback on first and intermediate drafts; instead, they were asked to use marking codes and marginal and end comments in order to promote problem-solving and revision strategies. Guidelines for peer review followed the same principles. It was made clear to students that, while this type of feedback was not only acceptable but also desirable, seeking outside help with editing or proof-reading was not allowed. At no point was there any reason to suspect that these guidelines had been ignored, and while it is acknowledged here that problems in this area may occasionally arise, the experience of those working on this project seems to indicate that the collaborative nature and the strong process orientation of portfolio assessment are important factors in the avoidance of breaches of trust, provided that the notion of authorship is properly defined and made explicit to students.

Having established that under the conditions described above portfolio assessment in the context of a full-time EAP course, although time-consuming and administratively complex, appeared to be feasible, we compared the marks given to the portfolios with the results of the timed end-of-term test which the students participating in the project were also required to take. The findings showed a high correlation between the marks for the two types of assessment. Out of the 22 students assessed by both methods, 20 (91%) were placed on the same band of a six-point scoring scale for the portfolio and the test. The other two students performed significantly better in the portfolio assessment than in the test, which in each case resulted in a one-point difference between the two types of assessment. In both cases, this appeared to be mainly due to the non-completion of one of the two tasks in the end-of-term test, which reflects the difficulty these students had in writing under time constraints.

5. The Portfolio as a Tool for Self-Assessment

The third purpose of the pilot project was to investigate whether portfolio assessment can enhance learning. We intended to explore this issue by considering the use of portfolios as self-assessment tools and their role in the development of metacognition. The compilation of a portfolio enables student writers to reflect on the work they have produced over a period of time. This is why many portfolio assessment schemes include a self-assessment task in the form of a letter, essay or questionnaire. We chose to use a guided self-assessment task, to be carried out on completion of the portfolios in the last week of term. The task asked students to answer the following questions about their writing:
1. What are your strengths?
2. What are your weaknesses?
3. In what aspects of the work have you made progress
   this term?
4. What aspects of your work need further improvement?
This proved to be a highly successful way of dealing with self-assessment, as it forced students to reflect on the positive aspects of their performance as well as areas of difficulty. Despite having been given a checklist of aspects of writing to consider, most students initially found it difficult to identify their strengths and a few could think of no positive comments about their own writing other than the ability to use capital letters or punctuation accurately.

But when encouraged to look through their portfolios for evidence of strong points in their work, they were soon able to note some down. Examples include:

- *I have many good ideas.*
- *When I write an essay, I can cover most of the main points.*
- *Generally speaking, my language is mostly good in grammar, cohesion, spelling and punctuation.*
- *I think that I am better at writing descriptive essay. The reason for this may be that there aren't lots of pressure: I don't have to think about defeating other people's point of view. Therefore I do it in a more relaxing way.*
- *My strength is that, when I understand the subject clearly and make a clear plan for it, then I think I can write quite clear and simple discussion.*
- *Bring detailed facts to support my points, to argument: bring ideas together; to organise my work, my plan.*

These comments indicate an understanding of the importance of the composing process. It is interesting that, apart from a few references to surface features of grammar, spelling and punctuation, most observations refer to aspects of composition. Had the writing teacher not provided positive feedback on these aspects through marginal and end comments, it is unlikely that these students would have demonstrated such an awareness of their strengths as writers. And without this awareness they would probably have been incapable of making a realistic self-assessment of their competence and progress.

Students were less reticent when asked to write about their weaknesses. Here, all aspects of writing, from mechanics to high level processes, were represented. However, as was the case in the answers to the first question, most comments referred to problems with composition, as the examples below show:

- *Very poor organisation. Sometimes I have some ideas in my mind but I don't know how to put them in order.*
- *Content of my essay sometimes is not relevant to the topic.*
- *Support opinions are very weak; lack of information and examples in many essays.*
- *Argumentative essay is my nightmare.*

- *When interpreting data I cannot control the information and therefore use more data than appropriate.*
- *When time is limited, I'm thrown into confusion, so I can't write clear discussion.*
- *I make things too simple so often need expansion.*
- *There are repetitions – problems of organisation.*
- *My writing is not reader friendly. possibly, I am too absorbed in my own subjectivity to think about my readers.*

The answers to the first two questions in the self-assessment task strongly suggest that portfolios which include appropriate, fair and sensitive responses from teachers have considerable potential as tools for self-assessment and the development of metacognition.

Further evidence of this is provided by the answers to the third question in the self-assessment task, which asked students to comment on the aspects of their work in which they had made progress. In general, students felt that they had improved a great deal. Only one student was negative about his progress: *'I don't think I have some progress in this term'*, and one was very cautious: *'I may have made progress in the development of ideas'*. But most recognised that they had made progress, often in more than one area:

- *I have found it much easier for me to write an introduction this term.*
- *I do think I made progress this term. Because I hardly received any training in English writing before I came here. I learned a lot in writing academic essay from this writing class.*
- *I used to have many sentences in essay that were very complicated; however, I think that I managed to simplify them, compare to previous term.*
- *I believe that I improve my organisation skill to compare with last term and graph and tables are really improved. Before I studied it, I could not write at all.*
- *Writing clearly and putting more details; write fast and fluently; the style of my work have improved.*
- *I introduce the topic easier for the reader to follow than before.*

Equipped with a good understanding of their strengths and weaknesses as writers, and empowered by the knowledge that they had made progress, students were able to answer the final question in the self-assessment task, which required them to indicate what aspects of their work needed further improvement. They wrote:

- *My argument is not clear in that which side I am supporting. Therefore, my work need further improvement on presenting clearer argument.*
- *Generally, I feel necessary to improve in all the point, especially I need great care in spelling and grammar.*
- *I think I have to improve the use of reference.*
- *How to organise the paragraph more easily and clearly.*
- *Acquire a more formal academic writing style.*
- *I still find difficulties to organise whole discussion, especially in a conclusion.*
- *Work fast.*
- *Strategies for planning.*
- *To avoid introducing irrelevant information.*

The ability to set realistic objectives for further improvement is an essential condition of independent learning. In demonstrating that they were capable of identifying specific areas in which more work was needed, these students provided additional evidence of the usefulness of writing portfolios as tools for self-assessment and learner training.

When asked to evaluate the experience of compiling the portfolios, the majority of students showed considerable enthusiasm, as the following statements illustrate:

- *I think it is good idea to file what we have done because we can remind ourselves what we have to improve more, what progress we had, etc by looking at portfolio. In fact, I could see a lot of difference between beginning of this term and now in each work from portfolio. We'd be better to do this next term.*
- *I think that it is very useful. Because by looking at our improvement we can get incentive to get better and better.*
- *I think I have been improving my writing a lot this term, but it is never enough. I hope I could improve more in next term.*
- *I think it is useful for me. I can realise what should I improve in next term.*
- *It was useful for me. Because I could know which skill improved and which skills need more.*

- *It is very useful. I can learn or notice what I should change and in what point I am good at.*
- *I suppose it's useful as well, we can find our improvements and also problems by looking through our previous work. We often miss such things at the time but after a while, we can look at them more objectively.*

Their comments highlight the awareness-raising element of portfolio assessment schemes. While immersed in the day-to-day work of their course, student writers may have a somewhat fragmented understanding of their ability, but the writing portfolio and the self-assessment task that accompanies it can help them to build a more coherent picture. A one-to-one tutorial with the writing teacher once the self-assessment task is completed may help to complete a balanced picture. Equipped with an awareness of their strengths and weaknesses, and empowered by the knowledge that they have made progress, students have the basic tools to direct their own learning.

6. Conclusions and Implications

This paper has examined the use of writing portfolios for two different – although not mutually exclusive – purposes. As an alternative to timed essay tests for the assessment of writing, portfolios can provide a more accurate reflection of the learning that has taken place and a richer picture of the student's ability as a writer. However, the implementation of a large-scale portfolio assessment scheme is administratively complex and makes considerable demands on those involved in marking the portfolios, even if procedures are kept as simple as possible. There is some indication in the data that portfolio assessment may benefit students who find writing under time constraints difficult; nevertheless, the marks for portfolio assessment show a high correlation with the results of the timed essay test, suggesting that a change to portfolio assessment would not necessarily lead to fairer or more accurate scores.

As tools for self-assessment and learner training, writing portfolios have much to offer. It is the aim of general EAP programmes to give students a foundation in academic writing skills that will enable them to cope with the writing requirements of their own discipline. To do this successfully, they will need to continue to develop their writing skills, often without the help of a language tutor. The learner training aspects of portfolio assessment can provide useful preparation for this. Furthermore, there are other ways in which portfolios can enhance future learning: the data gathered through the compilation of student work, teacher feedback and self-assessment can help teachers to construct an informative student profile for use by the receiving academic department and language tutors on other courses the student may join at a later date. This could ease the transition from the general EAP course to other programmes and enable both academic and language tutors to respond more readily to the needs of their students.

The case for a change to large-scale portfolio assessment is not wholly proven. As a method of assessment, it places a greater administrative and possibly financial burden on the programme and the institution running it. Furthermore, on the basis of this small study, the results of portfolio assessment are similar to those of timed essay tests. More research is needed in this area. For the time being, the main strength of portfolio-based assessment appears to be its potential for self-assessment and learner training. In this respect, results are sufficiently impressive to justify the introduction of small-scale, in-class portfolio assessment schemes. Such an approach would not only have considerable pedagogical benefits but would also contribute to the development of expertise in portfolio-based assessment and provide the conditions necessary for further research.

References

Anson C and R Brown (1991) 'Large-scale portfolio assessment: ideological sensitivity and institutional change', in Belanoff P and M Dickson (eds) *Portfolios: Process and Product*, Portsmouth, NH: Boynton Cook

Belanoff P and M Dickson (eds) (1991) *Portfolios: Process and Product*, Portsmouth, NH: Boynton Cook

Belanoff P and P Elbow (1991) 'Using portfolios to increase collaboration and community in a writing program, in Belanoff P and M Dickson (eds) *Portfolios: Process and product*, Portsmouth, NH: Boynton Cook

Condon W and L Hamp-Lyons (1991) 'Introducing a portfolio-based writing assessment: progress through problems', in Belanoff P and M Dickson (eds) *Portfolios: Process and product*, Portsmouth, NH: Boynton Cook

Flower L (1979) 'Writer-based prose: a cognitive basis for problems in writing', *College English* 41, pp 19 – 37

Flower L (1994) *The Construction of Negotiated Meaning: A social cognitive theory of writing*, Carbondale, IL: Southern Illinois University Press

Flower L and J Hayes (1981) 'A cognitive process theory of writing', *College Composition and Communication* 32, pp 365 – 387

Hamp-Lyons L (1996) 'Applying ethical standards to portfolio assessment of writing in English as a second language', in Milanovic M and N Saville (eds) *Performance, Testing, Cognition and Assessment*, Cambridge: Cambridge University Press

Hamp-Lyons L and W Condon (1993) 'Questioning assumptions about portfolio-based assessment', *College Composition and Communication* 44, pp 176 – 190

Larson R (1991) 'Using portfolios in the assessment of writing in the academic disciplines', in Belanoff P and M Dickson (eds) *Portfolios: Process and Product*, Portsmouth, NH: Boynton Cook

Milanovic M and N Saville (eds) (1996) *Performance, Testing, Cognition and Assessment,* Cambridge: Cambridge University Press

Mills-Court K and M Rae Armiran (1991) 'Metacognition and the use of portfolios', in Belanoff P and M Dickson (eds) *Portfolios: Process and Product,* Portsmouth, NH: Boynton Cook

Peyton J, J Staton, G Richardson and W Wolfram (1990) 'The influence of writing task on ESL students' written production', *Research in the Teaching of English* 24, pp 142 – 147

Tedick D (1990) 'ESL writing assignments: subject matter knowledge and its impact on performance', *English for Specific Purposes* 9, pp 123 – 143

Tierney R, M Carter and L Desai (1991) *Portfolio Assessment in the Reading-Writing Classroom,* Norwood, MA: Christopher Gordon.

Wauters J (1991) 'Evaluation for empowerment: a portfolio proposal for Alaska', in Belanoff P and M Dickson (eds) *Portfolios: Process and Product,* Portsmouth, NH: Boynton Cook

White E (1994) *Teaching and Assessing Writing,* Second Edition, San Francisco: Jossey Bass

White E (1995) 'An apologia for the timed impromptu essay test', *College Composition and Communication* 46, pp 30 – 45

Zamel V (1983) 'The composing processes of advanced ESL students: six case studies', *TESOL Quarterly* 17, pp 165 – 187

M I Freeman

A Self-Evaluation Instrument for the Measurement of Student Proficiency Levels

1. Introduction

This paper presents a self-evaluation instrument designed to measure student proficiency levels. As several versions of this instrument were developed, it will be referred to as SEI4 (Self-Evaluation Instrument 4). It was adapted from Spolsky's (1989) can-do scales during my doctoral research (for a more complete description, see Freeman, 1996: 156). The instrument is a communicative measure of all four skills and takes about five minutes to administer. Its main feature is that it combines 4 can-do scales with performance criteria, that is, it not only asks the question 'Can you do this task?' but also 'How well can you do it?'. The performance criteria for reading/listening are expressed in percentages, whereas speaking/writing performance is evaluated using a 5-point scale. These criteria allow students to indicate how well they perform on a range of tasks.

This paper reviews relevant literature, describes the instrument, outlines the results of some experimental trials, and presents a speculative discussion of the value of such an instrument as a low cost/readily available standard of language proficiency.

2. Literature Survey

Four major types of assessment were identified by Thomas (1994: 307) in a review article:

- impressionistic judgement
- institutional status as a proxy for proficiency level
- research-internal or in-house measures of proficiency
- standardised test scores

Each type of assessment has its own advantages and disadvantages. Standardised tests (for example, TOEFL and IELTS) are often expensive to use and time consuming to administer and mark, but give results that are seen to be comparable with other studies and credible. Institutional course grades are often of unknown reliability and validity, and difficult to compare with other measures. SEI4 is a research-internal instrument, based on impressionistic judgement. Some research-internal instruments lack credibility, but SEI4 was adapted from Spolsky's scales which have been tried and tested. Dickinson (1987) and Oskarsson (1989) mention a range of advantages for self-assessment, including improved goal-orientation, shared assessment burden, raised level of awareness and promotion of learning. Brown and Hudson (1998) review a range of 'alternatives' in language assessment, and point to four possible advantages: administration speed, student involvement, student autonomy and increased motivation.

Many different types of self-assessment instrument are to be found in the literature (see Blanche and Merino, 1989 and Oskarsson, 1978 for review articles; Harris, 1997 and MacIntyre et al, 1997 provide recent examples). Many of these instruments can be administered quickly, effectively and at low cost. Let us look first at some of the drawbacks mentioned in the literature, before reviewing more positive aspects. Self-assessment and self-report instruments are sometimes viewed as defective because of lack of objectivity, possible social desirability response bias (Ehrman and Oxford, 1995; Blue, 1994, 1988), acquiescence effect (Heilenman, 1990) and possible dependence on age, cultural and personality factors (Blanche and Merino, 1989).

It is widely recognised that learners may find it difficult to be objective about their own language level, or that they may not have the necessary expertise and experience to make judgements of this sort (Blue, 1994: 18)

The degree of confidence seems to be a key factor here. MacIntyre et al (1997) found that 37 anglophone students tended to overestimate their language skills when they were self-confident, but to underestimate when their disposition was more anxious. Evidence for overestimation was also found by Heilenman (1990), particularly for less experienced learners. The effectiveness of self-assessment will depend upon the type of learner and the type of scale used; it may be that in some cases the type of self-assessment instrument used was inappropriate to the learners, or that the scales themselves were unreliable.

Despite the possible disadvantages of self-report and self-assessment, many researchers have found that in practice, with sufficient precautions, these techniques can provide reliable and valid data more rapidly and easily than traditional methods.

> Several studies included quantitative comparisons between self-appraisals and more objective measures of proficiency, usually in the form of Pearson product-moment correlation coefficients. Values ranging from 0.5 to 0.6 are common, and higher ones not uncommon. What this means is that a set of self-assessments (such as answers to a questionnaire) tend to carry about the same weight as any of the various parts (subtests) of a standardised testing instrument... (Blanche and Merino, 1989: 315)

More recently, Shameem (1998) found quite strong correlations between performance test and self-report data (r = 0.63 to 0.70). Ross (1998) carried out a meta-analysis of 10 studies, including Bachman and Palmer (1982), Buck (1992) and LeBlanc and Painchaud (1985), covering a wide range of contexts: with sample sizes from 32 to 878, languages including ESL, Dutch and French, and subjects of many nationalities, including Chinese, Japanese and Swiss. The average of 60 correlations was found to be r = 0.63, p = 0.0001, providing ample support for the Blanche and Merino study. Ross also found evidence that self-assessment worked best when the learners had experience of the tasks mentioned in the instruments used.

> The crafting of self-assessment scales requires considerable finesse, and they have to involve language skills that learners have had enough instruction or language contact to develop ... (Ross, 1998: 5)

Another criterion for well-designed scales is the amount of detail and the degree of clarity of the tasks. When the scales are poorly defined it is likely that the instrument will be more unreliable. However, if the language is too complex for the users of the scales to understand, then this is also likely to lead to lower reliability. Spolsky's (1989) can-do scales were adapted from Clark's (1981) scales, which contained more complex language. SEI4 contains items which are more clearly defined than Spolsky's, but using language which even lower-intermediate level students can understand (SEI4 was designed for use with students from band 4 to 7 on the IELTS scale).

3 Methodology

3.1 Instrument: the development of SEI4

Three early versions of SEI (1–3) were tried out on groups of Turkish, pre-sessional and case-study students at Sussex University. These instruments were designed to make them more suitable for the sample of students being investigated and to improve the characteristics of Spolsky's scales. In particular, the validity of Spolsky's scales was felt to be unsatisfactory. Spolsky, for example, does not give any predictive validity coefficients for his can-do scales. To summarise, the main changes made to Spolsky's scales were:

- the addition of a writing scale,
- the deletion of items relating to the Israeli school situation (for example, describe school, read prayer book),
- the inclusion of items relating to university language students,
- greater definition of texts, tasks and performance criteria.

SEI4 contains 40 items including a wide range of authentic tasks; students have to rate their own performance in all four skills.

3.2 The reading and listening tests

Both reading and listening are rated according to percentage of comprehension of a variety of texts, sufficiently graded to cater for elementary, intermediate and advanced level students at university level. Two sample items from the reading scale are shown below:

Please assess your language proficiency by placing one tick against each item. Try to estimate how you would do alone, *without any help*, without dictionaries etc.

READING SLOWLY (say, 5 minutes per page)	% COMPREHENSION				
	0-20%	21-40%	41-60%	61-80%	81%+
Personal letter using short, simple sentences, ~ 1 page long	....	....	....	....	....
Complex research article in international journal ~ 10 pages long	....	....	....	....	....

Students have to estimate how good they are at the reading tasks shown. For example, for the first task, a tick on the far right indicates that they would comprehend more than 81% of a one page personal letter, written in short simple sentences, given five minutes to complete the task.

3.3 The speaking and writing tests

Speaking and writing were rated on a five-point performance scale defined in terms of fluency, accuracy, difficulty and comprehensibility. Three sample items are shown below, preceded by the performance scale used:

For speaking, indicate your level by circling a number from 1-5 after each task. Please use the following scale:

1 = No, I cannot do it; my message would not be understood at all.
2 = Yes, I can do it, but with extreme difficulty, very slowly and with many errors.
3 = Yes, I can do it, but with some difficulty; my message is generally understood.
4 = Yes, I can do it, with little or no difficulty, occasional inaccuracies and rather slowly.
5 = Yes, I can do it easily, fluently and accurately.

SPEAKING   NO   YES, EASILY

Introduce self	1	2	3	4	5
Talk about future plans	1	2	3	4	5
Give paper at conference	1	2	3	4	5

For the second task, if students circle number 5, this indicates that they can talk about their future plans easily, fluently and accurately. In this way, students estimate their language skills on a wide range of tasks and in each case they have the choice of 5 performance levels. On each task students score more points for better performance. Thus, it is possible to obtain a numerical total of 50 points for each major skill (reading, writing, listening and speaking), and a grand total out of 200 for language proficiency. Further definition of the scales and performance criteria are desirable from a theoretical point of view, but the present instrument represents an effective compromise between simplicity and complexity. The model of language embodied in the instrument is essentially functional, and skills based (Alderson and Clapham, 1992). This instrument is a communicative measure of proficiency as the main emphasis is on meaning and task completion. The scale for each skill was designed so that the items were on an incline of difficulty (Harrison, 1983: 27), so that the instrument would work with a wide range of proficiency levels.

3.4 Sample

The sample consisted of 118 language students from the Universities of Brighton and Sussex. In terms of target language, about half were students of French and half students of EFL. The groups were chosen so that there would be a wide range of proficiency levels for each language, roughly from elementary to advanced, but also so that the vast majority would easily comprehend the forms used.

3.5 Data collection

Data were collected by questionnaire and interview. University of Cambridge Local Examinations Syndicate (UCLES) examination results were obtained from the university authorities, with the permission of all students concerned. The instrument SEI4 took about 5 minutes to administer, the EFL students taking a little longer. About 20% of the sample of 118 were interviewed. The main purpose of these interviews was to check the data collected. Selected reading, writing, listening and speaking tasks from SEI4 were assessed during the interviews by a qualified examiner. These scores were compared with the student assessments. In order to calculate test-retest reliability coefficients, the students were asked to reassess their proficiency level with SEI4 after an interval of a couple of weeks.

4. Results

4.1. Reliability and validity of SEI4

SEI4 seems very reliable, with a Cronbach alpha internal consistency reliability coefficient of 0.942 for the whole instrument. This reliability coefficient is comparable with the can-do scales used by other researchers:

Gardner et al (1989):	Alpha = 0.80 – 0.93
Weltens and Cohen (1989):	Alpha = 0.86 – 0.88
Spolsky (1989):	Alpha = 0.982
Gardner and MacIntyre (1993):	Alpha = 0.77 – 0.90
Clément et al (1994):	Alpha = 0.79

The test and retest reliability coefficient of SEI4 was found to be 0.898 ($p < 0.001$). This result is comparable with Spolsky's (1989) test-retest reliability coefficient of 0.92, and indicates that the instrument is of acceptable reliability for research purposes.

Concurrent validity coefficients for SEI4 ranged from 0.810 to 0.875 ($p < 0.001$), whereas the predictive validity coefficients for students of EFL were slightly lower: $r = 0.778$, $p < 0.001$, for students of CAE. The EFL groups were chosen for this study so that their University of Cambridge Local Examinations Syndicate results could be used to validate SEI4. These examinations were taken approximately three months after the main data collection.

5. Discussion

The following discussion includes a summary of the main advantages and disadvantages of SEI4, an indication of possible improvements, possible uses of SEI4, and an argument in favour of different types of national proficiency standard.

5.1 Advantages

The results shown above indicate that SEI4 was sufficiently reliable and valid using the sample of 118 students of EFL and French at the Universities of Sussex and Brighton, but could probably be used with similar results for British university students studying any language. It is fast to administer (~ 5 mins) and score (~ 3 mins), and relatively easy to check selected items. As this instrument is a communicative measure of all four skills, it appears to have reasonable face validity, and should have a positive backwash effect. In addition, the language used is simple and the tasks are easily recognisable; SEI4 can be used with EFL students of FCE level and above.

This instrument avoids many of the disadvantages of some standardised tests: time pressure/unpleasantness, high cost, the necessity for good performance and high test motivation on the day, very limited proficiency range, reliability of coursework, waiting for test results etc. (see Harris, 1997 and Oskarsson, 1989 for other advantages).

It is also a good way of helping students to take control of their own learning, and to manage their own progress or lack of it.

> self-assessment can facilitate their learning by helping them develop strategies to enhance their linguistic skills (MacIntyre et al, 1997: 266)

Traditional can-do scales such as those used by Spolsky (1989) and MacIntyre et al(1997) simply ask if the task can be completed or not, for example, 'Can you talk about your future plans?' They only allow for a yes/no response. This gross oversimplification reduces the accuracy and sensitivity of the instrument. The addition of performance criteria to a can-do scale seems to make a considerable improvement.

5.2 Disadvantages

The main disadvantage of this instrument is that it requires students to be honest, independent and accurate judges of their own proficiency levels (see Heidt, 1979: 35; Blanche, 1988). The students at the Universities of Sussex and Brighton took this task seriously and co-operated to the full. It is possible, however, that other groups may be biased, uncooperative or poorer judges. For these reasons, self-assessment cannot replace standardised tests where important decisions are taken on the outcomes.

Another disadvantage is that the performance criteria, as they stand, do not take into account more sophisticated concepts such as appropriateness, style, register and vocabulary range, nor is the concept of comprehension clearly defined. In addition, the tasks and performance criteria do not emphasise interactive skills. It would be possible to take these issues into account, but only at the expense of speed, simplicity and comprehensibility.

5.3. Possible uses of SEI4

SEI4 was used during the present author's doctoral research, in conjunction with other tests, as a measure of student proficiency levels. It could also be used as a diagnostic instrument, as part of data collection for needs analysis. It would quickly yield an overview of the students' perceived communicative strengths and weaknesses; this ties in with Ingram's (1985) 'response to felt need' principle in syllabus design. Furthermore, this simple instrument could be used as part of a placement test (see Ward Goodbody, 1993), as it is very fast to administer and score. Many course organisers avoid any measure of speaking during the placement process, as it is so time consuming. This could provide a compromise, as well as allowing students to take a more active role in the placement procedure.

> ... evaluating self-perceptions of competence is an efficient mechanism for placing students at appropriate levels saving both

the time and expense of formal testing ... (MacIntyre et al, 1997: 266)

However, the most valuable use of this instrument may be as a personal standard of proficiency used to guide students in their learning, similar to the GUME tests. It would be as a rough, but readily available, instrument used at any time, anywhere. Students could assess their own level, and using a simple conversion chart convert the SEI4 raw score into ESU levels, and then decide which examinations were most appropriate for them. It could also help them to formulate and develop their own communicative goals. This suggestion is best situated within the context of a more general discussion of the present availability of national standards and future needs.

5.4. National standards for proficiency levels

In a recent survey of British and European university-level language learning, Coleman (1996) recommended that universities adopt common standards for language proficiency.

> This study provides evidence to support a call from students, parents, employers and educationalists for universities to clearly state proficiency levels in all course documentation. In addition, to defining linguistic objectives, level descriptors and assessment criteria, universities should be encouraged to adopt agreed national or international standards. (Coleman, 1996: 11)

Students' GCSE and 'A' level grades are often an inaccurate guide to student proficiency levels at university, as these examinations do not only measure communicative competence, and students may have taken these examinations some time in the past. Coleman (1996) also remarked upon the wide spread of levels at 'degree level'.

> There are such immense discrepancies in levels of foreign language proficiency across British universities that labels such as

'first-year level' or 'foreign language to degree level' are meaningless. (Coleman, 1996: 7)

The situation is somewhat clearer for students of EFL thanks to the 'gold standard' of the IELTS test, but even here not all students take this test. Partly due to the high cost of IELTS, and partly due to the 3-month rule, it is not a test which is taken frequently. Therefore, the students who do take IELTS are likely to notice changes in their own proficiency levels with time, and they may well wonder where they stand at any particular point in time. It would be useful to have an instrument such as SEI4 to give them some guidance.

The ALTE framework of tests covering a range of European languages and levels (ALTE, 1994) has helped to map out the proficiency field, but it does not include EAP examinations and only includes one examination board from each country. These tests are arranged in tabular form and divided into 5 levels: Waystage, Threshold, Independent, and two higher levels. Unfortunately, the relationship between levels and languages is unclear. Are the proficiency levels of equal band width? Is grade 'A' in FCE higher or lower than grade 'très bien' in the Diplôme de Langue Française? How can two examinations be equivalent when they do not test the same skills, and the skills which are the same are not given identical weightings? It seems possible that a self-assessment instrument, which is not limited to testing language itself, can help to overcome such interlanguage difficulties.

The Languages Lead Body (1993 and 1995) has also produced a five level framework of proficiency levels. Each level is criterion referenced using descriptors, and a detailed series of tasks, texts and performance criteria define what standards the individual can achieve in each of the four skills at each level. Once again, these standards are not designed for students learning languages at university, but for a variety of vocational purposes. These standards could be adapted for university use, but at present the performance criteria are somewhat vague. They are described as '... a nationally accepted yardstick or benchmark of language competence,' (Languages Lead Body, 1995: 2) but there is no mention in the performance criteria of degree of fluency, which is an important aspect of language proficiency.

Furthermore, the degree to which information is accurately transmitted or received is also not taken into account. How can these 'standards' be a benchmark of proficiency without clearly defining fluency and accuracy? It seems that there is a need for greater definition, and possibly some real examples of what is acceptable at each level and what is not, before these standards can become really useful. The characteristics of standards should reflect the use for which they are designed. These standards lack sufficient precision to be considered as a national benchmark. Even a 5-point scale such as the one used in SEI4 would be a considerable improvement.

There is clearly a need for a range of standards:

- Rough and Ready: low cost, fast, easily accessible, giving a rough estimate of proficiency, as a guide to students and teachers such as SEI4 or similar
- Clearly Defined Behavioural Scales: criterion referenced, with precise definition of texts, tasks and performance criteria, like those of the Languages Lead Body, but more precise
- Standardised Tests: such as the UCLES examinations over the full proficiency range, in order to take important decisions, such as university entrance
- Precise Instruments: for research purposes and the measurement of progress or 'value added' during language courses

As mentioned in the ILTA (1995) report on standards, the term 'standard' is used in many different ways. Perhaps, these four types of instruments could be referred to as: guideline standards, performance standards, test standards, and high-precision standards.

What are urgently needed are instruments of low and high accuracy. SEI4 could easily be developed into an acceptable form at the low accuracy end of the scale. The development of very precise, sensitive and objective instruments, essential for the measurement of small changes in proficiency levels, is a far more challenging objective. Until we are able to measure proficiency, the most important outcome of the teaching/learning process, with a more satisfactory range of instruments, we shall continue to grope in the dark more often than we would like to admit.

References

Alderson J C and C Clapham (1992) 'Applied linguistics and language testing: a case study of the ELTS test', *Applied Linguistics* 13.2, pp 149 – 167

ALTE (1994) European Language Examinations, Version 2, Cambridge: UCLES

Bachman L and A Palmer (1982) 'The construct validation of some components of communicative proficiency', *TESOL Quarterly* 16, pp 449 – 465

Blanche P (1988) 'Self-assessment of foreign language skills: implications for teachers and researchers', *RELC Journal* 19, pp 75 – 96

Blanche P and B J Merino (1989) 'Self-assessment of foreign-language skills: implications for teachers and researchers', *Language Learning* 39.3, pp 313 – 340

Blue G M (1994) 'Self-assessment of foreign language skills: does it work?', in Blue G M (ed) *CLE Working Papers 3*, Southampton: University of Southampton Centre for Language in Education

Blue G M (1988) 'Self-assessment: the limits of learner independence', in Brookes A and P Grundy (eds) *Individualization and Autonomy in Language Learning*, Modern English Publications in association with the British Council

Brown J D and T Hudson (1998) 'The alternatives in language assessment', *TESOL Quarterly* 32.4, pp 653 – 675

Buck G (1992) 'Listening comprehension: construct validity and trait characteristics', *Language Learning* 42, pp 313 – 357

Clark J L D (1981) 'Language', in Barrows T S (ed) *College Students' Knowledge and Beliefs: A survey of global understanding*, New Rochelle, New York: Change Magazine Press

Clément R, Z Dörnyei and K A Noels (1994) 'Motivation, self-confidence, and group cohesion in the foreign language classroom', *Language Learning* 44.3, pp 417 – 418

Coleman J A (1996) *Studying Languages: A survey of British and European students. The proficiency, background, attitudes and motivations of students of foreign languages in the United Kingdom and Europe*, London: CILT

Dickinson L (1987) *Self-instruction in Language Learning*. Cambridge: Cambridge University Press

Ehrman M E and R L Oxford (1995) 'Cognition plus: correlates of language learning success', *Modern Language Journal* 79.1, pp 67 – 89

Freeman M I (1996) *Time Factors as Predictors of Success in Language Learning. A study of background variables and language learning activities*, unpublished PhD Thesis, University of Surrey

Gardner R C, R Moorcroft and J Metford (1989) 'Second language learning in an immersion programme: factors influencing acquisition and retention', *Journal of Language and Social Psychology* 8.5, pp 287 – 305

Gardner R C and P D MacIntyre (1993) 'On the measurement of affective variables in second language learning', *Language Learning* 43.2, pp 157 – 194

Harris M (1997) 'Self-assessment of language learning in formal settings', *English Language Teaching Journal* 51.1, pp 12 – 20

Harrison A (1983) *A Language Testing Handbook*, London: Macmillan

Heidt E (1979) *Self-evaluation in learning. A report on trends, experience and research findings*, Paris: UNESCO

Heilenman L K (1990) 'Self-assessment of second language ability: the role of response effects', *Language Testing* 7.2, pp 174 – 201

ILTA (1995) 'Report of the task force on testing standards to the ILTA', www.surrey.ac.uk/ELI.

Ingram D E (1985) 'Assessing proficiency: an overview on some aspects of testing', in Hyltenstam K and M Pieneman (eds) *Modelling and Assessing Second Language Acquisition*, Clevedon: Multilingual Matters

Languages Lead Body (1995) *Implementing the National Language Standards: A guide to best practice*, London: Crown Copyright

Languages Lead Body (1993) *National Language Standards: Breaking the language barrier across the world of work*, London: Crown Copyright

LeBlanc R and G Painchaud (1985) 'Self-assessment as a second language placement instrument', *TESOL Quarterly* 19, pp 673 – 687

MacIntyre P D, K A Noels and R Clément (1997) 'Biases in self-ratings of second language proficiency: the role of anxiety', *Language Learning* 47.2, pp 265 – 287

Oskarsson M (1978) *Approaches to Self-Assessment in Foreign Language Learning*, Oxford: Pergamon (published for and on behalf of the Council of Europe)

Oskarsson M (1989) 'Self-assessment of language proficiency: rationale and applications', *Language Testing* 6.1, pp 1 – 13

Ross S (1998) 'Self-assessment in second language testing: a meta-analysis and analysis of experiential factors', *Language Testing* 15.1, pp 1 – 20

Shameem N (1998) 'Validating self-reported language proficiency by testing performance in an immigrant community: the Wellington Indo-Fijians', *Language Testing* 15.1, pp 86 – 108

Spolsky B (1989) *Conditions for Second Language Learning*, Oxford: Oxford University Press

Thomas M (1994) 'Assessment of L2 proficiency in second language acquisition research', *Language Learning* 44.2, pp 307 – 336

Ward Goodbody M (1993) 'Letting the students choose: a placement procedure for a pre-sessional course', in Blue G M (ed) *Language, Learning and Success: Studying through English*, Modern English Publications in association with the British Council

Weltens B and A D Cohen (1989) 'Language attrition research', *Studies in Second Language Acquisition* 11.2, pp 127 – 133

George M Blue

Self-Assessment and Defining Learners' Needs

1. Introduction

Since Oskarsson carried out his pioneering work for the Council of Europe over twenty years ago (Oskarsson, 1978) self-assessment has gradually assumed more and more importance in the language learning field and in education generally. In the last few years in particular, there has been a surge of interest in the subject. My own interest goes back to the mid-1980s, and I have been using self-assessment questionnaires with my students since then, in the belief that self-assessment can have positive benefits for students' learning, providing 'the opportunity for learners to assess their own progress and thus help them to focus their own learning' (Harris, 1997). In a previous BALEAP publication (Blue, 1988) I looked at students' self-assessment using a global descriptive rating scale, and compared this with assessment by tutors. I found that there was an overall tendency to overestimate ability, and that this varied considerably depending on cultural background. Generally speaking, the measure of association between self-assessment and tutor assessment was positive but not very strong. More recently (Blue, 1994), I compared students' self-assessment using the same global rating scales with their scores in internationally recognised language tests (IELTS and TOEFL). Again, I found a positive measure of association, but it was neither strong nor significant. However, other studies (for example, Bachman and Palmer, 1989; LeBlanc and Painchaud, 1985; Ward Goodbody, 1993; Freeman in this volume) have found self-assessment to be generally more accurate.

Even if students are inaccurate in their self-assessment, the fact that they have begun to think about what they can and cannot do in English is very helpful when it comes to setting goals, and if we can help them to become more accurate, this is likely to be even more beneficial. In 1994 I suggested two hypotheses, which were supported by my data:

- Hypothesis 1: Learners with low self-ratings tend to persevere with language learning, provided their self-ratings are not too low.
- Hypothesis 2: Learners with realistic self-ratings tend to set and achieve realistic language learning goals (Blue, 1994: 29 – 30).

If, as I believe, these hypotheses are valid, it is clearly important to guide learners towards more accurate self-assessment. Although global rating scales are extremely useful as a means of encouraging students to think globally about their language proficiency, they do seem to be very difficult for many students. As well as the complexity of the judgement being made, students may find that they agree with one part of a descriptor but disagree with another part. This can be seen in figure 1 for level 3 writing (on a 0 to 5 scale):

Figure 1. Rating scale requiring complex judgements

I can formulate written messages or give a coherent account of things connected with my studies and interests or my needs and wishes, but I make some mistakes in both grammar and spelling. I sometimes cannot find the words for what I want to express. I can write down from dictation a normal prose text about a familiar subject, without too many errors.

As a result, I decided to break the task down into more manageable chunks. Drawing on the work of LeBlanc and Painchaud (1985) I produced a series of statements about specific tasks that learners can perform in English (ten statements for each language skill) and asked them to agree or disagree with these on a five-point scale.

2. Self-Assessment and External Measures of Proficiency

The self-assessment questionnaire starts with some general questions about students' previous experience of learning English, their own opinion of their language skills, and what they hope to gain from their courses. Students are encouraged to write as much as they can, partly so that they will have given the matter some thought by the time they get to the statements and partly so that tutors will have a reasonable amount of writing to judge when they come to discuss the questionnaires with the students.

This questionnaire has been used with students registering for in-sessional courses in EAP at the University of Southampton. It has not generally been used with ERASMUS/SOCRATES or other visiting students, as there is insufficient time to interview them and discuss the completed questionnaire. Nor has it been used with students who have attended pre-sessional courses, who have already completed a similar questionnaire (but with global rating scales) on the pre-sessional course.

By the time incomplete questionnaires were rejected, there were 123 questionnaires from the current academic year that could be used in this study. These questionnaires were completed by students from 42 different countries, including five or more from each of China (5), France (9), Germany (9), Greece (9), Hong Kong (10), Italy (9), Malaysia (13), and Spain (7).

The majority of those who completed questionnaires were postgraduate students, who were supposed to have met the University's English language entrance requirements. A few were visiting students or visiting members of staff, who were not required to produce evidence of language proficiency. These were the tests that had been taken:

IELTS	44
TOEFL	32
GCSE equivalent	12
NEAB UETESOL	3
CPE	4
FCE (not accepted)	5
Other test	2
Degree from British university	5
None	16

In a few cases the test had been taken some time before the beginning of the academic year, and in these cases there could have been considerable improvement or, less likely, considerable deterioration in the intervening period. Thus we would not necessarily expect a perfect match between test scores and self-assessment, though the number of such cases is relatively small and should not distort the overall result unduly.

In order to give a numerical score to the self-assessment profiles I have allocated a score of 1 to 5 for each of the 40 statements in the questionnaire, with 5 being the most positive ('always') and 1 the least confident ('never'). Total scores could therefore vary theoretically between 40 and 200. If we look at the students who rated themselves most highly we find the following:

Table 1. Students with the highest self-assessment scores

Country of Origin	Test Score	Self-Assessment Score
Finland	IELTS 7.0	186
Germany	GMAT	176
Italy	TOEFL 657	175
Greece	FCE	175
Indonesia	IELTS 6.5	174
Spain	FCE	171
Costa Rica	IELTS 6.0	165
Germany	British university degree	164
India	IELTS 6.5	164

The two cases that stand out here as possible mismatches are the students from Greece and Spain, who each awarded themselves scores of over 170, yet had failed to meet the University's admission criteria, having only passed Cambridge First Certificate in English. At the bottom of the scale, by contrast, the picture shown in Table 2 emerges.

The three cases that stand out here are the Korean, Swiss and Indonesian students, all with scores in recognised tests that are well above the minimum required for admission to the University, yet all with very low overall self-assessment scores.

IELTS and TOEFL scores were compared with self-assessment scores, and the Pearson product-moment correlation coefficient was calculated. The results are reported in Tables 3 and 4 below.

Table 2. Students with the lowest self-assessment scores

Country of Origin	Test Score	Self-Assessment Score
Italy	No test	100
Malaysia	FCE	100
Korea	IELTS 7.5	100
Taiwan	TOEFL 570	98
Russia	No test	94
Switzerland	TOEFL 620	90
Indonesia	IELTS 7.0	79
China	IELTS 6.5	77
Malaysia	IELTS 6.5	71

Table 3. Comparison of IELTS and self-assessment scores

Country	IELTS	SelfAss	Country	IELTS	SelfAss
Spain	8	117	Greece	6.5	110
Turkey	8	154	Indonesia	6.5	174
Netherlands	8	125	Hong Kong	6.5	141
Korea	7.5	100	Austria	6.5	146
Denmark	7.5	155	Portugal	6.5	146
Germany	7.5	137	Malaysia	6.5	150
Italy	7.5	139	India	6.5	164
Italy	7.5	141	Greece	6.5	123
Malaysia	7.5	150	Greece	6.5	109
Japan	7.5	158	Malaysia	6.5	71
Hong Kong	7.5	112	China	6.5	77
Oman	7	122	Nepal	6.5	125
Indonesia	7	79	Malaysia	6.5	128
Denmark	7	141	Argentina	6.5	139
Germany	7	122	Sweden	6.5	158
Finland	7	186	Malaysia	6.5	121
Denmark	7	162	Venezuela	6.5	130
Mexico	7	136	Hong Kong	6.5	115
France	7	151	Malaysia	6.5	143
Belgium	7	117	Costa Rica	6	165
Malaysia	7	107	China	6	108
Colombia	6.5	126	Syria	5.5	126

The Pearson product-moment correlation coefficient was found to be 0.07, which indicates that there is almost no correlation. The IELTS scores are in descending order, but no equivalent descending order can be discerned in the self-assessment scores.

Table 4. Comparison of TOEFL and self-assessment scores

Country	TOEFL	SelfAss	Country	TOEFL	SelfAss
France	677	144	France	603	121
Germany	660	157	Greece	600	122
Italy	657	175	China	600	131
Finland	633	142	Germany	593	155
Germany	627	125	Sweden	590	120
Switzerland	620	90	Taiwan	570	98
Greece	620	157	Taiwan	567	140
Italy	620	107	Italy	567	145
Hong Kong	620	188	Norway	553	131
France	617	145	Korea	550	115
Italy	613	137	Korea	550	150
Malaysia	613	109	Ethiopia	540	104
Mexico	610	153	Syria	540	159
Greece	607	145	Macau	540	127
Italy	607	151	Syria	527	147
Greece	603	140	Malaysia	no score	116

The Pearson product-moment correlation coefficient was found to be 0.23, which suggests that there is a slight positive correlation. However, this is not significant, and when one looks at Table 4 there is no obvious relationship between the TOEFL scores and self-assessment scores. TOEFL scores are given in descending order, but the ordering of the self-assessment scores appears almost to be random.

3. The Self-Assessment Instrument

In this section we shall consider the self-assessment questionnaire in a little more detail. As has already been mentioned, it starts off with some general questions and then proceeds to ask students to agree or disagree (expressed on a 5-point scale: 'always ... never') with 10 statements for each of the four language skills. We shall first look at one section (reading) in a little more detail. This reveals something of the difficulty of framing statements that represent the right degree of challenge and that are sufficiently straightforward for the students. Generally speaking, students rated their reading ability quite highly, as can be seen from the following mean scores:

Table 5. Mean self-assessment scores in reading

	Mean
21 I can understand headlines and articles in popular newspapers.	3.9
22 I have a very good understanding of articles on current affairs in quality newspapers, and can recognise what is fact and what is the author's opinion.	3.7
23 If I have to fill in a detailed application form (eg for a grant) I understand what information is required and where.	4.2
24 I have a wide range of vocabulary which enables me to understand general as well as specialised texts.	3.2
25 I can look through an article quickly to pick out the main lines of argument without getting lost in the detail.	3.4
26 I know the language well enough to be able to spot mistakes and misprints in a text.	3.1
27 I understand exactly what is required when I am faced with examination or essay questions in English.	3.7
28 My reading speed is not unduly affected by the fact that I am reading in a foreign language.	3.3
29 When I look at a detailed table of contents of a book, I can tell whether the book will be useful to me or not.	4.1
30 I have a full understanding of books or articles dealing with my own discipline or related fields of study.	4.1

Some of these mean scores are quite surprising, though different people will probably be struck by different statements. Personally, I would not have expected statements 21, 23, 27 or 30 to be so highly scored, though I was not really surprised by the statements which received lower scores.

Reading was in fact the skill in which students generally rated themselves most highly, and, as might be expected, the lowest self-assessment scores are to be found for writing. The mean scores for each of the skills were:

> Reading   36.5
> Listening 34.9
> Speaking 32.9
> Writing   30.0

The results were generally slightly weighted towards the positive end of the scale, but that is perhaps only to be expected for a population of fairly advanced EAP students like this. Most students used the full range of possibilities, and everybody varied their scores for different statements, suggesting that they had all thought about which boxes they were ticking. Informal questioning of some students during the interviews suggested that they had not found the task too difficult or time-consuming.

If we now look at the way individual students assessed themselves in each of the four skill areas we find that their ratings appear in the following bands:

Table 6. Individual students' self-assessment scores

	Listening	Speaking	Reading	Writing
46–49	7	6	9	–
41–45	18	9	30	8
36–40	36	30	32	17
31–35	28	29	27	35
26–30	22	32	21	31
21–25	9	15	3	18
16–20	2	1	1	12
11–15	1	1	–	2

For writing, only eight students rated themselves above 40 overall, whilst 14 rated themselves 20 or below. For reading, on the other hand, 39 gave themselves a score above 40, whilst only one was in the 11–20 range (with a score of 18). If we turn now to consider the individual statements we find that the average score in most cases was between 3.0 and 3.9. The following statements fell outside of this range:

Table 7. Statements for which students rated themselves most highly

		Skill area and mean score	
11	I can make myself understood in simple everyday situations, eg asking directions, asking the time, ordering food.	Speaking	4.3
23	If I have to fill in a detailed application form (eg for a grant) I understand what information is required and where.	Reading	4.2
5	I can understand the essential points in everyday conversations.	Listening	4.1
29	When I look at a detailed table of contents of a book, I can tell whether the book will be useful to me or not.	Reading	4.1
30	I have a full understanding of books or articles dealing with my own discipline or related fields of study.	Reading	4.1
6	I can understand instructions from my lecturers without asking for repetition or clarification.	Listening	4.0
7	When listening to a lecture I can recognise when one point finishes and the next point starts, and can therefore make adequate notes.	Listening	4.0

It is perhaps unsurprising that there are no statements from the writing section which received average scores of 4 and above. Indeed, six of the seven statements in this category apply to the receptive skills of reading (3) and listening (3). As well as the reading scores referred to above, I was also quite surprised that statements 6 and 7 received such high average scores. Overall, though, these are the sorts of statements that one might expect students to agree with by and large, and all of these statements received large numbers of ticks in the 'always' column and hardly any in the 'never' column.

Table 8. Statements for which students rated themselves least positively

		Skill area and mean score	
3	I can understand speech in unfavourable conditions, e.g. through loudspeakers outdoors.	Listening	2.9
15	I have a good control of the grammatical structures of the language, and use them accurately in my speech.	Speaking	2.9
20	If asked to give a talk on an aspect of my subject to a group of students I could do so without reading from my notes.	Speaking	2.9
32	My grammatical control of the language is very good, and I write accurately and correctly.	Writing	2.9
34	I have a good knowledge of punctuation, abbreviations and other conventions of the language.	Writing	2.9
38	I have a good command of the language used for linking ideas together.	Writing	2.9
2	I can understand local people even when they speak in dialect or slang.	Listening	2.7
4	I have a very wide vocabulary, and can understand the meaning of less common expressions.	Listening	2.7
13	I have a wide vocabulary, so I seldom have to hesitate or search for words.	Speaking	2.7
35	I have a wide vocabulary and have no difficulty in finding the right words to express my meaning.	Writing	2.7
36	I have a good command of academic style.	Writing	2.6

This time there are no statements from the reading section. There are equal numbers from listening and speaking, whilst half of all the statements from the writing section appear among the least positively rated statements. It is interesting to note that many of the statements about which students appear to be least confident involve not only the language skill but also another factor or skill, for example,

20   involves speaking plus memory plus self-confidence;
34   involves writing plus a knowledge of conventions;
36   involves writing plus a knowledge of academic style.

A deliberate policy decision was taken to include a statement mentioning vocabulary in each of the four sections of the questionnaire, as a way of testing for consistency. It was not anticipated that three of the four statements where vocabulary appeared (4, 13 and 35) would produce an identical mean score (2.7). However, the fact that they did so is very encouraging, as it suggests that there is a great deal of internal consistency in the way students have completed the questionnaire. In other words, even if students may tend to over- or under-estimate their overall level, they do seem to have quite a clear idea of what they are better at and worse at, and to be fairly consistent in their reporting of what they see as their strengths and weaknesses. Although there are some inconsistencies that can be pointed out in individual interviews, there is a great deal of fairly consistent self-assessment that can be built on in tutorials.

There was a statement including vocabulary in the reading section as well (statement 24, mean score 3.2), and it is worth noting that although the mean score is higher than for the other statements including vocabulary it is one of the lowest scores in the reading section. Presumably understanding vocabulary in the written mode presents fewer problems than either producing the right word or understanding it in the spoken mode, where there is usually no time to re-read, stop the flow or guess at the meaning by reviewing the context. Thus the fact that the average score for this statement was slightly higher does not imply any inconsistency in the students' self-assessment.

The general principle applied in devising the statements in the questionnaire was to keep them as straightforward as possible. A few responses revealed that I had not always been successful in this. For example, one student pointed out in relation to statement 21 (I can understand headlines and articles in popular newspapers) that he could generally understand the articles but not the headlines. Occasionally, though, it is good to recognise that language cannot always be divided up into discrete skills and that part of proficiency in a language is being able to combine skills. Thus, the questionnaire includes a few more complex statements such as:

10   If a fellow student has missed a lecture I can summarise the
contents for them, referring to my notes to supply some of the
details.

Although this statement was included in the listening section, it draws
on all four language skills. Despite the seeming complexity of this
combination of skills, the average score was 3.5, the same as the
average for listening as a whole.

4. Conclusion: The Value of Self-Assessment

We have already spoken about the way in which self-assessment of
this kind can be used as a tool for placing students in in-sessional
classes. The overall level of proficiency is relatively unimportant, and
in any case tutors can gain an idea of students' overall level from the
interview, from tests that students have taken previously and from the
writing that they do in the earlier parts of the questionnaire. What is
perhaps more important is that students will in the process of
completing the self-assessment questionnaire start to think about
which skills they wish to improve and which aspects of those skills. It
may be a very good tool for helping students to decide on their
priorities even if it is not reliable enough to be used for placement
purposes on a pre-sessional course, where a more objective
assessment of language proficiency may be needed to place students
into the correct proficiency level group.

For students working independently in a self-access language
resources centre self-assessment questionnaires of this type would
seem to have great potential as a preliminary stage in needs analysis.
If learners can think about their strengths and weaknesses in a
structured way this is an important first step in determining their aims
and objectives. It would be very useful to have a number of
questionnaires at different levels so that self-assessment could be a
regular part of the independent learning process.

Finally, the use of this self-assessment questionnaire has proved
to be a very good way of gathering information about students, what

they feel confident about and the areas where they are least sure of their ability. Although there is always the problem of finding the time to analyse the results for a given class, it can be an excellent tool for use in course design, and priorities can be set in consultation with the students. Again, one can imagine that with a range of different questionnaires at different levels, perhaps focusing on different skills for different classes, this could become an important component in the negotiated syllabus (see Bloor and Bloor, 1988).

There remains a great deal of work to be done, and perhaps some of the earlier concerns about the accuracy of self-assessment (compared with either tutors' assessment or test scores) are still valid. Nevertheless, self-assessment can be a very useful formative stage in the language learning process, and it can have a very important role to play in helping to define learners' needs.

References

Bachman L F and A S Palmer (1989) 'The construct validation of self-ratings of communicative language ability', *Language Testing* 6.1, pp 14 – 29

Bloor M and T Bloor (1988) 'Syllabus negotiation: the basis of learner autonomy', in Brookes A and P Grundy (eds) *Individualization and Autonomy in Language Learning*. Oxford: Modern English Publications in association with The British Council

Blue G M (1988) 'Self-assessment: the limits of learner independence', in Brookes A and P Grundy (eds) *Individualization and Autonomy in Language Learning*, Oxford: Modern English Publications in association with the British Council

Blue G M (1994) 'Self-assessment of foreign language skills: does it work?', in Blue G M (ed) *CLE Working Papers 3*, Southampton: University of Southampton Centre for Language in Education

Harris M (1997) 'Self-assessment of language learning in formal settings', *ELT Journal* 51.1, pp 12 – 20

LeBlanc R and G Painchaud (1985) 'Self-assessment as a second language placement instrument', *TESOL Quarterly* 19.4, pp 673 –687

Oskarsson M (1978) *Approaches to Self-Assessment in Foreign Language Learning*, Oxford: Pergamon (published for and on behalf of the Council of Europe)

Ward Goodbody M (1993) 'Letting the students choose: a placement procedure for a pre-sessional course', in Blue G M (ed) *Language, Learning and Success: Studying through English*, London and Basingstoke: Macmillan

Appendix

SELF-ASSESSMENT QUESTIONNAIRE
(for international students registered for a University of Southampton degree)

Name ....

Date ....

In order to gain a better understanding of you as a language learner, we would like you to tell us about your experience of learning English, your own opinion of your language skills, and what you hope to gain from your courses. Please write as much as you can to help us to help you.

Previous Experience of Learning English

1. Describe your previous experience of learning English. You may mention, for example, size of class, type of English (reading, writing, grammar, discussion, etc.), organisation of learning (pairs, groups, whole class) and the role of the teacher.

2. What has been your most helpful language learning experience so far inside or outside the classroom?

Language Skills and Learning

1. How confident do you feel about your skills in
   - listening
   - speaking
   - reading
   - writing
   - grammar?

2. How do you think you learn best?

Aims for your English Courses

1. What do you hope to get out of these courses?

2. Which language skills do you particularly feel you need to improve and why?

Self-Assessment

Please read through the following statements. If a statement is always true please put a cross in the far left box, if it is never true in the far right box, and if it sometimes true somewhere in between.

LISTENING

always   ...   never

1   I can understand news or discussion
     programmes on the radio.   ☐ ☐ ☐ ☐ ☐

2   I can understand local people, even when they
     speak in dialect or slang.   ☐ ☐ ☐ ☐ ☐

3   I can understand speech in unfavourable
     conditions, e.g. through loudspeakers outdoors. ☐ ☐ ☐ ☐ ☐

4   I have a very wide vocabulary, and can
     understand the meaning of less common
     expressions.   ☐ ☐ ☐ ☐ ☐

5   I can understand the essential points in
     everyday conversations.   ☐ ☐ ☐ ☐ ☐

6   I can understand instructions from my lecturers
     without asking for repetition or clarification. ☐ ☐ ☐ ☐ ☐

7   When listening to a lecture I can recognise
     when one point finishes and the next point
     starts, and can therefore make adequate notes. ☐ ☐ ☐ ☐ ☐

8   I can understand how examples (or jokes)
     relate to the main point the lecturer is making. ☐ ☐ ☐ ☐ ☐

9   I can understand most of the content of lectures
     or television programmes on subjects outside
     of my discipline.   ☐ ☐ ☐ ☐ ☐

10   If a fellow student has missed a lecture I can
     summarise the contents for them, referring to
     my notes to supply some of the details.   ☐ ☐ ☐ ☐ ☐

SPEAKING

		always	...	never		

11   I can make myself understood in simple everyday situations, e.g. asking directions, asking the time, ordering food.   □ □ □ □ □

12   I can participate fully in discussions about current affairs.   □ □ □ □ □

13   I have a wide vocabulary, so I seldom have to hesitate or search for words.   □ □ □ □ □

14   My pronunciation is clear, and people usually understand me without having to ask me to repeat things.   □ □ □ □ □

15   I have a good control of the grammatical structures of the language, and use them accurately in my speech.   □ □ □ □ □

16   I can make myself understood without difficulty on the telephone.   □ □ □ □ □

17   I can participate fully in a discussion with other students on a subject related to my discipline.   □ □ □ □ □

18   If something is unclear in a lecture I am happy to ask a relevant question so as to clarify matters.   □ □ □ □ □

19   In a tutorial situation I am confident about answering a lecturer's questions and giving my own opinions where appropriate.   □ □ □ □ □

20   If asked to give a talk on an aspect of my subject to a group of students I could do so without reading from my notes.   □ □ □ □ □

READING

		always	...	never

21   I can understand headlines and articles in
      popular newspapers.
      ☐ ☐ ☐ ☐ ☐

22   I have a very good understanding of articles on
      current affairs in quality newspapers, and can
      recognise what is fact and what is the author's
      opinion.
      ☐ ☐ ☐ ☐ ☐

23   If I have to fill in a detailed application form
      (e.g. for a grant) I understand what information
      is required and where.
      ☐ ☐ ☐ ☐ ☐

24   I have a wide range of vocabulary which
      enables me to understand general as well as
      specialised texts.
      ☐ ☐ ☐ ☐ ☐

25   I can look through an article quickly to pick
      out the main lines of argument without getting
      lost in the detail.
      ☐ ☐ ☐ ☐ ☐

26   I know the language well enough to be able to
      spot mistakes and misprints in a text.
      ☐ ☐ ☐ ☐ ☐

27   I understand exactly what is required when I
      am faced with examination or essay questions
      in English.
      ☐ ☐ ☐ ☐ ☐

28   My reading speed is not unduly affected by the
      fact that I am reading in a foreign language.
      ☐ ☐ ☐ ☐ ☐

29   When I look at a detailed table of contents of a
      book, I can tell whether the book will be useful
      to me or not.
      ☐ ☐ ☐ ☐ ☐

30   I have a full understanding of books or articles
      dealing with my own discipline or related
      fields of study.
      ☐ ☐ ☐ ☐ ☐

WRITING

		always	...	never

31 I am confident about my ability to write letters
    or short notes to third parties.   □ □ □ □ □

32 My grammatical control of the language is
    very good, and I write accurately and correctly.   □ □ □ □ □

33 My spelling is accurate, and I only rarely have
    to check spellings in a dictionary.   □ □ □ □ □

34 I have a good knowledge of punctuation,
    abbreviations and other conventions of the
    language.   □ □ □ □ □

35 I have a wide vocabulary and have no
    difficulty in finding the right words to express
    my meaning.   □ □ □ □ □

36 I have a good command of academic style.   □ □ □ □ □

37 When writing about my subject I can organise
    my ideas clearly and logically.   □ □ □ □ □

38 I have a good command of the language used
    for linking ideas together.   □ □ □ □ □

39 I am confident about my ability to paraphrase
    or summarise other people's ideas in my own
    words.   □ □ □ □ □

40 I can write clearly and accurately at speed, e.g.
    when taking notes from lectures or in
    examinations.   □ □ □ □ □

Part Five:

Students' Views of Assessment

Barbara Atherton

Developing Accuracy in Academic Writing

1. Introduction

The large number of students attending voluntary, academic writing classes bears witness to the importance our students place on developing this aspect of their language skills. Many come from educational systems where accuracy, both in the reproduction of facts and in the use of language, is fundamental to the assessment process. Logic tells them that, if they can become more accurate in their use of English, their chances of academic success will be enhanced. A review of the assessment criteria used across their subject disciplines will show that this perception is not wholly misplaced. Nearly all the written assignments given to students will contain reference to the need for accurate spelling, punctuation and grammar, with penalties levied for 'poor' or 'inaccurate' expression.

Writing, even in one's mother tongue, can be a long and difficult process during which errors will inevitably be made. However, for second language learners errors are, as Kroll (1990: 141), drawing on work by Shauhnessy, notes '... neither attempts to deliberately sabotage language in reckless disregard of its rules nor necessarily careless inattention to details' but an integral part of the language learning process. As such, errors and their correction play an important part in the on-going assessment of our students. However, the same positive attitude cannot necessarily be found in the assessment of subject-discipline assignments. Whilst it is probably impossible to judge objectively the effect of regularly occurring grammatical errors on subject-specialist markers, error correction can take on a negative connotation and the criticism of 'careless inattention to details' may well be levelled.

This paper describes a project (Atherton, 1996) which was generated by the concern that, despite the generally high level of students' motivation, despite the wide range of writing programmes and activities now available and the use of many and varied methods of feedback and error correction, accuracy within written discourse appears a difficult and distant objective for many students. Students spend time writing their essays, teachers discuss, correct and mark them, the essays are returned and the process starts again – another topic, another script but all too often the same errors requiring the same correction. It was decided to look more closely at the steps students take in their quest for accuracy and how they respond to the assessment of their written work. As the techniques of teaching writing have changed, so too the relationship between the teacher and student writers has come to be seen as far more of a partnership. However, it is possible that there may be a degree of imbalance in this partnership, particularly in the areas of giving and responding to feedback and error correction; much has been written about what teachers should do but what of the students?

2. Student Approaches to the Writing Process

The first stage of the project was the administration of a questionnaire to 80 students, which sought information on which aspects they found most difficult when writing, which errors they thought they made most often, if and when they revised their work and what they checked for, the type of feedback they personally felt was most helpful to them and their reactions on the return of their assignments. 68 students, representing 25 different nationalities replied, giving a response rate of 85%.

2.1 Areas of difficulty and the revision process

20 students cited the difficulties of either expressing or translating their ideas within the framework of the English grammatical system, and two

more expressed their frustration with this process. A further 27 identified difficulty with specific aspects of grammar (especially tenses) or with grammar generally. 17 saw their main difficulty as a lack of vocabulary and eight students identified spelling. 13 felt that essay style, format and organisation posed a problem; an interestingly small number when we consider how long we necessarily spend on these important elements in our classes.

The majority of respondents (79.4%), claim to check their work as they are writing. 53 checked grammar and 44 were concerned with spelling. However, there was a disappointingly low degree of checking self-confessed areas of difficulty or error at any time. 50 students read through their work again as a final check, one for 'obvious mistakes' and one student replied, 'as I read I underline things I think they (? sic) need to improve'. Use was made of the spell and grammar checker facility on a PC and those who responded that they read their work aloud had been influenced by previous work with the researcher. Two students asked native speaker friends, a low but perhaps not surprising number, possibly indicating that although the use of peer correction strategies is popular and widely advocated, this is not always an easy or comfortable choice for the international student. Seven students stated that they checked, 'for everything (or anything) at the same time', a strategy which as Zamel's (1985) research into the accuracy of teachers' corrections showed, can lead to errors being corrected inconsistently or inaccurately, so hardly an approach which should be encouraged in our students!

2.2 How helpful is teacher error correction?

It is probably not surprising that 38% of students think that it is most useful having all errors corrected by their teacher, with responses such as, 'It's nice because I see my mistakes corrected' and 'I prefer my written work corrected so I can learn from my mistakes'. Also interesting was the comment from a German student, using the 'system' in an ideal way, 'I sometimes use expressions I'm not sure of therefore I'm interested to see the corrected work'.

A significantly smaller number (16%) found the use of symbols and indications of error of benefit, and yet this is the only method which actively requires the student to use the feedback they are given and to consider their errors in the light of their grammatical knowledge and the context it is being applied to. 12 students wrote that having mistakes corrected is, 'the only way to learn' or 'it's the way to improve'.

Comments written in, or at the end of, an essay and relating to both structure and style, were seen as useful by 43%. If we are in any doubt that time spent on such marking is unappreciated, then remarks such as 'At least he spent some time on it' and 'disappointed if the teacher doesn't give an opinion', must surely counter this. As one student wrote, 'I feel he/she read it. It's useful because it helps me identify my weakness. When I don't agree with my teacher at least I know him/her a little better'. By contrast, responses from other students indicate a less robust reaction to error correction. They admit to being anxious (two) – but only a little (one), curious (two), 'sad ... that I didn't learn so much' (one) or 'it's like sitting in an electric chair!' (one).

Whilst 82% of students claim to be aware of previous feedback in completing subsequent writing tasks, the constructive attitude demonstrated by these findings does not appear to translate itself into more accurate written work as effectively as might be hoped. A more detailed examination of students' reactions to their returned work and the procedure they adopted when processing the various markings and comments was therefore needed.

3. Student Responses to Feedback

As it was considered important to gain as spontaneous a response as possible to the returned piece of work, it was decided to use an introspective technique for gathering the data. Ten students were asked to speak their reactions and thoughts on the immediate return of a piece of corrected work, in private, into a tape recorder. Whilst they were aware of the broad area of my research this was to be 'self-initiated introspection' (Faerch and Kasper, 1987: 17) with no specific questions set. Subsequent small group discussions took place informally after the recordings had been made. Essays were marked in the accustomed manner, using the marking code issued to students at the beginning of their courses, together with comments on both content and form and a grade. The comments would often suggest that the student ask the teacher for further clarification or help with re-writing a phrase or sentence where meaning was unclear. It has previously been noted that this is a suggestion that is very rarely taken up.

3.1 The recorded reactions

Analysis of the tape transcripts revealed that most of the students appeared to agree with the comments and corrections made and to understand the feedback given. Disagreement came from a French student, expressing frustration with the English use of full stops (points) and commas. She appeared to quickly skim through her essay (probably too quickly to read the comments written on it), before exclaiming in a tone of anguish, 'Oh, no! ... points ... you use such short sentences. We don't write like this ... I'm always being corrected for this but I can't write in this way'. Later discussion with her revealed that she was fully aware of the punctuation rules but preferred the French style. She insisted that to punctuate in the English way would alter her intended meaning. An example, maybe, of a change resistant learner as identified by Graham (1994).

A significant feature of the tape transcripts was that in all cases it was only the feedback on *mistakes* and *errors* which were read onto tape, with all the positive comments on content or the use of a particularly well structured or complex sentence left un-remarked upon. This is of concern as it is important to sustain the motivation of our students and to provide a balance between positive and negative reinforcement. Here, the students appear to be only concentrating on the negative aspects of the feedback procedure, perhaps reflecting their personal concern for the need for accuracy. No comments were made on the grade awarded, although responses to the questionnaire had shown that a grade was found to be helpful by 98% of students.

Particularly noticeable was that the corrections were noted but not questioned – yes the articles were missing, yes the tense was wrong – but there was no indication that any student sought further clarification, or indeed to explain why they had made the mistake in the first place. Perhaps the answer lies in one student's comment that, 'if I'd known it was wrong I wouldn't have done it!' or perhaps the action of recording prevented a further, deeper analysis. One student, who after reading through a lengthy list of corrections relating to the use of tenses and omitted or incorrectly used articles, typified the general reaction with a sigh and the comment, 'Finally, it wasn't that bad!'

Follow-up discussions supported the findings of the questionnaire, with nine out of the ten students saying they always read through my comments and noted the corrections, but this was done by making a 'mental note'. When asked what this involved, reactions varied from sheepish expressions to 'by reading it'. One student admitted to sometimes just checking the final comment and mark and 'that was that'. They all said they would try not to make the same mistakes again but no one had any strategy for suggesting how they might learn from their mistakes.

It would therefore appear that it is the feedback itself that ends the process, rather than the student acting upon that feedback. Students may be using our error correction as a benchmark for progress, for example in terms of the number and type of errors made, but the level of reasoning apparently applied to their corrected work is so small as to make only the slightest contribution to the development of accuracy.

3.2 Errors or mistakes?

The complexity and variety of demands that the writing process places on our students can make the distinction between errors and mistakes difficult for the teacher of writing to recognise. Ellis (1992: 214) has identified the notion of 'backsliding': the situation where students perform a particular structure accurately in the context of controlled language practice but fail to do so in applied tasks such as essay writing. At times retrieval may be at fault, with the writer struggling to express an opinion or idea within the framework of his/her adopted grammatical system. We may have an effect similar to that found in elicited translation tasks, which research (as reported in Larsen-Freeman and Long, 1991: 32) has shown, can produce a higher level of error which can be traced back to the influence of the mother tongue. However, it cannot always be said that retrieval of the rule is at fault, nor that the rule is partially or incorrectly learnt. Indeed at times it appears that the rule is not even considered. Rather, we are referring to 'mistakes' or perhaps 'inaccuracies' – the grey area which lies between the accepted definitions of mistakes and errors. Although possibly subject to the influences of interlanguage variability (Ellis, 1992: 122), and the effects of the learner's L1, these cannot truly be said to be 'errors of competence' after the definition given by Corder (1981).

The high level of 'inaccuracies' rather than 'errors' is indicated when one works through a draft with a student and adopts the technique of reading up to the error and stopping. On a significant number of occasions it is found that the student can then identify and correct the error made, especially in areas such as use of articles, subject/verb agreement and verb form. It therefore seems that the difficulty for the student might be that of moving from writer to reader/editor (Smith, 1982), as well as trying to control the number of processes which are being called upon at any one time (Bereiter and Scardamalia, 1987). As one student remarked, 'I know what I'm meant to be looking for but what I don't know is how to find it!'

Students at this level do have good, and often very good, listening and spoken skills which could be utilised in the re-drafting and editing procedure: to raise the consciousness of the writer to their own mistakes and to assist in the necessary shift from writer to reader. It was decided to try and harness these skills by asking students to make a tape recording of one of their essays, to listen to this recording and then to make any corrections they felt necessary.

4. From Writer to Reader

Students were set an essay as part of their normal academic writing class, following the usual planning, draft, re-draft protocol. Essays were of 250 – 300 words, judged to be a reasonable length as the distillation and integration of source material was not an area for consideration in this part of the research project. Writing time was also not considered as a significant variable (Kroll, 1990: 144 – 153). Copies of the essays were made, marked, and the number and type of errors counted. The unmarked original was returned to the students who read exactly what they had written onto tape. They then worked with the recording and their script to make any corrections they felt necessary. The amended scripts were collected and instances of students' own corrections and incorrect amendments collated. Finally both the teacher-marked and student-marked scripts were returned to the students for comparison and discussion. Due to academic commitments only five students were available for the full programme. This small number obviously reduces the possibility of any conclusive results being drawn.

4.1 Students' own error correction

Whilst Leki (1990: 59) states that unlike native speakers, L2 writers do not automatically correct their written errors when reading their texts aloud, it would appear that by adding the additional step of listening to themselves, students were able to identify and correct an average of 65% of errors, although obviously this result must be treated with caution. There were more corrections made to the areas which students themselves identified as causing difficulty. 90% of the errors made in the use of articles, 83% of singular/plural errors and 80% of prepositional errors were corrected. The 44% correction rate for verb form and verb choice, although resulting from a very small sample size, may indicate that further use of this technique could aid self-correction here. Against this, instances of over-correction and mis-correction were noted in the work of three students and such cases must be addressed when the self-corrected and teacher-marked scripts are compared. Significantly lower success was noted for correction of punctuation (40% of a very small sample), spelling (16%) and capital letters (0%).

The participants' attempts to aid clarity by restructuring a phrase, substituting more appropriate vocabulary and re-organising paragraphs were most effective. It was noticeable with all the students, including those whose results could not be included in the research, that their awareness of the effects of their writing on the reader was substantially increased. Also noticeable was the attention given to the returned, teacher-marked scripts. Each student worked through comparing what they had done with the teacher's marking, acknowledging, questioning and considering both comments and symbols, with the general reaction being one of, 'I should have noticed that'. This close attention to the feedback provided by the teacher was an unanticipated bonus from this element of the research.

Within the time scale of the research period it was not possible to address the longer term effects of this technique, although in subsequent discussions with the participants all said that it had raised their awareness of the likely areas of mistakes and they would make greater efforts to check for these. They also felt it had helped them by reinforcing the need for the final 'proof reading' stage of the writing process. Widdowson (1990: 98) has stated that, 'Learners need to realise the function of the [grammatical] device as a way of mediating between words and context, as a powerful resource for the purposeful achievement of meaning'. Perhaps these students were moving a little closer to this understanding.

This method does have practical constraints. It is time consuming in a subject and type of class where time is at a premium. Equally, one questions how many students would be prepared to take the necessary time and effort to tape and listen as part of their normal procedure. However, the students did find the method highly motivating. It allows for private reflection and respects cultural and age differences and might therefore be regarded as a suitable activity for guided learning or independent study programmes.

5. Conclusions

One of the stated objectives of many degree courses is to encourage students to take responsibility for their own learning and to develop skills which can be transferred and applied in the future. The ability to handle feedback, both positive and negative, to benefit from it and apply it to future tasks is an important element here. Both the responses to the questionnaire and the introspective study have shown that many of our learners, whilst aware of their problems with writing in their L2, appear unprepared, and possibly as yet unwilling, to use the feedback and error correction they receive to its fullest advantage.

Whilst it is accepted that the different notions of error require and respond to different types of feedback and correction, it is also apparent that our students require strategies and time to raise their own consciousness, as well as encouragement and opportunity to act on the feedback given. It is tentatively suggested that the technique outlined above may be of some assistance in helping to achieve these objectives and a step towards making error correction a more effective part of the assessment process.

References

Atherton B S (1996) *Developing Accuracy in Second Language Writing: The effectiveness of error correction techniques*, Unpublished MA Dissertation, St Mary's University College, University of Surrey

Bereiter C and M Scardamalia (1987) *The Psychology of Written Composition*, Hillsdale, New Jersey: Lawrence Erlbaum Associates

Corder S P (1981) *Error Analysis and Interlanguage*, Oxford: Oxford University Press

Ellis R (1992) *Second Language Acquisition and Language Pedagogy*, Clevedon: Multilingual Matters

Faerch C and G Kasper (eds) (1987) *Introspection in Second Language Research*, Clevedon: Multilingual Matters

Graham J G (1994) 'Four strategies to improve the speech of adult learners', *TESOL Journal*, Spring, pp 26 – 28

Kroll B (ed) (1990) *Second Language Writing: Research insights for the classroom*, Cambridge: Cambridge University Press

Larsen-Freeman D and M H Long (eds) (1991) *An Introduction to Second Language Aquisition Research*, Harlow: Longman.

Leki I (1990) 'Coaching from the margins: issues in written response', in Kroll B (ed) *Second Language Writing*, Cambridge: Cambridge University Press

Smith F (1982) *Writing and the Writer*, London: Heinemann.

Widdowson H G (1990) *Aspects of Language Teaching*, Oxford: Oxford University Press

Zamel V (1985) 'Responding to student writing', *TESOL Quarterly* 19.1, pp 79 – 101

R R Jordan

Is the Customer Sometimes Right?
Students' Views of Assessment in EAP

1. Introduction

1.1 Background

In broad terms, as applied to students' language learning, assessment involves some kind of measurement of the students' knowledge of the language and ability at using it. Probably the most common forms of assessment, in general, are by means of tests or examinations. The type of test used will depend upon its purpose; the main types are as follows:

- Proficiency – which measures how much of a language a student has learned (regardless of which syllabus, course or books are followed). Such a test may be used for admission or placement purposes.
- Achievement – which measures how much a student has learned from a language course (or syllabus, material, method, teacher, etc.). For example, a progress test may be used at intervals during a course and an end-of-course test to conclude.
- Diagnostic – which identifies which aspects of language, knowledge or skills, a student knows or does not know, for example, vocabulary and pronunciation. A diagnostic test is often used as part of an achievement test.

Full discussions of the different types of test, with appropriate examples, are contained in a number of works, for example: Hughes (1988, 1989), Alderson et al (1995), Bachman and Palmer (1996), Genesee and Upshur (1996).

Apart from tests, there are a number of ways in which students' language ability can be assessed. Basically, they are part of needs analysis and include the following: observation and monitoring, interviews and discussions, self-assessment by means of questionnaires and checklists, and the keeping of journals or diaries. These aspects are discussed and exemplified in West (1994), Brindley (1995), Genesee and Upshur (1996), and Jordan (1997). Self-assessment, in particular, will be looked at more closely later.

1.2 The survey

In all the research and discussions about assessment, very little has been said about the students' point of view and preferences. In an effort to redress part of the balance, a questionnaire survey of 212 international students, predominantly postgraduates attending pre-sessional EAP courses, was conducted at the Universities of Leeds, Manchester, Reading and Southampton. The purpose of the survey was to explore students' views of assessment in EAP: their preferred types of assessment and priority areas for assessment, the effect that assessment has upon them, and their experience of assessment in EAP. This bottom-up approach was one small step in the direction of providing data to throw some light on the subject.

The questions to be included in the questionnaire were decided upon after trying out a pilot version with MEd students (native and non-native English speaking) at Manchester University, and then discussing the questions and their purpose with the students. It was agreed that to encourage responses, most questions should list options and request students to tick their choices. In several cases, however, students were asked to make brief comments.

The 212 students who completed the questionnaires were from a total of 45 countries. The vast majority were from Asia (55%) and Europe (31%), with 11% coming from the Middle East and 3% from Latin America. Postgraduates accounted for 81% of the respondents while undergraduates accounted for 17% ('others' were 2%).

Erratum

In Table 1 on p. 273 the percentage figures have been omitted.
The Table should read:

1	interview	63 %
2	coursework/classwork	63 %
3	homework	61 %
4	judgement of teachers	50 %
5	course test	42 %
6	class test	38 %
7	formal, external exam	38 %
8	self-assessment (by questionnaire)	32 %
9	peer-assessment	12 %

2. Survey Results and Comments

2.1 Types of assessment preferred

The students were asked (Yes/No) if they thought it was useful to have some kind of assessment during an EAP course and for course directors and teachers to have information about their language achievements and difficulties in order for appropriate help and advice to be given. 94% thought that this information would be useful.

The students were then given a list of nine assessment types and asked to tick those that they thought were the best for giving information. They could tick as many of the choices as they wished. A follow-on question asked which kind of assessment they preferred to have. There was an exact correlation between choices of types of assessment and preferences.

Table 1. Types of assessment preferred

1	interview
2	coursework/classwork
3	homework
4	judgement of teachers
5	course test
6	class test
7	formal, external exam
8	self-assessment (by questionnaire)
9	peer-assessment

It can be seen from the information above that the students overwhelmingly agreed with the idea of some kind of assessment. A clear majority favoured an informal approach, covering interviews, classwork, homework and judgement of the teachers. This is, perhaps, understandable during a course, as such methods give an all-round view and are less stressful for the students. About 40% selected a test of some kind, but only one-third selected self-assessment as an indicator of achievement. This has implications for the notion of independence in learning and will be discussed further at the end of this paper. Peer-assessment, or the judgement of other students, did not find favour with many (see Lynch, 1988, for examples of this technique).

2.2 Course components to be assessed, and how frequently

The students were given a list of the four language skills that might feature as course components. They were asked to tick those that they thought it was important to assess. In addition, they could add their own items in a blank section – 'others' – or tick that no assessment of components was necessary. Separately, regarding frequency of assessment, the students were asked to tick those statements that they agreed with. These were as follows:

There should be assessment
(a) At the beginning of a course (to decide which group I go in),
(b) At the end of a course (to indicate my achievements and difficulties and to assess whether I am ready for academic studies in English),
(c) At regular intervals on a course.

Table 2. Course components to be assessed, and how frequently

Components				Frequency of assessment		
1	writing	90%		1	At the beginning of the course	84%
2	speaking	74%		2	At the end of the course	67%
3	listening	71%		3	At regular intervals	58%
4	reading	58%				
5	others	9%				
6	none	0%				

Not unexpectedly, students attached most importance to writing as a component to be assessed. Doubtless this is because they feel that all their work at university will be judged by their writing through essays, reports, examinations, dissertations, theses, etc. It is, therefore, important that they obtain independent assessment of this productive skill. Speaking and listening were both considered important to assess, probably because many students have difficulty with these skills in an academic context. For example, when listening to lectures and note-taking, making oral presentations, and discussions in seminars, etc. They probably need assurance that they are making progress.

Although a lower percentage considered it important to assess reading, it was still more than half. They are almost certainly aware of its importance on a university course, with numerous books and journals to be read. Possibly some of the students think that they may be able to judge their own ability at this receptive skill and, therefore, do not require assessment of it.

Less than 10% of the students added their own suggestions for assessment. In fact, several of the proposals could be subsumed under speaking and listening, for example, oral presentations and discussion. The traditional test items of vocabulary and grammar were also included by some. More unusually, a few listed speed at working in English. This might have been prompted by an awareness of slow reading speeds, and the anticipation of spending a long time writing essays and the need to write exam questions against the clock.

Not a single student opted for 'no assessment of course components'. With regard to frequency of assessment, it is understandable that a large proportion of students believe that there should be assessment at the beginning of a course. In order to be placed in the most appropriate group will certainly be one reason for this but also the need to obtain information about aspects of language and skills that need to be concentrated on during the course.

A significant number also considered it necessary to be assessed at the end of a course for the reasons indicated in the questionnaire, namely, to indicate achievements and difficulties and to assess if their level of language proficiency is sufficient to proceed with their studies. More than half the students were in favour of assessment at regular intervals during a course. Presumably the reasons for this are linked with their comments contained in Table 4.

2.3 Experience of English course tests; preferred maximum length

The students were asked to tick the kind of tests that they had usually taken on English courses in the past – objective, subjective, or none. They were not asked if they had any experience of taking external tests such as IELTS. If there were to be tests on courses, the students were asked what they thought the maximum time should be.

Table 3. Experience of English course tests and preferred maximum length

a) Type of tests taken on English courses in the past

1	objective (e.g. multiple-choice)	87%
2	subjective (e.g. essay)	52%
3	none	4%

b) Preferred maximum length of tests on EAP courses

1	1 hour or less	28%
2	1-2 hours	47%
3	2 hours or more	15%
4	blank	10%

Most students have experience of multiple-choice-type English tests on courses and just over a *half* have experience of writing essay-type questions. This indicates that nearly a half have no experience of subjective-type tests on courses. Consequently, careful explanation is needed if such assessment is used on courses, otherwise students may wrongly assume that they will take an objective test. Continuous assessment was not asked about, therefore if it is used on courses it would need explanation.

It is not surprising that shorter tests (two hours or less) preferred by 75%, should be much more popular than longer ones (2 hours or more) on EAP courses. Even if the 10% who did not express an opinion had done so, it would not affect the overall emphasis.

2.4 Effect of assessment

Based upon their own experience (current or previous courses), the students were asked to tick the appropriate comments about assessment that applied to themselves. The comments are summarised in Table 4.

Table 4. Effect of assessment

1	gives a useful indication of progress	70%
2	motivates learning	58%
3	gives a short-term objective	32%
4	removes enjoyment from learning	14%
5	causes unnecessary worry	7%
6	wastes time	3%

The question was asking about the students' reaction to assessment in a general sense. It did not refer to the different types of assessment referred to at the outset of this paper, that is proficiency or achievement. However, the type of assessment associated with the students' views may be deduced from the list of preferred types in Table 1, that is, informal.

The vast majority of students clearly found assessment to have positive effects with regard to indicating the progress they had made and providing motivation and objectives. Fortunately, the negative aspects, such as removing enjoyment from learning and causing unnecessary worry, were only felt by a relatively small minority. However, some of the negative aspects could probably be removed by carefully briefing the students as to the purposes of the assessment and the types to be used.

2.5 Experience of assessment in EAP

A very general question was asked about the students' current experience of assessment in EAP. 'Has it helped you to receive appropriate help and advice?' The students were asked to tick an appropriate response, as listed in the table below.

Table 5. Experience of assessment in EAP

Has it helped you to receive appropriate and helpful advice?

1	Sometimes	51%
2	Yes	34%
3	Don't know	9%
4	No	4%
5	Blank	2%

The general question elicited a generally favourable reaction: 85% of the students felt that they had either definitely or sometimes received appropriate help and advice. Only 4% were definitely negative. A useful follow-on question might have been to ask which kind of assessment had prompted the help or advice, and what kind of help or advice had been offered and found useful. In addition, what kind of help or advice might the students prefer to receive. This could be a useful dimension for further research.

2.6 Students' own comments

The questionnaire concluded by asking an open question: 'Are there any other comments that you would like to make about assessment?' 19% responded to this and their comments provide the meat on the bare bones of statistics and provide food for thought! They certainly include some useful pointers for course directors and teachers. A selection only is included below.

(a) 'At the beginning of the course, the *type* and *standard* of assessment should be carefully explained.'
(b) 'After assessment students should be given the results and recommendations as soon as possible.'
(c) 'I'd like to know the results of assessment and tests in detail eg which questions were wrong, also which skills are weak.'
(d) 'Personal interviews are needed to discuss the results of assessment.'
(e) 'Depending on the results of assessment, students should be put in groups according to each skill.'
(f) 'In order to be really informative, there should be several assessments over a period, not just one at the end. A variety of forms of assessment should be used.'
(g) 'Assessment is part of the learning process and should be used much more to help students learn rather than just to evaluate them.'
(h) 'Assessment should be done informally as it is more effective.'
(i) 'Assessment should not become the aim of the course.'
(j) 'Students want to be appreciated not just evaluated.'

Overwhelmingly, what emerges from the comments is a need for careful explanation at the beginning of a course of the types of assessment to be used and their purpose. That would help to forestall comments like 'I don't need official assessment' and 'Everyone knows their own level, therefore it's unnecessary'. In addition, an effort should be made to alleviate some students' apprehensions. This might be done by explanation, using informal methods of assessment where possible, and follow up with interviews in order to reassure and encourage. In assessing students, it is necessary to be sensitive and to motivate them not discourage them. Finally, one student commented that 'learning English takes time'. This may be a truism but a reminder to students of this obvious fact might help to dispel the notion that courses can perform miracles!

3. Conclusions

In Table 1 it was noted that only a third of the students favoured self-assessment. This is quite possibly because they have had little experience of it in their own countries and probably do not know what is involved. Some evidence for this is contained in Grierson (1995) who conducted a small survey of immigrant students in Australia. None of the students 'chose either self- or peer-assessment as a preferred method' (p 219): about half the students had never used self-assessment or peer-assessment in their country of origin.

There are various forms of self-assessment that may be utilised, including questionnaires, checklists, self-rated rating scales, progress profiles (which may consist of portfolios or collections of work), and diaries or journals. Different aspects of self-assessment have been well researched and reported on. Useful overviews are provided by Oskarsson (1980), Sheerin (1989 and 1991), Cram (1995).

The benefits of using a self-assessment, placement questionnaire at the beginning of an EAP course have been reported by Ward Goodbody (1993). It helped the students to focus on the aims and content of the course and was used in conjunction with teachers' assessments. Blue (1988) had used a descriptive rating scale for self-assessment at the beginning of a pre-sessional EAP course. He found that there was some variation between cultures regarding overestimation and underestimation of ability in language skills. Learner diaries 'can be used as a way of gaining insights into students' learning experiences, as they are based upon introspection. They can be used to supplement, in a qualitative way, the often quantitative information supplied by end-of-course questionnaires' (Jordan, 1997: 34). Jordan then reported on an analysis of student diaries made on a pre-sessional EAP course at Manchester University.

Genesee and Upshur (1996: 46) have spoken in favour of self-assessment utilising journals as they 'can assist students and teachers in monitoring student progress' as students 'can monitor their own language performance in any and all settings that call for the use of the target language, especially outside instructional periods'. They added a note of caution: 'the information garnered from self-assessment should always be used in conjunction with data from other assessment methods'.

Overall, there is considerable support for the principle of student involvement in assessment. 'Self-assessment can increase learners' involvement in and responsibility for their own learning' (Genesee and Upshur, 1996: 45). In the context of using self-access materials and encouraging students to become independent learners, their involvement is important (see Sheerin, 1989; McNamara and Deana, 1995).

The results of the survey suggest that more needs to be done on courses to explain to students the value of self-assessment procedures and to bolster their self-confidence in using them. This does not imply that self-assessment should be the *only* form of assessment. It is important to have an accurate assessment of students' abilities and this can best be done by combining forms of assessment. One overall conclusion of the survey, apart from noting and bearing in mind students' views and preferences, is that whatever forms of assessment are used on courses, they need to be carefully explained in advance. In addition, students should be adequately informed of the results of their assessment.

The survey indicated that further research could usefully be carried out in a number of areas, some of which are listed below:

(1) A comparison of students from different countries or continents and at different levels (undergraduate/postgraduate) and their attitudes towards different kinds of assessment.

(2) An analysis of the different kinds of assessment that students have found most helpful in indicating the areas for them to focus on for language improvement or development.

(3) An analysis of the kind of help or advice that students find most useful as a follow-on to assessment results.

(4) A survey of the types of self-assessment that students have experience of (if any) in their own countries, compared with the country in which they are now studying, and which type they prefer and for what reasons.

References

Alderson J C, C Clapham and D Wall (1995) *Language Test Construction and Evaluation*, Cambridge: Cambridge University Press

Bachman L F and A S Palmer (1996) *Language Testing in Practice*, Oxford: Oxford University Press

Blue G M (1988) 'Self-assessment: the limits of learner independence', in Brookes A and P Grundy (eds) *Individualization and Autonomy in Language Learning*, ELT Documents 131, London: Modern English Publications in association with The British Council

Brindley G (1995) 'Assessing achievement in a learner-centred curriculum', in Alderson J C and B North (eds) *Language Testing in the 1990s: The communicative legacy*, Hemel Hempstead: Phoenix ELT

Cram B (1995) 'Criterion-based assessment: a classroom teacher's perspective', in Brindley G (ed) *Language Assessment in Action*, Sydney: NCELTR, Macquarie University

Genesee F and J A Upshur (1996) *Classroom-Based Evaluation in Second Language Education*, Cambridge: Cambridge University Press

Grierson G (1995) 'Classroom-based assessment in intensive English centres', in Brindley G (ed) *Language Assessment in Action*, Sydney: NCELTR, Macquarie University

Hughes A (ed) (1988) *Testing English for University Study*, ELT Documents 127, London: Modern English Publications in association with the British Council

Hughes A (1989) *Testing for Language Teachers*, Cambridge: Cambridge University Press

Jordan R R (1997) *English for Academic Purposes: A guide and resource book for teachers*, Cambridge: Cambridge University Press

Lynch T (1988) 'Peer evaluation in practice', in Brookes A and P Grundy (eds) *Individualization and Autonomy in Language Learning*, ELT Documents 131, London: Modern English Publications in association with the British Council

McNamara M J and D Deana (1995) 'Self-assessment activities: toward autonomy in language learning', *TESOL Journal* 5.1

Oskarsson M (1980) *Approaches to Self-Assessment in Foreign Language Learning*, Oxford: Pergamon

Sheerin S (1989) *Self-Access*, Oxford: Oxford University Press

Sheerin S (1991) 'Self-access', *Language Teaching* 24.3

Ward Goodbody M (1993) 'Letting the students choose: a placement procedure for a pre-sessional course', in Blue G M (ed) *Language, Learning and Success: Studying through English*, Hemel Hempstead: Phoenix ELT

West R (1994) 'Needs analysis in language teaching', *Language Teaching* 27.1

Acknowledgements

My thanks are due to: Richard West, Manchester University, for arranging for his MEd students to complete a pilot version of the questionnaire; the following BALEAP members for giving my questionnaire to their pre-sessional course students in 1996: June O'Brien, Manchester University; Penny Adams, Leeds University; Pauline Robinson, Reading University; Alasdair Archibald, Southampton University.

Notes on Contributors

J Charles Alderson

J Charles Alderson is Professor of Linguistics and English Language Education at Lancaster University. His involvement in ESP includes teaching and writing ESP materials and tests in Mexico and the UK, and acting as Director of the Project to Revise the ELTS test, which resulted in the new IELTS test. He has been consultant to a number of ESP projects, most notably in Brazil, and latterly he was consultant to the PROSPER Impact Study in Romania.

Barbara Atherton

Barbara Atherton is a Senior Lecturer and English Language Support Co-ordinator in the School of Languages, Kingston University, London. She is responsible for the design and delivery of pre and in-sessional EAP courses across the university and also teaches on the Applied English Language degree programme. Her research interests centre on reading and writing for academic purposes.

George Blue

George Blue works at the University of Southampton, where he teaches and co-ordinates EAP classes, contributes to individual tutorial support, promotes independent learning and the use of the language resources centre, and teaches on the MA course in Applied Linguistics. His main research interests are in aspects of ESP/EAP and in autonomy and individualisation in language learning.

Moira Calderwood

Moira Calderwood is a Lecturer in the EFL Unit at the University of Glasgow. Over the years she has developed a wide range of EAP courses and is currently Course Director for the pre-sessional course. She is particularly interested in academic writing and testing and has recently become involved in the training of IELTS examiners.

Alicia Cresswell

Alicia Cresswell is a Lecturer in English as a Foreign Language at the Language Centre, University of Newcastle upon Tyne. She teaches courses in EAP, general English and applied linguistics and co-ordinates the in-sessional English programme. Her interests include discourse analysis and second language writing.

Joan Cutting

Joan Cutting is a Senior Lecturer in EAP at the University of Sunderland. She runs the in-sessional EAP and English for Business Studies modules, lectures on Pragmatics, and designed and runs the Linguistics and Research Methods modules on the MA TESOL programme. Her interests are pragmatics and discourse analysis, and academic writing.

Esther Daborn

Esther Daborn is a Lecturer in the EFL at the University of Glasgow. She has led a project with the Electrical Engineering department for the last three years. She runs in-sessional classes and designed the core of the university pre-sessional course. Her research interests are genre studies, corpus linguistics, and communicative norms in cross cultural communication.

Lynn Errey

Lynn Errey, Senior Lecturer in the International Centre for English Studies at Oxford Brookes University, has wide experience of designing and teaching EAP programmes and now co-ordinates the Oxford Brookes MA in Teaching EAP and ESP. Her research interests are academic writing and strategic learning in EAP.

Paul Fanning

Paul Fanning is a Senior ESOL Lecturer at Middlesex University in North London. He is Curriculum Leader for courses in TEFL and English Language and British Culture, and provides EAP support for students of Computing and Engineering. His current interests are EAP grammar, issues in ESP, and the teaching of academic reading.

M I Freeman

Mike Freeman is a Research Associate at the University of Portsmouth. He is working on the Residence Abroad Project, and is one of the Course Leaders for the MA in Teaching and Learning in Higher Education. His interests are in language learning strategies, ID research, prediction of success in language learning, self-assessment, and the teaching of languages for specific purposes.

Katie Gray

Katie Gray is Director of Language Studies at Oxford University Department for Continuing Education. Her interests are in course design and evaluation, language awareness and the cultural aspects of teaching and learning. The common aim for all her courses is to develop her students' ability to engage in intellectual debate and critical thinking, within the context of the British academic culture.

Rita Green

Rita Green was, at the time of writing, a member of the Testing and Evaluation Unit at the University of Reading. She is now a freelance language testing consultant teaching and working overseas. Her research interests include the relationship between academic reading and academic listening, portfolio assessment and test data analysis.

Lynne Hale

Lynne Hale is a Principal Lecturer in ESOL and Head of English Language and Learning Support at Middlesex University, responsible for non-modular in-sessional and pre-sessional EAP courses, and academic writing for native speakers. Research interests include academic literacies, ESP, and collaborative teaching and learning.

Julie Hartill

Julie Hartill is a Teaching Fellow in the EFL Unit at the University of Essex. She is currently responsible for undergraduate EAP and directs the August pre-sessional course. She teaches on the Unit's range of EAP and teacher education programmes. Her research interests include EAP, course design and qualitative research methods in ELT.

R R Jordan

Bob (R R) Jordan is an Honorary Fellow of the Faculty of Education, University of Manchester, where he took his PhD in EAP (1998). He was a founder member of BALEAP in 1972 and is now an Honorary Member. His resource book for teachers, *English for Academic Purposes*, appeared in 1997 (Cambridge University Press); the third edition of *Academic Writing Course* was published in 1999 (Pearson Education: Longman).

Gill Meldrum

Gill Meldrum is a Lecturer in EAP at the University of Nottingham. She has taught and course directed on pre-sessional and in-sessional programmes there since 1987. Previously she taught at Glasgow University and in Greece. Her particular interest in EAP is in developing students' evaluative and critical approach to reading and writing.

James Milton

James Milton is Director of the Centre for Applied Language Studies in the University of Swansea and a Fellow of the British Institute of ELT. One of the Centre's principal roles is the preparation of students for academic courses and student support during courses. Current research work centres on computer-mediated teaching and testing, especially of vocabulary knowledge, and on language aptitude testing.

John Morley

John Morley teaches on and directs EAP courses at the University of Manchester. He has taught in Spain, Indonesia, Singapore and more recently in Australia. He holds an MEd (Hons) degree from the University of New England. Research interests include genre analysis, independent language learning and the role of corrective feedback.

Jane Saville

Jane Saville is a Senior Lecturer in the School of EFL and Linguistics at the University of the West of England, Bristol. She has designed, managed and taught a wide variety of EAP courses at different levels and is currently Award Leader for an MA in TEFL and Linguistics.